DIALOGUE AND DESIRE

DIALOGUE AND DESIRE
Mikhail Bakhtin and the Linguistic Turn in Psychotherapy

On behalf of the United Kingdom Council for Psychotherapy by

Rachel Pollard

Routledge
Taylor & Francis Group
LONDON AND NEW YORK

First published 2008 by Karnac Books Ltd.

Published 2018 by Routledge
2 Park Square, Milton Park, Abingdon, Oxon OX14 4RN
711 Third Avenue, New York, NY 10017, USA

Routledge is an imprint of the Taylor & Francis Group, an informa business

Copyright © 2008 by Rachel Pollard

The rights of Rachel Pollard to be identified as the author of this work have been asserted in accordance with §§ 77 and 78 of the Copyright Design and Patents Act 1988.

All rights reserved. No part of this book may be reprinted or reproduced or utilised in any form or by any electronic, mechanical, or other means, now known or hereafter invented, including photocopying and recording, or in any information storage or retrieval system, without permission in writing from the publishers.

Notice:
Product or corporate names may be trademarks or registered trademarks, and are used only for identification and explanation without intent to infringe.

British Library Cataloguing in Publication Data

A C.I.P. for this book is available from the British Library

ISBN13: 9781855754492 (pbk)

Edited, designed, and produced by
Florence Production Ltd, Stoodleigh, Devon
www.florenceproduction.co.uk

For Aileen and Lyn

CONTENTS

ACKNOWLEDGEMENTS   ix

ABOUT THE AUTHOR   xi

INTRODUCTION   xiii

CHAPTER ONE
Who was Mikhail Bakhtin?   1

CHAPTER TWO
Bakhtin, Dialogism, and European Philosophy   21

CHAPTER THREE
Bakhtin, the Dialogical Self and Dialogical Psychotherapy   33

CHAPTER FOUR
Some Limitations of Dialogism as a Model for
Psychotherapy   65

CHAPTER FIVE
Interdividual Psychology and the Dialogical Self   89

CHAPTER SIX
Towards a Further Integration of Interdividual Psychology and Dialogical Consciousness via Developmental Psychology, Cognitive Neuroscience, and Linguistics 123

CHAPTER SEVEN
Bakhtin's Ethics and Psychotherapy 155

CHAPTER EIGHT
Towards a Bakhtinian Practice of Psychotherapy 185

BIBLIOGRAPHY 217

INDEX 235

ACKNOWLEDGEMENTS

This book is partly a development of some of the themes that emerged when doing research for a doctorate in the sociology department at the University of Manchester. I would therefore like to express my gratitude to my PhD supervisor, Nick Crossley, for his guidance and support throughout. I also remain indebted to the many people who helped me when researching and writing my thesis, by suggesting reading, sending me books and papers and discussing ideas about Bakhtin and psychotherapy. I am grateful to the following people: Fazila Bhimje, Sarah Lucas, Ian Parker and Jan Wright, who have read and commented on various chapters, and am particularly indebted to Elizabeth Kemp for her careful reading of the first draft of this book and the many corrections and improvements she suggested. Any remaining errors are entirely my own. Last but not least I would like to thank my partner, Izzat, for his continued encouragement, practical support and patience over the past seven years.

ABOUT THE AUTHOR

Rachel Pollard currently works as a psychotherapist in private practice, specialising in cognitive analytic therapy and has previously worked in the NHS and in higher education. She graduated from the University of Wales and studied social and community work in Zimbabwe. She has an MA in counselling studies and a PhD in sociology from the University of Manchester.

INTRODUCTION

This book is an exploration of the relationship between the Russian philosopher, Mikhail Bakhtin, and contemporary dialogical psychotherapy. This exploration led me to consider how two central and inseparable dimensions of human experience, language and desire, could be thought about differently by bringing the thinking of Bakhtin into a dialogical relationship with the thinking of the controversial French anthropologist and cultural critic, René Girard. The radical difference between these two original thinkers is illustrated in their differing interpretations of Dostoevsky's novels; while Bakhtin finds in Dostoevsky an author who allows his characters the freedom to speak for themselves without passing judgement on them, Girard finds an author who is both sympathetic and critical towards his characters because they are consumed with passionate desires that often lead to violence.

Bakhtin is becoming increasingly well known in psychotherapy as one of the main inspirations for what is known as the Dialogical Self, a self that can be conceived of as different "voices" in conversation with each other, and one that is in tune with the complex and fragmentary aspects of postmodern subjectivity. Girard is less well known in psychotherapy but I will argue that his original and provocative theory of human desire can illuminate diverse aspects of human social and emotional life in a way that is complementary to a dialogical understanding of the self. Girard insists that desire, like language, is central to human social life and is also the source of our most intense and disturbing emotions as well as our propensity for violence. However, contemporary psychotherapy often neglects to account for desire in the way it formulates subjectivity and in its understandings of human distress. Crucial to understanding how desires trouble their patients is psychotherapists' acknowledgement and understanding of their own desires, particularly the desire to be a therapist, and for many, the desire to do research, write books and papers and formulate new theories and models.

This book is also an attempt to grapple with some of the difficulties in using Bakhtinian ideas in psychotherapy. It oversimplifies Bakhtin to claim him exclusively for any one school of thought, political persuasion or religious belief, however tempting that might be. Bakhtin wears his political views and religious beliefs lightly and ideological generalisations of any kind are always subordinated to the particular features of each situation. Because of this and the diversity and apparent flexibility of his thinking, Bakhtin can easily be moulded to suit our own purposes, which means acknowledging that we are choosing from a range of possible interpretations. I have tried to be impartial in presenting some of the debates about Bakhtin in the first two chapters and have drawn on commentators from Russian and Western traditions with widely divergent perspectives. However while not discounting in any way the wisdom of experienced Bakhtin scholars, I think it is important to approach Bakhtin as far as possible without preconceptions and see what we can find in his writing for ourselves.

What I found was an account of embodied human intersubjectivity that coincided neither with conventional "psychological" theories nor with the radical opposition to them in Marxist and post-structural critiques. I also found an ethical approach to intersubjectivity that could form the basis of an ethical practice of psychotherapy that is not constrained by theories or preconceived ideas about the person. With psychotherapy in mind, the non-dogmatic openness of Bakhtin's thinking means that his insights can be enhanced rather than compromised by bringing him into dialogue with other perspectives.

The first chapter introduces Bakhtin and discusses some of the difficulties encountered in using his ideas in psychotherapy, given the highly contested interpretations of his work in the wider field of Bakhtin scholarship. The second chapter discusses dialogism, Bakhtin's most significant concept for psychotherapy, drawing attention to the many shades of meanings that dialogism has acquired and relating these to the philosophical context in which Bakhtin developed his ideas. Chapter Three describes the concept of the Dialogical Self and discusses two contrasting dialogical approaches to psychotherapy, including some of their limitations: the first brings Bakhtinian ideas into interaction with Object Relations theory and the second attempts to demonstrate congruence between Bakhtin's ideas and those of Lacan, whose psychoanalytic and linguistic conception of the self makes him an obvious and interesting subject of comparison with Bakhtin. The fourth chapter draws attention to some further possible limitations of a Bakhtinian dialogical approach, drawing on some of Bakhtin's critics and briefly outlines a critique of Bakhtin from a Girardian perspective, introducing Girard's key concept of mimetic desire: this is followed by a discussion of how Girard and Bakhtin could be brought into a complementary dialogical relationship with each other. Chapter Five presents a more detailed overview of Girard's ideas including his critique of the Freudian Oedipus complex and Freud's account of narcissism. Bakhtin's "dialogue" with Girard involves holding two mutually exclusive versions of the self viewed from very different perspectives; one that is unique, indeterminate and resistant to closure and one who, far from being unique and indeterminate, is indistinguishable from other selves in the way it experiences desire.

Both Bakhtin and Girard are brought into dialogue with some contemporary scientific discourses in Chapter Six, which discusses how recent research in developmental psychology and cognitive science seems to lend support to the concept of a Bakhtinian dialogical self that is also Girardian desiring self. This research also demonstrates not only the embodied nature of dialogical interaction, that is the inseparability of physiological and mental processes, but also the embodied nature of the conceptual systems that structure human consciousness. These are findings that give retrospective credence to the importance of the body in Bakhtin's philosophy: for Bakhtin, our shared experience of incarnation is the basis of the moral obligations that we have towards our fellow human beings. It is also the basis of his key concept of "outsideness", a term that denotes how our relationships with other people and our perceptions of them are both unique to ourselves and constrained by the limitations of the body. Some of the implications of Bakhtin's ethics of intersubjectivity are discussed in Chapter Seven and related to his later work on "carnival" that, from a psychotherapy perspective, could be seen as modifying his emphasis on individual difference with the universalising aspects of embodied experience. The concluding chapter brings the discussions in the previous chapters together and maps out a possible direction for a practice of psychotherapy that is informed by Bakhtinian ethics; an ethics that takes full account of the social origins of individual mental distress and that recognises the complex ways in which desires are expressed in language. Such an approach to the practice of psychotherapy should be predicated on the capacity and willingness of its practitioners to consciously reflect on and acknowledge the origins and nature of our own desires and how these interact with our identity and our activities as psychotherapists.

Author's note: Readers who are not familiar with Bakhtin may find some of the references in the text to Voloshinov, a member of Bakhtin's circle of intellectuals, confusing. Voloshinov is sometimes invoked by theorists of the Dialogical Self interchangeably with Bakhtin, as it was widely thought that Bakhtin published some of his own writing using Voloshinov's name. It is now generally recognised that Voloshinov was the author of the works published under his name, whose ideas both overlapped with and influenced those of Bakhtin and whose thinking, even where it differs from Bakhtin, can usefully inform understandings of dialogical subjectivity.

CHAPTER ONE

Who was Mikhail Bakhtin?

Although little known during his lifetime, since his death in 1975 this Russian philosopher and cultural theorist has achieved immense popularity among academics in the West as his influence has extended beyond literary criticism and philosophy across the humanities and even further to psychotherapy. In stark contrast to Bakhtin's penury and relative domestic obscurity, his ideas have become the springboard for many notable Western academic careers. Scholars from diverse perspectives, from Marxists to theologians, from feminists to postcolonial theorists, from sociologists to linguists, and literary theorists to psychologists, have all declared an interest in Bakhtin. As Graham Pechey (1989) observed, one of the interesting characteristics of Bakhtin's ideas is their capacity to migrate across national and disciplinary boundaries and make themselves at home in very different fields of intellectual endeavour. However, Edward Said (2001) warns that when theories travel beyond their original and temporal context, they can lose some of their radical power. One of the central arguments of this book is that the Bakhtin invoked in psychotherapy is a much tamer and less controversial figure than the Russian Bakhtin and that the radical implications of his thinking for psychotherapy extend far beyond the notion of the "Dialogical Self". Moreover, outside the field of psychotherapy, Bakhtin's thinking is highly contested, making any unitary or monologic interpretation problematic.

Problems with the use of Bakhtin in psychotherapy

It can be tempting to romanticise or even idealise Bakhtin: compared to many of his relatively comfortable contemporaries in Europe, he can be seen as having led a heroic life in tragic circumstances, enduring persecution and exile under Stalin, while continuing to develop his ideas in isolation from mainstream intellectual life. And where other theorists of the psyche from Freud to the present day have been subject to continual critical debate, Bakhtin or interpretations of Bakhtin used in psychotherapy are rarely challenged. This may be because he never set out to be a theorist of psychotherapy, even less to found a new school or movement, and is not therefore a potential threat to existing models. Another reason could be the apparent simplicity of some of his ideas that can obscure the complexities of interpreting Bakhtin for practitioners of psychotherapy in the West. Bakhtin's reputation seems in some ways to have eclipsed the content of his work. However, before even beginning to think about a critical engagement with Bakhtin, there is the problem of which Bakhtin to critically engage with, as there is no central or definitive interpretation of his work.

When I first began to read Bakhtin and what others had written about him, I was both surprised and fascinated by the range and volume of work he has inspired, of which writing concerning Bakhtin and psychotherapy is only a minor sideshow. A major problem for psychotherapists interested in Bakhtin is deciding how to read him: do we read all the texts for ourselves and form our own conclusions about how to interpret them, or do we rely solely on the interpretations and appropriations of established theorists of the dialogical self and dialogical psychotherapy? If we decide to read Bakhtin for ourselves, how do we get round problems of inaccurate translation, if we are not Russian speakers, or the fact that some of his earlier work is an amalgamation of fragments put together by others? A further complication is that he may have plagiarised other philosophers or felt obliged to disguise his real beliefs to evade censorship. If we turn to the secondary literature for guidance, we face the apparently insurmountable problem of what to read and whose opinion to trust given the enormous output of Bakhtin scholarship and the lack of any consensus within it. The volume of critiques of Bakhtin far exceeds what even the most dedicated Bakhtin scholar could read in a lifetime. Those writing about Bakhtin have not read most of what has already been written about him and so, as Anthony Wall (1998a) observes, many are not writing in dialogue with each other but merely "chattering" to themselves. As my primary interest is in psychotherapy rather than Bakhtin, I have been guided in my own reading by a few long established Bakhtin scholars, by no means all in agreement with each other, such as Caryl Emerson, Kenneth Hirschkop, Charles Lock, Michael Holquist and David Shepherd, following up writers who they refer to who seem to be addressing areas that I felt might be of relevance to a psychotherapy perspective. The more I read, the more I felt I needed to exercise my own critical judgement, about the unstated assumptions that seemed to inform the appropriations of Bakhtin in psychotherapy theory. Bakhtin is far too complex and contested a figure to take any single judgement or interpretation on trust. I imagine that, while Bakhtin would have welcomed the interest that psychotherapists have shown in his ideas, he would have also much preferred a critical and questioning engagement with them.

In order to engage with Bakhtin critically, we need to attempt to understand him in the social, political and intellectual context of 20th century Russia and the Soviet Union, as well as in the context of the field of contemporary Bakhtin studies and to consider why his ideas have become so important to many practitioners of psychotherapy. A major question is the extent to which Bakhtin's work was shaped or even distorted by events in the Soviet Union as explored by Hirschkop (2001). One of the problems with appropriations of Bakhtin is that he is often treated as if he were a thinker in isolation, whereas he developed his ideas in dialogue with a vast tapestry of past and contemporary thinkers. He is also seen as having paved the way for later developments in European philosophy, which have probably underpinned his current popularity. In a broad sense his thought seems to evolve through a process of internally persuasive discourse, a process that has continued after his death as Bakhtin has been brought into dialogue with other strands of thought. One way of understanding internally persuasive discourse is the capacity to hold two or more contradictory "positions" (beliefs, opinions or perspectives) simultaneously: however, unlike dialectical reasoning it does not supersede these contradictions with a synthesis of ideas, but continues to throw up new contradictions. Internally persuasive discourse is one of Bakhtin's least referred to but most important concepts, although it can be challenging and disturbing to cherished beliefs. It is the antithesis of dogma and received wisdom. Bakhtin (1981) defines internally persuasive discourse against authoritative discourse, a prior discourse that brooks no discussion or questioning. Authoritative discourse is never "double voiced" as it is always spoken from a single, closed perspective. Internally persuasive discourse by contrast has no special privileges, is backed up by no authority and is a hybrid open-ended discourse:

> When thought begins to work in an independent, experimenting, and discriminating, way what first occurs is a separation between internally persuasive discourse and authoritarian enforced discourse ... Internally persuasive discourse—as opposed to one that is externally authoritative—is, as it is affirmed through assimilation, tightly interwoven with "one's own word". In the everyday rounds of our consciousness, the internally persuasive word is half ours and half someone else's. Its creativity and productiveness consists precisely in the fact that such a word awakens new and independent words ... it enters into interanimating relationships with new contexts. [Bakhtin, 1981, 345–6]

The previous discourses with which it engages with may be deemed monological and authoritative, though not necessarily in absolute terms, due to their having gained a certain degree of acceptance and respectability. While I am aware that this book could also be accused of augmenting what Wall (1998a) dismisses as the meaningless babble that characterises much that is written about Bakhtin, it is offered as a dialogical response to some previous discourses and an attempt to bring previously unrelated discourses into a dialogical relationship.

Internally persuasive discourse demands that nothing is sacred and everything is open to question and critique, including its own presuppositions. When I first started to read Bakhtin, one of my conclusions was that psychotherapy is not Bakhtinian enough; as I read more I realised that Bakhtin's thought alone is insufficient and that to use Bakhtin as a mode of critique while leaving him outside the scope of the critique is unsatisfactory. A Bakhtinian dialogue with Bakhtin demands a critical and questioning approach. Only in this way can he be brought into dialogue with others and remain a dialogical thinker. While it is suggested that psychotherapy could be enhanced by a more inclusive reading of Bakhtin, a more inclusive reading of Bakhtin and some of his critics reveals gaps in his own thought, which, from a psychotherapy perspective, can be used creatively to bring him into dialogue with other thinkers. The principal dialogue in this book is with the highly controversial French anthropologist and literary critic René Girard, who dares to supply the emotional "content" that seems to be missing in Bakhtin's social conception of self. Girard's ideas, like Bakhtin's, were developed in dialogue with a range of other thinkers and particularly, from a psychotherapy perspective, in response to Freud.

The initial concerns that led to this study were the problems of how subjectivity, consciousness and selfhood are understood in psychotherapy and the implications of these understandings for practice. Although these issues are central to the concerns of psychotherapy, they are in general taken as self-evident, as well as being poorly defined (Erwin, 1997). Bakhtinian concepts are often grafted on to other models or theories which may, themselves, be integrations of previous theories (e.g. cognitive analytic therapy) or have an implicit Cartesian model of the self (e.g. cognitive behavioural therapy). One problem with integrating ideas from different schools and disciplines is the difficulties this poses for their evaluation by non-specialists; hence the scarcity of critical studies of the use of Bakhtin or ideas derived from Bakhtin in psychotherapy. How the self is understood and the ideological and political implications of this understanding should logically be the starting point for psychotherapy rather than something retrospectively inferred. This apparently strange state of affairs reflects the fact that theories do not account for their own existence, for their own mutations, permutations and variations or the rivalry that can arise between them.

Bakhtin has often been appropriated in a selective way that does not fully reflect the potential contribution of his thought to psychotherapy. A Bakhtinian socio-historical self with a dialogical consciousness is in direct conflict with the monadic self of traditional cognitive therapy and partially in conflict with psychoanalytic models. A further complication was the, probably erroneous, attribution to Bakhtin of works actually written by Valentin Voloshinov, a member of the "Bakhtin Circle" and the assumption that their ideas do not merely overlap but are entirely shared. This particular interpretation of Bakhtin (e.g. Leiman, 1992; Ryle, 1994) has probably led to an over-emphasis on semiotics and a neglect of other, potentially more radical aspects of Bakhtin's thinking; however, even when these more radical implications are taken on board, Bakhtin remains silent on crucial aspects of human emotional experience and how this is reflected in human behaviour.

Bakhtin has implicitly been used to justify a particular ideological model of self that is social and largely structured by linguistically mediated intersubjective relationships. It is a self without any specific or fixed meanings, content, sexuality or gender, and without desire. It is a self that is by omission disembodied. It is a model of the self that is only universal to the extent that it is pitched at a level of abstraction that renders it uncontentious. It is a self that is in tune with post-modern academic tendencies to promote the local, secular and particular rather than the universal. It is accepted here that human consciousness is far too complex and uncertain for any theory of psychotherapy to claim or even attempt a final account. Consciousness continues to elude all human attempts to fully define and understand it. Despite all these points, it is argued that a more inclusive reading of Bakhtin could advance the understandings of self and consciousness in psychotherapy as well as opening it up further to other influences. Such a reading of Bakhtin could enhance the practice of "dialogical" psychotherapy as it also provides a basis for thinking through the ethics of practice.

The introduction of Bakhtin into psychotherapy also raises philosophical questions about the nature of the knowledge base in psychotherapy. Bakhtin was neither a psychologist nor a psychotherapist and did not consider how psychoanalytic theory might interact with his ideas about subjectivity, even though psychoanalysis was gaining increasing influence during his lifetime and was the subject of a critique by Voloshinov. This study aims to demonstrate that Bakhtin has a considerable amount to offer to the practice of psychotherapy beyond the idea of the dialogical self, but as his potential contribution comes from very different perspectives to mainstream psychological thinking, this opens gates to many other kinds of knowledge, potentially making psychotherapy a truly multi- or cross-disciplinary undertaking. Moreover, since psychotherapy in Bakhtinian terms could only be conceived of as a human social practice and, as such, be infinitely variable and unrepeatable, such a psychotherapy directly challenges the relevance and appropriateness of "scientific research" into its effectiveness.

As we have seen, the complexity of interpreting Bakhtin means that not only is it necessary to be transparent about how we choose to interpret him, it is also necessary to defend or justify the particular interpretation chosen. In conclusion, it is necessary to make a judgement and as there is so much uncertainty surrounding Bakhtin that judgement can only be made with explicit reference to the values that influenced it.

The enigma of Bakhtin

During most of his lifetime, Bakhtin was on the margins of Russian intellectual life and was almost unknown in the West. Born in 1895, he lived through the communist revolution of 1917, the Second World War, the tyranny of Stalinism, and the Cold War, alongside the unprecedented and rapid transition from Russian feudalism to a modern, centralised and industrialised Soviet Union that in 1961, two years before the publication of the revised version of Bakhtin's influential book *Problems of Dostoevsky's Poetics*, made a hero of cosmonaut Yuri Gagarin, the first person to go into space. Until recently, the uncertainties surrounding the facts of Bakhtin's life and the authorship of some of the texts associated with him lent him an air of mystery. Bakhtin's biographers in the West, Clark & Holquist (1984), note that he suffered from osteomyelitis from an early age, which eventually led to him having a leg amputated in 1938. Illness and pain often confined him to bed for months at a time and his classes were often conducted from a couch. He led what appears to have been a profoundly insecure, impecunious and unsettled domestic and professional life, working variously as a school teacher, an accountant (while in exile) and a lecturer. He was persecuted by the Soviet authorities under Stalin; he was arrested in 1928 while involved with a quasi-Masonic religious sect (Brandist, 2002) and sentenced to five years in a concentration camp, later commuted to exile in Kazakstan on the grounds of ill health after representations from his wife and friends.

After his return from exile in 1936, Bakhtin returned to Moscow and was appointed to a lectureship in literature in Saransk: he was dismissed a year later for "bourgeois objectivism" in his teaching. Even though he was appointed Head of the Department of World Literature at the Mordivinia Pedagogical Institute in 1945, his doctoral dissertation on Rabelais was rejected the following year for being subversive and was only accepted in 1952 following substantial revision. In the 1960s, Bakhtin finally achieved recognition in the Soviet Union after students from the Gorky Institute in Moscow discovered that he was still alive and assisted him in revising and publishing some of his work.[1] The Bakhtin "industry" in the West originated two decades later, in 1981, with the publication of *The Dialogical Imagination* (Hirschkop, 1999), to coincide with the widespread interest in "literary theory" (the application of Saussure's structural linguistics to literary texts and the discarding of hermeneutic interpretations in favour of semiotic analysis) that began during the 1960s, and which by the 1980s had become increasingly fashionable in Western academia, particularly in North America. Bakhtinian "linguistics" (or Western "translations" of them) had a more generalised appeal in this climate than they might otherwise have done, particularly as unlike the post-structuralists Bakhtin had apparently succeeded in decentring the subject while retaining a distinctly humanist perspective.

The collapse of the Soviet Union and access to the Bakhtin archives have thrown much previous Bakhtin scholarship into question, particularly regarding the author's relationship to his sources: Bakhtin did not leave an established and complete body of work on his death in 1975 as much of his work was not published during his lifetime and, since those works that were published posthumously were not done so chronologically, his work has only become available to Western scholars in a fragmented way. And, as no piece of work contained all his key concepts (Morris, 1994), those interested in his work have been largely dependant on secondary sources. A leading Bakhtin scholar, David Shepherd, implied that one of the major collections of Bakhtin texts for Western scholars,

The Dialogical Imagination (1981), was translated so as to make Bakhtin seem compatible with the "theory boom" in North American academia and, in so doing, omitted the philosophical side of those texts (Hitchcock, 1998). Another serious concern is the evidence uncovered in the Bakhtin archive by Brian Poole (1998, 2001) of plagiarism by Bakhtin and Voloshinov, both of whom copied the work of German philosophers Ernst Cassirer and Max Scheler into their works without acknowledgement. Shepherd freely admits that Bakhtin could ultimately turn out to be a charlatan (Hitchcock, 1998), which may be a source of fascination for Bakhtin scholars but for theorists who harness his ideas to further their understanding of the human psyche and to refine their techniques for healing it, this must be a cause for concern.

Archival research has shown that Bakhtin falsely claimed descent from minor nobility and lied about his education by claiming degrees that were awarded to his brother, Nicolae, and Matvai Kagan, a member of the "Bakhtin Circle" (Hirschkop, 1998, 2001, Poole, 2001). Expediency or exigency perhaps meant that Bakhtin fabricated degrees he did not have, wrote things he did not believe or even published under other peoples' names in order to survive under conditions of Stalinist censorship and terror. The account by Nikolae Pan"kov (2001) of *Bakhtin's Dissertation Defence* shows how Bakhtin struggled to gain acceptance in Soviet academia. From what little is known, it would appear that Bakhtin studied, wrote and taught under conditions of hardship unknown to most contemporary scholars in the West—he wrote using only a pencil and soft paper and most of a major work he wrote on the *Bildungsroman* was lost to posterity; he used his back-up copy to roll his cigarettes during the poverty-stricken war years and the original was destroyed when a bomb hit his publishers during the Second World War (Emerson, 1997).

The uncertainty about Bakhtin's life, the confusion and controversy about the interpretation of his ideas and even about what texts he actually authored begs the question as to why Bakhtin has been embraced so enthusiastically by academics in the West, and the wisdom of Western appropriations of Bakhtin must be open to question when the Bakhtin canon is so unstable. This confusion and uncertainty allows for Bakhtin to be read and interpreted in different ways; to become all things to all people. There is no dominant authoritative reading of Bakhtin, which means that unlike other significant thinkers of the 20th century, there is no significant opposition to him either, but a multitude of incommensurable interpretations (Lock, 1991):

> In the secondary literature we encounter Bakhtin in fragments—the linguist, the semiotician, the deviant Formalist, the categorist of genres, the instigator of such terms as dialogic, heteroglossia, carnivalesque—and if all these fragments or aspects are brought together, synthesised, dialectically resolved, we find, at best, a panoptic guru. [Lock, 1991, reprinted in Emerson 1999, p. 285]

This means that however little we know or understand Bakhtin, we can make him mean what we want him to mean and the greater the historical and epistemological distance we are from him, the less likely we are to be challenged.

Bakhtin's contested legacy

As discussed above, psychotherapists cannot afford to ignore the fact that, with his increasing popularity, Bakhtin's legacy has become highly contested, not least between those who wish to claim him for Western philosophy and some Russian scholars who believe his rightful place is in the Slavic tradition. As Rachel Falconer (1997) suggests:

> ... do we approach Bakhtin as a historical critic, or do we approach him historically? Do we address him as a Renaissance critic or a critic of the modern era; alternatively do we place his writing historically, in the era of Russia's transformation to a totalitarian state? Or do we place him in a tradition of metaphysical philosophy, in which case the periods of literature he chose to study are of secondary importance? And if we agree on this, where in this tradition do we place him? Should he be allied with Descartes, with Kant, with Heidegger, with or against Derrida? Or taken as a whole, does his work constitute a work of pure philosophy and, if so, how do we interpret his pragmatism? What are the connections between Bakhtinian theory and Marxism? And a slightly different question, how does a Marxist critic

approach Bakhtin? Or, does the theory of dialogue constitute a polemical rejection of Marxist dialectics? Does Christian philosophy and theology help us to make sense of Bakhtin's definition of "otherness", his emphasis on individual "answerability." [Falconer, 1997, p. 32]

The almost insurmountable difficulties faced by anyone attempting to categorise Bakhtin or place him in a particular disciplinary tradition are a source of apparently endless stimulation and productivity for dedicated Bakhtin scholars but a potential source of frustration for the practitioners of psychotherapy when it comes to evaluating Bakhtinian contributions to dialogical practice. While it may be of little consequence whether Bakhtin was a Marxist, a Christian, a philosopher, a literary theorist or all of these, the disputed interpretations and therefore the implications of key concepts such as dialogism, polyphony, and carnival[2] are of considerable importance when attempting to apply these concepts to an understanding of human consciousness, self-hood and social functioning. There is no agreement either as to whether Bakhtin's works form a coherent whole or whether he even intended them to be regarded in that way. Makhlin (1997) sees an overall unity in Bakhtin's work, as a new philosophical programme for the humanities, which he terms a "social ontology of participation" that is nevertheless a dialogical response to the existential pre-occupation of 20th century philosophy. Anthony Wall (1998b) disagrees with any attempt to impose an overall coherence on Bakhtin. Some of his earlier works, which have only recently become available, were disconnected fragments put together by editors to give the appearance of wholeness. Wall sees no connection between the early fragments, for example those welded together to produce the essay *Toward a Philosophy of the Act*, and Bakhtin's later work. He argues that these were "broken" pieces of thought that could have developed in numerous directions and that it is doing Bakhtin a disservice to impose such a unity when none exists:

> Let us not mistake Mikhail Bakhtin for some philosophical Humpty Dumpty whom we might somehow put back together if we could recruit enough king's horses and enough king's men to the task. [Wall, 1998b, p. 677]

In a similar vein, Bernard-Donals (1994) argues that there is an irreconcilable division between two versions of Bakhtin that reflects divisions in the literary academic community; the phenomenological Bakhtin and the Marxist/materialist Bakhtin. Both agree on the boundlessness of language; however the former interpret this as meaning that there can be no certain access to material conditions because language is so messy and unpredictable and that knowledge can only be pursued by unscientific hermeneutic methods, while the latter insists that a scientific study of objective material reality and of the economic conditions which determine social interaction, including language, is possible.

Rather than force Bakhtin into the straightjacket of either philosophy or sociology, Hirschkop (1997) maintains that he was both a philosopher and a sociologist and that his thinking was incomplete rather than inconsistent. Although his various writings were superficially diverse, they were all attempts to resolve the same issues, although he never succeeded in doing so. The reason for this, according to Hirschkop, was that Bakhtin could not reconcile his ideal of intersubjectivity with historical realities; that intersubjectivity has historical limits:

> Bakhtin's historical moment gave rise to both a desire for redemption and the circumstances which frustrate it, a vision of reciprocal and mutual intersubjectivity and the fissures and unevenness which render it impossible, a search for philosophical meaning in history and a dawning awareness of the contingency of history itself. [1997, p. 55]

When measured by the number of books, publications and the financial advantages that many Western scholars enjoy in comparison to their Russian counterparts, the greater productivity of Bakhtin scholarship in the West has given rise to understandable resentment, particularly when this promotes interpretations of Bakhtin that are alien to Russian scholars:

> The native (Russian) researcher ... who becomes acquainted with foreign textual and extra-textual "discourses" in general and with interpretations of Bakhtin in particular at times feels as though he is in a dream. [Makhlin, 1995, cited in Adlam, 1997, p. 5]

While the biggest cleavage in Bakhtin scholarship is between East and West, neither school presents a monolithic version of Bakhtin. Russian scholars are far more inclined to regard Bakhtin as a philosopher and are critical of Westerners who read him too literally, failing to realise that he was constrained by his political circumstances to dress up his philosophical concepts as literary criticism (Falconer, 1997). Vadim Kozhinov, one of Bakhtin's literary executors, claims that Bakhtin described himself as a philosopher, not a literary scholar (Rzhevsky, 1999) while Bosenko (1993/4, cited in Adlam, 1997) attributes Bakhtin's popularity in the West to a decline in general philosophical culture and the deceptive ease with which his work can be understood. Western scholars are sometimes seen as colonising Bakhtin in the service of Marxism, feminism or post-structuralism. Makhlin (1997) is particularly scathing of any attempt to interpret Bakhtin from a standpoint of post-modernity, arguing that this assumes a finalised version of the world, the very opposite of what Bakhtin stood for. Similarly Gasparov (1984) argues that Bakhtin's reputation has outstripped him[3] and that his work has to be understood in the context of the Soviet Union in the 1920s, a time when Russian scholars were reacting against past cultural assumptions (Emerson, 1999):

> The irony of Bakhtin's fate was that he thought in dialogue with the 1920s but was published, read and respected at a time when his colleagues had already left the scene and strangers gathered around him. . . . The overthrower of every kind of piety has himself become the object of piety. His followers have come too late and made a research programme out of his programme for creativity. [Gasparov, 1984, p. 85]

Russian scholars are more likely to find or emphasise a spiritual dimension in Bakhtin's work: Kozhinov (1999) is adamant about his allegiance to Russian Orthodoxy, maintaining that Bakhtin said that freedom of thought was not possible without some kind of faith. Christian interpretations have also been promoted in the West: Bakhtin's biographers Clark & Holquist (1984) argue that Bakhtin was profoundly influenced by the spiritual practices of the Russian Orthodox Church although Holquist later modified his views in this respect. A more recent and subtlely argued account by Ruth Coates (1998) claims to find Christian themes throughout all the work of Bakhtin.

From a Western standpoint, Hitchcock (1997) argues that Russian ethical and Christian interpretations are partly a knee-jerk reaction by humanist intellectuals to their suppression under Soviet communism and partly a response to their more recent marginalisation under free-market conditions. From a Slavic perspective, Kozhinov (1999) criticises Western scholars for their fickleness of interpretation according to the vagaries of the "market" and he is highly critical of younger Russian scholars whom he accuses of looking to the West rather than valuing the work of native Russian thinkers.

The disputed texts

A long-running dispute amongst Bakhtin scholars has been over the authorship of texts, published under the names of V. N. Voloshinov, a prominent member of the "Bakhtin Circle" but which were often attributed to Bakhtin. Without clear evidence, opinions as to the authorship of these texts often seemed to reflect the writer's preferred interpretation of Bakhtin. The work of Brian Poole (2001) has apparently rendered these discussions obsolete but it is relevant to give a brief account of these disputes, as they illustrate the conflicts that abound in Bakhtin scholarship.

Two of the disputed texts, *Marxism and the Philosophy of Language (MPL)* and *Freudianism, a Marxist Critique (Freudianism)*, written by Voloshinov[4] but formerly often attributed to Bakhtin, are cited frequently by Mikael Leiman, a prominent theorist of dialogical psychotherapy. At the time of their publication in the 1920s, they attracted little attention and it was only when they started to attract more interest during the 1960s that the question of authorship became an issue of concern. A Soviet linguist, V.V. Ivanov, declared in 1971 that all the texts signed by Voloshinov were in fact written by Bakhtin (Morris, 1994, Titunik & Bruss, 1976), a view that has been advanced in the West by Clark & Holquist (1984). They point out that although these texts were published under Voloshinov's name, his widow later denied his authorship and finally Bakhtin claimed authorship for himself. According to Kozhinov, Bakhtin only acknowledged his authorship of the Voloshinov texts with great reluctance, as he wrote them *wearing a mask* at a time when he needed to earn money and did not want these works to be seen as representing his thinking (Rzhevsky, 1994).

Differing views as to the authorship of both texts inevitably became entangled with differing interpretations of Bakhtin and what he represented. Clark & Holquist, who regarded Bakhtin as promoting a form of Christian mysticism, argued that being recognised as the author of a text was less important for Bakhtin than getting it published. They suggest that the Marxist rhetoric in *Freudianism* and *MPL* was merely a device to appease the Soviet authorities and make them acceptable for publication. The translator and editor of the English version of *Freudianism*, I.R. Titunik, and the editor, Neil Bruss, refute Ivanov's account of Bakhtin's authorship of Voloshinov's works, arguing that Bakhtin's book *Problems in Dostoevsky's Art*,[5] published in 1929, at the same time as *MPL*, while sharing a similar orientation towards language, employs a very different terminology. Moreover, what they regard as the distinctly Marxist orientation in Voloshinov's work is absent in Bakhtin's work published at the same time. More recently two other prominent Bakhtin scholars, Gary Morson and Caryl Emerson (1989), have also refuted Bakhtin's authorship of Voloshinov's texts on the grounds that Bakhtin was consistently hostile to Marxism. In their view, Voloshinov is a creative and independent thinker whose Marxism is "organic" to his argument; he advances a Marxist interpretation of language and culture that not only influenced Bakhtin but challenged him to formulate a theory of language and culture that was social without being Marxist.

Psychotherapists could reasonably argue that these disputes are of little relevance to them but whether Bakhtin wrote the Voloshinov texts is a relevant consideration when considering the overall philosophical and ethical implications of his work for the enterprise of psychotherapy. And, if Voloshinov's contribution is a separate and distinctive one, then it should be acknowledged as such.

The collapse of the Soviet Union has had a profound effect on Bakhtin scholarship, which has led to greater contact between scholars in the former Soviet Union and scholars in the West. However, the opening up of previously unavailable archives has served to complicate even further the picture regarding the circumstances of Bakhtin's life and the authorship of the disputed texts. The revelations about the falsity of some of Bakhtin's claims about his own ancestry and educational record and his failure to fully acknowledge his intellectual debt to others makes his claim to have written the Voloshinov texts even more problematic.

Brian Poole, a Canadian scholar who has worked extensively on the primary sources used by Voloshinov and Bakhtin from the Soviet archive, has argued that while the neo-Kantian philosopher Ernst Cassirer was an unacknowledged source for both Bakhtin and Voloshinov, his influence in Voloshinov's texts is evident several years before it became apparent in texts authored by Bakhtin. On this basis Poole states categorically that:

> Bakhtin did not write Voloshinov's works (Poole, 2001, p. 127)

Poole's work has not only been a source of embarrassment for Bakhtin scholars who had failed to recognise his debt to German philosophy but has also added further complexities to the debates between Western and Russian scholars and between the "Westernisers" and "slavophiles" in Russia. In illuminating Bakhtin's sources, Poole demonstrates a continuity between his earlier "philosophical" works and his later "sociological" and linguistic work that confounds those critics who argue for a single interpretation. In drawing attention to Bakhtin's unacknowledged sources, Poole upsets those Russian scholars who wish to position him entirely within a Slavic tradition. But far more importantly, Poole exposes the readings of Bakhtin that:

> resemble pathological forms of identification and projection (Poole, 2001, p. 123)

and demonstrates how important it is to take account of his sources in any attempt to understand and interpret Bakhtin.

The appeal of Bakhtin for psychotherapists

Although Bakhtin cuts rather a romantic, even a tragic, figure to Western eyes, notwithstanding the uncertainties surrounding his life and the controversies over interpretation, the main appeal for psychotherapists is the priority given to intersubjectivity and dialogue in his writing. While he is not the only, or even the first, linguistic influence on psychotherapy, his account of subjectivity is altogether more benign and less alienating in comparison to post-structuralist and deconstructive influences in psychotherapy. The concept with which Bakhtin is most associated, dialogism, offers a warmer, more human alternative to what can seem like the cold anti-humanism of post-structuralism (Pollard, 2003). It allows for a "self" formed through social processes, which is at the same time embodied, dynamic, and creative (Gardener, 1998).

Psychotherapies influenced by post-structuralism draw attention to how language, in the broader sense of discourse, is a constraining force that limits the subject positions individuals can adopt, that limits what can be said and therefore what can be thought and that is therefore inextricably bound up with the exercise of power. Rather than discourse being the means whereby subjectivity is expressed, Foucault (1970) saw it as constitutive of subjectivity thereby undermining notions of human agency, individual responsibility as well as individual creativity. Similarly Derrida's deconstruction eliminated people entirely from the creation of meaning which is purely a product of the free play of signifiers (there is nothing outside of the text). For Derrida (1978), the ambiguity of language leads to a perpetual slippage between intention and meaning. Meaning is always changed by what follows in the chain of signification and is therefore always deferred. While this bears comparison with Bakhtin's (1984) well known aphorism that there is neither a first nor a last word, Bakhtin's account of the ambiguity of language can seem a far more optimistic one that stresses the formative role of human subjects in the continual creation and recreation of meaning, while also fully acknowledging the role of language in forming subjectivity. Deconstructive approaches focus on the workings of power and the consequent alienation that insinuates its way into the therapeutic relationship, while Bakhtin seems to offer the promise of freedom and self-actualisation through a benign intersubjective relationship with another.

Bakhtin appears to emphasise the active and unique use of language by its speakers. While the self is a social being formed in the network of social and communicative relationships, it is also an active, responsive self. Rather than discourses being static and constraining, they are constantly being re-created and so have the capacity to be heretical, subversive or radical and as such constitute a vital instrument in social struggles. It is easy to see how Bakhtin, in apparently emphasising both the social nature of consciousness and the creative dynamism of human language use, appeals to both psychotherapists and scholars of liberal and libertarian left persuasions, as it allows for both individual agency and the possibility of change, whether personal or political. However, Bakhtin's view of popular culture and the redemptive powers of language can seem overly optimistic as it takes no account of the differing amounts of linguistic capital that accrue to different groups thus conferring either advantage or disadvantage in the struggle over meaning and value (Lane, 1997).

Conclusion

Poole's research has lead to a "most interesting crisis" in Bakhtin studies (Lock, 1999), which will no doubt intrigue scholars for many more years. Poole underlines Russian scholars' emphasis on the importance of understanding Bakhtin in his context; when evaluating the appropriation of Bakhtinian ideas by psychotherapists, it is also important to understand these ideas both in the wider context of Bakhtin's fluctuating reputation and the social context in which psychotherapy is practised.

The increasingly complex debates about Bakhtin complicate attempts to appropriate some of his ideas in the service of psychotherapy for the following reasons:

If, as Makhlin (1997) argues, the state of Bakhtin scholarship demands a suspension of judgement about the meaning of his most important concepts, then how can psychotherapists justify the use of one meaning over any other?

If there is, as many scholars argue, an overall coherence in Bakhtin's works, psychotherapists cannot selectively appropriate particular concepts without distortion by removal from their wider context.

Bakhtin's complex relationship to his sources, which has only been briefly explored here, makes any interpretation of meaning more problematic and risks the erroneous attribution to Bakhtin of ideas that were derived from others.

While one of Bakhtin's central concerns was the relationship between self and other, he never addressed the question of this relationship in psychotherapy.

While the extent to which Bakhtin's Russian Orthodox faith influenced his writing is disputed, it raises questions about the incorporation of his ideas into a secular model of psychotherapy.

Notes

1 For a more detailed Timeline of events in Bakhtin's life and the lives of others in his circle see Brandist, C., Shepherd, D., & Tihanov, G. (2004)
2 Vitalli Makhlin (1997) advocates a suspension of judgement with regard to what he refers to as the most popular but least understood of Bakhtin's terms as part of a necessary reorientation if Bakhtin is to be *reconstructed* in the social, cultural and intellectual context of 1920's Soviet Union.
3 Sergei Bocharov (1995), a contemporary of Gasparov disagrees. He argues that the intellectual climate in Russia at the time the Dostoevsky book was first published in 1929 was unreceptive although it was better received abroad. It became *timely* when the revised version was published in 1963.
4 Voloshinov's Marxist approach to linguistics was apparently too sophisticated for his contemporaries under Stalin and *Freudianism* and *MPL* sank without trace until the 1960s, a fact that Matejka (1973) refers to as an intellectual tragedy. He is now considered to have been less influenced by Bakhtin than previously thought and his specialism as a post-graduate student was literature not linguistics. He was also a poet and musician He died of tuberculosis in his thirties (Shepherd, 2004).
5 Subsequently revised and republished in 1963 as Problems of Dostoevky's Poetics.

CHAPTER TWO

Bakhtin, Dialogism, and European Philosophy

The previous chapter introduced the field of Bakhtin studies, drawing particular attention to the potential problems of interpreting Bakhtinian ideas for the practice of psychotherapy. This chapter discusses dialogism, the Bakhtinian concept that has been most influential in psychotherapy theory. This necessitates some exploration of the many meanings that have been attributed to dialogism as well as the overall context in which Bakhtin developed his ideas. Bakhtin did not write in isolation but in dialogue with other thinkers as others have subsequently written in dialogue with him, so some acknowledgement is needed of Bakhtin's relationship with European philosophy in order to contextualise his thinking. As Hirschkop (1999) wrote, interpretations that put Bakhtin into *solitary confinement* (136) are both inaccurate and an oversimplification of his writing. Far from being a thinker in isolation, Bakhtin was swimming with some of the dominant philosophical currents of his time.

Although a classicist by training, Bakhtin and others of his generation wrote and studied under the reigning influence of Kant and is now considered by most scholars[1] to have been a fellow traveller with the diffuse but highly influential philosophical movement known as the neo-Kantians. Bakhtin's dialogism originates in his dialogue with Kant and is best understood, in this context, as a philosophical idea about nature of meaning rather than as a linguistic concept. An important aspect of Kant's influence on Bakhtin is Kant's concern with our relationship with the world, which led to Bakhtin's profound interest in how we interpret the world and our experience in it (Holquist, 1990). The second half of the 19th century saw a "return to Kant" in German philosophy in an attempt to recover a unity between philosophy, the natural sciences, and culture and as a reaction against individualism and psychologism.[2] Anyone struggling to relate Bakhtin's early works, with their concerns with aesthetics, authoring, and creative activity, to psychotherapy should bear in mind that the early Bakhtin was trying to overcome the separation of art from life and culture from science in an attempt to recover a unity of experience and being. Psychology, like the other human sciences, only emerged as a separate discipline with its own body of knowledge in the early 19th century, largely divorced from its parent discipline of philosophy. Since Freud, psychotherapy has traditionally been much more catholic in its knowledge base but, to the extent that it has relied on psychological theories, this has constrained its effectiveness in understanding and finding solutions to human problems and has led to a certain degree of introverted navel-gazing among its practitioners. In his emphasis on human difference and the uniqueness of each human being, Bakhtin exposes some of the limitations of approaching any encounter with another individual with preconceptions.

While Bakhtin shared Kant's ethical concerns with individual responsibility, he did not share Kant's belief that behaviour should be governed by *a priori* considerations such as duty and law. Instead, Bakhtin was concerned with the particular, unique, and therefore creative aspects of each situation. Greg Neilson (2000), who gives a useful overview of Bakhtin's relationship to Kant, points out that an ethics that relies on transcendental universals cannot also take into account cultural and other forms of individual difference. He argues that *by driving a wedge between knowledge and experience (41)* Kant obscures the possibility of the answerability that comes from an unmediated, intersubjective engagement with another. This has obvious implications for psychotherapeutic interventions that are driven by theory or protocol. The early Bakhtin wrote that psychology:

> ... is studied in complete abstraction from the axiological weight of the I and the other—in abstraction from their uniqueness ... The inward given is not something to be contemplated, but something investigated, without any value judgement, within the prescribed (to be attained) unity of psychological regularity conforming to psychological laws. [1990, p. 114]

As Neilson observes, answerability directs the focus away from the normative i.e. theoretical, to the creative aspects of the act. In psychotherapy, responsive understanding can be a creative activity only if it is not driven primarily by *a priori* theoretical considerations. Bakhtin recasts Kantian ethics in a phenomenological light that fully recognises the other's subjectivity and different point of view and that demands a dialogic and participatory engagement with no preconceptions. Bakhtin's first foray into Kantian ethics was in his earliest work *Towards a Philosophy of the Act*, in which he argued against a universal and recurrent theory of ethical action in favour of an ethics grounded in a responsiveness to the unique and unrepeatable aspects of each human encounter. As Holquist (1993) explains in his introduction, Bakhtin is trying to "detranscendentalise" Kant; whereas Kant's overarching principles are a safeguard against unbridled relativity in moral judgements, they are also abstract in the sense that they do not take any account of the local and specific. Bakhtin is trying to recover

> ... the naked immediacy of experience as it is felt from within the utmost particularity of a specific life, the molten lava of events as they happen. [1993, p. x]

The most influential group of neo-Kantians was based at the University of Marbourg in Germany. Bakhtin makes frequent reference to philosophers from this school, most notably two Jewish philosophers, Herman Cohen and his pupil Ernst Cassirer. Bakhtin was particularly influenced in this respect by Matvai Kagan,[3] one of the members of the "Bakhtin Circle" who, unlike Bakhtin, had actually met and studied under Cohen and Cassirer at Marbourg, which so impressed Bakhtin that he pretended to have done so himself (Shepherd, 2004). In his obituary of Cohen,[4] Kagan writes that the neo-

Kantians wanted to resurrect Kant as a central figure in philosophy so as to re-establish philosophy as a means of understanding the unity of all the different domains of life, as a theory of experience or being. In Cohen's thinking religion and philosophy were inseparable domains of experience that were themselves inseparable from the rest of life. Bakhtin (1990) adapted the neo-Kantianism of Cohen to work out his ideas about the relationship between self and other: thus Bakhtin believed that the sense of self is constituted in its inevitable relationship with the other and aesthetic activity is an expression of this relationship between self and other, not the result of a solitary consciousness (Dentith, 1995). When the term dialogism is used in this way, it does not refer to a description of speech but represents a philosophical idea concerned with the nature of meaning, derived from phenomenology (Hirschkop, 1999):

> Dialogism is indeed about the two-sided aspect of meanings, but not in any sense necessarily about two people. Rather it refers to what other writers would call the intersubjective quality of all meaning: the fact that it is always found in the space between expression and understanding, and that this space—the "inter" separating subjects—is not a limitation but the very condition of meaningful utterance. . . . it is no more than the philosophical working out of the idea of communication . . . as a social act rather than the monological expression of a solitary individual. [Hirschkop, 1999, pp. 4–5]

Cohen was concerned with the relationship between man and God as opposed to Kant's concern with the relationship between mind and the world, but he also shared Kant's transcendentalism in that the world can only be said to exist as a subject of thought (Holquist, 1990). Although both Cohen and Bakhtin tried to reconcile the dualism implied in Kant's division of mind and world, Bakhtin's concerns were materialist compared to Cohen's and grounded in the relationship of human beings with each other. Bakhtin and Cohen were both concerned with man's experience of God, but for Bakhtin meaning, including spiritual meaning, was found and created in the space between people. For Bakhtin there was no transcendental position; our awareness depends entirely on where we are situated. While both Cohen and Bakhtin were struggling to find a unity whether between the human and the divine or between I and thou, the most important attraction in Cohen's thought for Bakhtin was his emphasis on the fluidity of experience and on the *process* of activity rather than closure (Clark & Holquist, 1984).

In a subsequent work *Author and Hero in Creative Activity (Author and Hero)*, Bakhtin is concerned with understanding how the self can only be understood in relationship to another self and how consciousness itself is a relational phenomenon. *Author* and *Hero* are terms borrowed from literary theory but used by Bakhtin as philosophical categories (Nikolaev, 1998) to analyse the ethics of how two human beings relate to and co-create each other. If read as a description of what we should aspire to in psychotherapy, Bakhtin's early writing seems extraordinarily prescient:

> ... the author's loving removal of himself from the field of the hero's life, his clearing of the whole field of life for the hero and his existence, and—the compassionate understanding and consummation of the event of the hero's life in terms of real cognition and ethical action by a detached, unparticipating beholder. [1990, p. 15]

Bakhtin also writes about the importance of the *Author* separating his own values from those of his *Hero*:

> I must empathise or project myself into this other human being, ... see his world axiologically from within him as he sees his world; I must put myself in his place and then, after returning to my own place "fill in" his horizon through that excess of seeing which opens out from this, my own place outside of him. [1990, p. 25]

Although Bakhtin is almost seen as synonymous with dialogism in some contexts, he neither invented nor discovered the concepts of dialogism and intersubjectivity. It was Martin Buber who made the concepts of dialogism and intersubjectivity central to European philosophy in 1923, with his collection of essays entitled *The Dialogical Principle*. The I–Thou relationship was a major interest of several European philosophers in the early 20th century, including Buber, although their influence on Bakhtin did not become apparent until scholars were allowed access to the Bakhtin archives in the 1990s. While Bakhtin admired Buber, they had different conceptions of the I–Thou relationship, a subject that has led to considerable debate among Bakhtin scholars.[5] A major difference seems to be that, despite what most scholars now acknowledge was his Christian Orthodox faith, Bakhtin's concerns were secular compared to Buber's. Emerson (2000) observes that, for Bakhtin, God is a possibility not a given; unlike Kant or Buber, Bakhtin did not look upwards for moral authority but sideways, in and between people. There is no one who is supposed to "know" for us and to pretend otherwise is, in Bakhtin's terms, an "alibi for being", an abdication of our responsibility for our own conduct in the world.

Hirschkop (1999) maintains that Bakhtin's major achievement was not his interest in dialogism as such but his use of it to reinterpret European culture. Moreover, he argues that the importance of dialogism in Bakhtin's work has been overemphasised at the expense of his other ideas and that the concept of dialogism has been misinterpreted by some of Bakhtin's most ardent followers. According to Hirschkop, their mistake has been to invest it with mystical or redemptive qualities while overlooking the fact that dialogism is a historical development. Hirschkop is sceptical of the liberal view expressed by Morson and Emerson (1990) that dialogism is merely the rules of everyday conversation "writ large" and, as such, a paradigm for a moral and ethical community.

Bakhtin's turn to language

The philosophical and phenomenological concerns of Bakhtin's early work are displaced in his later work by concerns with language and sociology. Scholars disagree as to whether or not this is due to the harsh political realities in the Soviet Union that led to Bakhtin disguising his work to bypass censorship. Brian Poole's (2001) dating of Bakhtin's early work suggests otherwise: according to his chronology, Bakhtin was still writing *Author and Hero* when he began work on *Problems of Dostoevsky's Art*, the book that straddles both his early phenomenological concerns and his later concern with language. Hirschkop (2001b) argues that Voloshinov, who studied linguistics while Bakhtin was studying phenomenology and German aesthetics, profoundly influenced Bakhtin's own "linguistic turn". Voloshinov's

Marxism and the Philosophy of Language was published in 1928, the same year as *Problems of Dostoevsky's Art*. It was at this stage in his development that Voloshinov introduced Bakhtin to the German neo-Kantian, Ernst Cassirer. Cassirer's major work was concerned with "symbolising forms"—language, myth, religion—unique to mankind and considered by Cassirer to be of equal importance to understanding the world as science. These "symbolisations" are both created by human beings and constitute their reality. Bakhtin discovered that he could explore the same ethical concerns of his phenomenological work through the medium of language and stylistics and unlike phenomenology, which is rooted in the here and now, language has a history that both reflects and is created by social conditions. The different styles of language, such as parody, skaz (vernacular) and free indirect discourse can also reflect the relationships between *authors* and *heroes* in a way that is easy to understand (Hirschkop, 2001b).

Bakhtin was not alone in his interest in language, nor was he the first to make the "linguistic turn", which became the defining feature of 20th century European philosophy. He was part of a widespread turn to language in Russia and across Europe. Through his close collaboration with Voloshinov, Bakhtin could be said to have anticipated and influenced the later but crucial linguistic turn in French philosophy.[6] However, psychotherapy theorists have generally tended to see Bakhtin in isolation from the work of other linguistic theorists whose work is highly relevant to a critical appreciation of Bakhtin. For example, Mikael Leiman (2000a) apparently dismisses both structuralism and post-structuralism, in particular Lacan and Derrida, as having merely elaborated on or modified what he considers to be the Cartesian roots of Saussure's concept of the sign. Anthony Easthope (1991) argued the opposite case, that it is Voloshinov/Bakhtin who are unable to elude Cartesian dualism because of their rejection of the Freudian unconscious and in doing so attribute all non-conscious phenomena to the body or "animal instincts", thus perpetuating a mind/body dualism, and he considers that this problem is resolved in Lacan's reworking of Saussure and Freud. However, Easthope assumes Bakhtin and Voloshinov approach this subject from the same perspective and does not take account of the importance Bakhtin attached to the body in relation to self-hood.

Whereas some writers see Bakhtinian dialogism as in conflict with and by implication superior to post-structuralism (e.g. Birkett, 1998, Leiman, 2000a) they could also be regarded as complementary theories that arose in different social and political contexts. Bakhtin wrote under conditions of Stalinist repression and censorship in which the unpredictability and open-endedness of dialogism was more democratic than and a threat to Stalinist monologism. It has even been argued that Bakhtin's terminology and aesthetics cannot be understood in isolation from the dominant aesthetic, ideology and politics of the Soviet Union under Stalin (Zima, 1999). In Western liberal democracies under economic conditions often referred to as advanced or late capitalism, the notion of individual freedom and responsibility has become a cornerstone of the state and a justification for many of its activities. Formerly subversive and potentially revolutionary activities have been absorbed and commercialised. A post-structuralist critique that draws attention to the illusory aspects of this freedom and to the constraining and constitutive role of discourse is, in this context, arguably more subversive. For Bakhtin, it was the liberatory and creative potential of language that was more important, while for the post-structuralists it was role of discourse in both constituting and managing subjectivity.

Although dialogism is the concept with which Bakhtin is most widely associated, this term is never clearly defined by Bakhtin and seems to gather to itself a variety of meanings. At its simplest dialogism can refer merely to the presence of more than one voice in a literary text. It is closely related to heteroglossia, the interaction of different "social languages" often in ideological conflict with each other, and polyphony, the presence of different "voices" that are supposedly independent of the author who created them and are capable of answering back. There is considerable slippage and variation in the way these terms as well as the term dialogism and its antonym, monologism, are used in the writings of Bakhtin and his exponents. To get to grips with dialogism, it is necessary to understand Bakhtin's concept of the utterance. For Bakhtin, the utterance is the basic unit of analysis in a dialogical approach to language. An utterance is quite distinct from a grammatical entity such as a sentence or a phrase, as it is the speech of people in interaction with each other. Utterances are always spoken from a perspective and as such embody values or ideology. Each utterance generates a response and is itself shaped by the anticipation of a response and contains within it a response to previous utterances (Bakhtin, 1986, pp. 67–71).

Dialogism could be understood variously as: a relationship between utterances; the dual or multivoicedness of a single utterance; or a relationship between different intentions, values or ideologies. However, there is also ambiguity in Bakhtin's writing between dialogism in the novel and everyday speech, where it refers to the presence of two or more voices in an utterance, and in language, where it can be seen as the defining quality of all language and takes on a wider meaning. This would include: the echoes of past voices; the shared creation of meaning between speaker and listener; and the utterance as a response to past utterances. An important question is whether dialogism is to be understood as: a constant feature of the utterance; the relationship between utterances; a historical phenomenon concerning the clash of opposing genres, styles and ideologies; or perhaps all of these (Hirschkop, 1989). Dialogism in this sense is both a characteristic of all discourse and a particular argumentative practice within it (Hirschkop, 1986).

By the late 1990s Hirschkop had arrived at a more specific and limited account in which dialogism is an achievement of modern Europe as expressed in the generic form of the novel (Hirschkop, 1999). Bakhtin's own account in his essay *Discourse and the Novel*, in which he develops his mature sociological account of language, would suggest that all language is inherently dialogic but it is the ability to analyse it as such that is a historical development:

> It is precisely those aspects of any discourse (the internal dialogic quality of discourse, and the phenomena related to it), not yet sufficiently taken into account and fathomed in all the enormous weight they carry in the life of language . . . [Bakhtin, 1981, p. 269]

An even more dynamic account of dialogism is the oppositional forces found in the natural and social worlds based on the binary opposition of centrifugal forces that strive for difference, variety and change and the centripetal forces that strive for unity, stability and stasis (De Santis, 2001). Heteroglossia is reflected in the tension between centrepetal and centrifugal tendencies:

> ... alongside the verbal-ideological centralisation and unification the uninterrupted process of decentralisation and disunification go forward. Every concrete utterance of a speaking subject serves as a point of where centrifugal as well as centrepetal forces are brought to bear. The process of centralisation, of unification and disunification, intersect in the utterance. [Bakhtin, 1981, p. 272]

In Bakhtin's earlier writing there is an ideological and teleological progression from monologism to dialogism as distinct world views, while in his later work there is a dynamic as opposed to a static view of monologism and dialogism as being in active historical conflict, a conflict that would itself be dialogical (Crowley, 1996). The monological world view gives priority to the idea, which is either affirmed or repudiated, and therefore is unable to encompass consciousnesses in interaction (Bakhtin 1984, 79–81). In contrast the dialogical world view gives priority to the freedom and indeterminacy that Bakhtin (1984, 63) finds in the novels of Dostoevsky.

Another meaning or aspect of dialogism is the interaction of the contemporary social and historical contexts in an utterance, both of which are aspects of heteroglossia (Vice, 1997). However, as Vice suggests, this poses a problem; if dialogism is an inherent property of all language, how could any form of language use be monologic? Pechey (1989) seems to answer this question by suggesting that all discourse, even discourse which is monological in its outward form, is actually animated by the inner dialogism of all discourse. This observation is related to what Pechey refers to as the "migration" of the dialogism-monologism binary across different contexts in Bakhtin's writing or the dialogism of dialogism itself. Monologism could be understood as something that is only attributed retrospectively to a discourse or literary form:

> Monologism is, then, never an absolute: as the false consciousness of discourse it is both practically modified and theoretically exposed by the dialogism it vainly seeks to occlude. [Pechey, 1989, p. 50]

These complexities perhaps underlie the apparent confusion as to whether the term dialogical is descriptive (the way something is) or prescriptive (the way, it should ideally be). Crowley (1996) accuses Bakhtin of absolutism in his celebration of diversity and plurality as always ethically superior to the unity and systemacticity of Saussure's vision. For Crowley, Bakhtin employs his concepts at such a level of abstraction that historical specificity is lacking and so questions concerning the relationship between language and power are not fully answered. Pechey (1989) makes a similar point when he says that Bakhtin did not succeed in resolving the relationship between discourse and power, as any socio-political hegemony, however pluralist, always asserts itself against the centrifugal forces in ideology that are opposed to it. Bakhtin's assertion that English, French and German are democratic heteroglot languages may therefore be true to a point, but this ignores the historical reality of, for example, the role of these European languages in colonial exploitation and the lived experience of people who speak them. Similarly the heteroglot qualities of North American culture become a hegemonic monologism from the perspective of the majority of the world's population, who are exploited by and receive no benefit from global capitalism. Pechey (1989) suggests that a weakness in Bakhtin is inadequate theorisation of the historical organisation of monoglot hegemony and a consequent overestimation of the strength of the diverse and carnivalised forces opposed to it.

A related observation is made by Hirschkop (1986), when he comments on Bakhtin's overestimation of the subversive potential of the novel because he fails to consider adequately the institutional conditions that gave rise to its existence. As Pechey (1989) explains, Bakhtin's philosophical starting point was German idealism, which was inspired by the bourgeois revolutions of France and England, a phase of development never experienced in Russia, with the relatively quick transition from feudalism to Soviet-style communism. Bourgeois hegemony, as opposed to feudal and Stalinist hegemony, is actually nourished by the dialogism of the novel that, while offering new subject positions to its readers, either does nothing to challenge established power relations or incorporates opposing ideologies as part of a wider process of social hegemony that is itself dialogical (Pechey, 1989). In liberal democracies dialogism ends where repression starts, for example in the imperial relationship with colonised people or in one of its contemporary equivalents in the European states' treatment of refugees and migrants.

Conclusion

This chapter has attempted to give a brief overview of the philosophical and intellectual context in which Bakhtin developed his concept of dialogism and the many different ways in which the term can be understood both in Bakhtin's writing and in the writing of his exponents in order to facilitate a critical evaluation of the concept of the Dialogical Self and dialogical psychotherapy discussed in the next chapter.

It has also further clarified the relationship between Bakhtin and Voloshinov referred to in Chapter One: as well as being a considerable influence on the development of Bakhtin's ideas about language, Voloshinov was a separate and distinctive author in his own right. They were both young men when they wrote the works that were to become so influential to subsequent generations of scholars and the originality of their ideas and the prodigious breadth of the knowledge they demonstrate reflects the vigour and diversity of the intellectual circles in which they moved.

Notes

1 Hirschkop (1999) cites evidence from the Russian archives of the continued influence of Kant and the neo- Kantians both in Bakhtin's texts and records of interviews with Bakhtin in the 1970s (footnote 143). Poole(1995) argues that the neo-Kantian influence both extends into and increases in Bakhtin's later "carnival" phase with its social collectivity and eternal life in a cultural sense (cited in Emerson, 2000, 231).
2 This refers to experimental psychology's attempt to displace philosophy during the second half of the 19th century (Hirschkop, 2001).
3 Kagan's daughter, Iudif Kagan (1998), wrote an account of her father's friendship with Bakhtin from 1918–1921 that vividly conveys their intellectual collaboration and also the appalling constraints on intellectual activity of any kind, due to persecution under Stalin.
4 Printed in translation for the first time in Brandist, C., Shepherd, D. and Tihanov, G. (2004) The Bakhtin Circle.
5 For a summary of these debates, see Emerson, C. (2000), 225–232.
6 The important link is Roman Jakobson, a member of the Prague School of linguistics, who was considerably influenced by Voloshinov's *Marxism and the Philosophy of Language*.

CHAPTER THREE

Bakhtin, the Dialogical Self and Dialogical Psychotherapy

Just as interest in critical theory in North America created the conditions necessary for the reception of Bakhtin in literary studies (Wachtel, 2000), the development of a psychology of the "self", inspired by James Mead, both coincided with Bakhtin's dialogic conception of consciousness (Hermans, 2004) and paved the way for what has come to be known as the "Dialogical Self". The first part of this chapter will give a brief overview of the "Dialogical Self" and the importance of Bakhtin's analysis of linguistic style in the modern novel in his interpretation of dialogism. The second part of the chapter examines some of the ways in which dialogical concepts derived from Bakhtin have been used in conjunction with two different models of psychotherapy; the third part compares dialogical approaches with other linguistic approaches to psychotherapy.

In psychotherapy, Bakhtin has become associated with a concept of the self that is "dialogical" i.e. that consists of a number of different "voices" that speak to each other from different "positions" or points of view (Stiles, 1997, Hermans 1996, 2004). These voices may have a historical origin, for example the voice of a parent, or they could have a more general, societal origin such as social class or social expectations of women or men, or be the voices of groups in society that we belong to such as a political party, football club or a religious faith. William Stiles (1997) suggests that the concept of "voice" can be understood as akin to that of role, in a sociological sense, or as that of object, in the psychoanalytic sense, or even, from a Jungian perspective, as an archetype:

> Each of us seems to carry many voices, representing people or ideas or events that we've encountered ... Some voices such as belief systems or psychological theories may transcend individuals so that the same voice speaks within many of us. Psychological, intellectual, emotional, social and cultural development can be understood as conversations among such voices. [Stiles, 1997, p. 154]

Voices can be said to exist only in relation to other voices, for example a child voice in relation to a parental voice and vice versa, and in this way voices co- define one another. Some voices may be in conflict with each other and some voices may be much more powerful than others, a reflection of the institutionally, culturally and politically determined hierarchies in society. The more complex and heterogeneous a society is, the more numerous and varied the different voices that comprise the self are likely to be. Not all of these voices will necessarily be easily available for conscious reflection, partly because we can only be aware of a limited range of mental activities at any particular time and also because some voices may be repressed or submerged by other voices. These disallowed or disowned voices will, nevertheless, find a way of making themselves heard, which, in psychoanalytic terms, could be understood as the return of the repressed (Cooper, 2004).

The dialogical self, sometimes known as the "polyphonic" self, is inspired by Bakhtin's concept of the polyphonic novel and, in particular, the novels of Dostoevsky as described in *Problems of Dostoevsky's Poetics* (1984). This novelistic form encompasses a plurality of different and opposing points of view, embodied in independent characters that are not mere ciphers for the authorial voice but capable of answering back on their own terms (Hermans, 1996). The relationship between these different voices or viewpoints is dialogic: a dialogical relationship differs from a logical relationship in that the same words spoken by a different person or the same person from a different temporal or spatial position have a different meaning even though the words themselves may be identical. Bakhtin's particular interpretation of Dostoevsky's novels, especially in his later works, was that as an author Dostoevksy did not seek to determine, control or "finalise" the characters in his novels but allowed them the freedom to speak for themselves without being subject to a controlling, all seeing, authorial voice. Dostoevsky's artistic relation to the characters in his novels is described by Bakhtin as:

> ... a fully realised and thoroughly consistent dialogic position, one that affirms the independence, internal freedom, unfinalisability and indeterminacy of the hero. [1984, p. 63]

As Hermans (1996) points out, the inner world or dialogical consciousness of Dostoevsky's characters is revealed by transforming a thought into an utterance that is answered by another utterance of a real or imagined other, speaking from a different "position". In dialogical relationships the spatial "positioning" of characters or voices is as important as the narrative or temporal dimension. Dostoevsky depicts a plurality of simultaneous, independent heterogeneous consciousnesses and what is important, according to Bakhtin (1984), is their interaction and interdependence.

It follows from this that the polyphonic or dialogical self has no central "I" in the centre or in charge and is therefore a decentred or even fragmented self, as well as being a thoroughly social self suffused with the voices of others; a society of voices within a society of voices. It can even be conceived of as a multiple self, with each voice being the voice of a separate "self" within the self. The "I" can speak from different "selves" in different positions and with different experiences and stories to tell about those experiences at different times. These different "I" positions can both speak to each other in "internal" conversations and have external conversations with other external voices. The dialogical self, far from being a static or fixed entity, is therefore a self in a process of constant movement between different positions in dialogue, both internally and externally, evolving in interaction with the social environment. Its boundaries are permeable, constantly exchanging meanings with other voices and other "selves". Consciousness is therefore not a property of the individual but a shared social phenomenon:

> To be means to be for another and through the other, for oneself. A person has no internal sovereign territory, he is wholly and always on the boundary; looking inside himself, he looks into the eyes of another or with the eyes of another. [Bakhtin, 1984b, p. 287]

The modern novel and psychotherapy

Hirschkop (1999, 2001) has drawn attention to the importance of the modern novel in the evolution of Bakhtin's thought. He argues that without the novel, Bakhtin would have had difficulty translating his phenomenology of the relationship between author and hero into a linguistic relationship or dialogism. As discussed in the previous chapter, the modern novel itself is an artistic form uniquely adapted to capture both the ways in which human actions bring about the accelerating pace of change that characterises societies under capitalism and how human consciousness and actions are themselves affected by those changes. The distinctiveness of the modern novel that sets it apart from previous literary forms such as the classical tragedy or epic is the medley of styles expressed by different voices, which allows the movement between different subjective positions (Lodge, 2006) and the intermingling of the authorial voice with the thoughts and speech of the characters. Unlike other artistic forms such as theatre, cinema, music and the visual arts, the novel permits a representation of consciousness from the "inside". Apart from our most intimate conversations, it is from the novel that many of us learn about and reach a greater understanding of the intricacies of human consciousness and how this is inextricably bound up with social interaction and the pace of social change. The gifted novelist is able to use acute powers of observation of other people refracted through an awareness of their own "inner" experience to depict the workings of consciousness and its interaction with the world in a way that other artistic forms can only hint at, allowing us a window on life that was unavailable to many earlier generations. The rapid advances in cognitive neuroscience over the past two decades may have gone a long way towards the demystification of consciousness but, as David Lodge (2002) observes, neuroscientists can explain how consciousness works but they cannot tell us what it feels like, something that is inaccessible to scientific investigation.

Modern prose stylists are admired and enjoyed partly because in the process of writing well they use their powers of imagination to tell us what it is like to be someone else, allowing us to extend our awareness of things happening elsewhere beyond our own direct experience. Not all novels approach the depiction of consciousness in the same way and there is considerable variation in the ways authors position themselves in relation to their "heroes" which is an aspect of novelistic style. More complex novels show us different and opposing consciousnesses represented on the page by various stylistic devices. Bakhtin (1981) and Voloshinov (1986) identified some of these stylistic devices, which are themselves both inventions of modern prose fiction and indicative of the social changes they depict. As Lodge (1990) points out, the fully dialogic novel with multiple viewpoints, not dominated by an authorial voice, is a modern phenomenon.[1]

It is a struggle for anyone whose awareness extends beyond the everyday and parochial to comprehend the sheer variety and complexity of human lives and consciousnesses in the 21st century as well as those of earlier times. Reading novels is one way of trying to ground our own experiences in this overwhelming reality, which is so much bigger than we are. Imperfect though it is, the novel seems to be the best means available to us to imagine what it is to be someone else, to stand in someone else's shoes and see the world and their own relation to it, from their own point of view, including their attempts to conceal their thoughts and feelings from others, their self-deceptions and their necessarily partial understandings of the worlds they inhabit. As readers, we are not passive consumers of novels but creatively involved in evaluating and attributing meaning to the words on the page. To read actively is to enter into a dialogical relationship with what we are reading and hence to be changed by what we read.

I find it surprising therefore that psychotherapy has not so far drawn more fully on this rich resource of insights into the human psyche and its relationship with the social world so as to enhance its own understanding, as well as deepening its understanding of its own interventions and their impact. Bakhtin's early phenomenology and its evolution into dialogism were both attempts to defend philosophy against the encroachments of an individualising psychology and of the social sciences into its territory (Hirschkop, 2001). Psychotherapy that draws on a Bakhtinian understanding of a dialogical self and a consciousness that is dialogical, as processes in movement, could begin to reclaim psycho-therapy as a human social practice, rescuing it from the stranglehold of psychological theories that categorise, normalise and marginalise.

I and Thou

Despite the importance of the novel in Bakhtin's formulation of linguistic dialogism and its value as a repository of human consciousness, to reach a better understanding of Bakhtin's concept of the self, we need to go beyond the metaphor of the dialogical self as a collection of voices and back to its phenomenological origins in the I–Thou relationship in Bakhtin's earlier work: here we find not just the presence of the other in the self but our absolute need of the other and the other's need of us. For Bakhtin, without the other we are in a void and cannot exist. We can see ourselves only in what the other reflects back to us and we are entirely dependant on the other's transgredient position or outsideness in relation to us to "complete" us.[2] In this respect, the individual self is insufficient and a precondition of its existence is interdependency on other selves:

> ... we evaluate ourselves from the standpoint of others, and through others we try to understand and take into account what is transgredient to our own consciousness. Thus, we take into account the value of our outward appearance from the standpoint of the possible impression it may produce on the other ... In short, we are constantly and intently on the watch for reflections of our own life on the plane of other peoples' consciousness, and, moreover, not just reflections of particular moments of our life, but even reflections of the whole of it. [Bakhtin, 1990, pp. 15–16]

Bakhtin confined his analysis of interdependency to the Author-Hero or I–Thou relationship. This can give the misleading impression that we only need one other person to "complete" us; undoubtedly two people can see and understand more than one person on their own but this does not mean that this pairing is then self-sufficient. Far from it, incompleteness and interdependency extend outwards from our selves like the ripples when a stone is thrown into a pond. There is no point at which we become complete and could not learn more about ourselves from another perspective we have not encountered before. Like dialogicality, interdependency carries with it responsibility for our selves and towards others. As Leszek Koczanowicz (2000) explains, Bakhtin's concept of the social/dialogical self does not mean a self at the mercy of social forces without self-determination: on the contrary free will is paramount and consequently we have an ethical responsibility to and are accountable to others for our own conduct in the world. Some of the implications of this for the practice of psychotherapy will be discussed in the final chapter.

The dialogical self and dialogical psychotherapy

Psychotherapists from several different orientations invoke the concept of the dialogical self and endeavour to identify and work with different "voices" in the client's discourse. Some draw on several different influences at once and are therefore hard to classify. This ecumenical state of affairs is both interesting and confusing as different language is used to refer to the same phenomena, which can be conceptualised in different ways, and different methodologies deriving from these different conceptualisations can analyse the same data and come up with very different results (Selgado, 2004). Bakhtin is also invoked in conjunction with other dialogical theorists as well as with theorists who hold a very different position in relation to language. As in Bakhtin studies, there has been a proliferation of literature on the dialogical self and dialogical psychotherapy so the following account is necessarily highly selective: my focus here will be on how Bakhtin has been invoked by two different traditions within psychoanalytic thinking, Object Relations theory and Lacanian psychoanalysis. This choice was made because of their respective emphasis on need and desire, a theme that will be explored further in the following chapters.

Object Relations theories encompass a broad tradition within psychoanalysis in which there is an understanding of the self formed, from early infancy, in relationship with other selves that then become internalised and a template for future patterns of relationships, both intra-psychic and interpersonal. Significant relationships that meet the needs of the infant/child for nurture, attachment, social acculturation, emotional learning and validation are seen as creating the right conditions for optimal personality development and mental well-being in adult life. Conversely depriving, neglectful or abusive relationships are strongly associated with later depression, personality difficulties and mental distress. In contrast to traditional Freudian accounts that emphasised the Oedipus Complex and the role of the father in psycho/emotional development, there is a particular emphasis on the mother-child relationship and the father's role is often marginalised. While the emphasis on mothering has been seen as giving due recognition to the importance of the female contribution to child-rearing, it has also been seen by feminists as reinforcing women's role as mothers at the expense of other aspects of their lives, as well as perpetuating the psycho/emotional deprivation of girls and women in relation to boys and men from one generation to the next. Even so, given the right social conditions, for example if men and women were to share childcare equally, Object Relations theory holds out a glimmer of hope for relationships that can actually meet the needs of the child (Chodorow, 1978). In Object Relations theory, the emphasis on how the self is formed in relationship with the other lends itself particularly well to a dialogical approach.

Bakhtin and cognitive analytic theory

Cognitive analytic therapy, a relatively recent development in psychotherapy theory and practice, incorporates Object Relations theory into a structured, focused and relatively short-term therapy. It differs from more traditional psychodynamic approaches in its use of descriptions of observable phenomena rather than interpretations of unconscious processes. Cognitive analytic therapy has, perhaps to a greater extent than other schools, attempted to integrate dialogical concepts into a psychodynamic model and in the process has allowed Bakhtinian concepts to modify its original theoretical assumptions. Dialogical thinking has been assimilated to the extent that Anthony Ryle, the founder and principle theorist of cognitive analytic therapy, subsequently referred to it as having become a "semiotic object relations theory" (Ryle, 2000). Ryle sees the concept of the dialogic self both as an alternative to the Kleinian emphasis on instinctual drives and to cognitive models with their Cartesian assumptions of the psychological monad.

It is largely due to the work of Mikael Leiman and his collaboration with Ryle that the Bakhtinian influence in cognitive analytic theory has become particularly strong (Leiman, 1992, 1994a, 1994b, 1997, Ryle, 1991, 2001). Drawing on Vygotsky (1978), who proposed that meaning, which is contained in signs, is fundamental to the human mind and that the ability to use socially created signs in communication and in the regulation of mental processes is the defining aspect of human consciousness, Leiman (1995) then argued that the study of mental phenomena should never lose sight of meaning and the social and interpersonal origins of mental life. However, Leiman (1992) saw Vygotsky's concept of the sign as unduly linguistic and as benefiting from Winnicott's account of the early development of signs and their materiality. Similarly Winnicott's (1971) account of the creative nature of subjectivity, the concept of transitional objects and the origins of object use in intersubjective space, is enriched by Vygotsky's conceptions of sign-mediated activity. In a further synthesis of ideas, Leiman brings in the work of Bakhtin/Voloshinov. In Voloshinov's account, the universality of signs and their materiality—anything in human life can be a sign in that it can represent or signify something outside of itself—overcomes the limitation of Vygotsky's arbitrary distinction between tools and signs and his adoption of the Western epistemological distinction between signs and their representation. A basic property of the sign is its ability to mediate between two realities. Another property is that signs can only arise between two or more individuals who are organised socially in relation to each other. There is therefore a dialectical relationship between signs and socially organised persons, in which both signs and persons define each other and neither can be understood without the other.

Leiman's (1992) description of Bakhtin/Voloshinov's conception of language is summarised as follows: the word's entire function is being a sign and its meaning is created and develops within communication; the word is neutral as it can carry out any ideological function because it is the primary tool of human interaction and as a specifically human production is the ...

semiotic material of inner life—of consciousness. [Voloshinov, 1973, p. 14]

At this point Leiman sees a convergence between Voloshinov and Winnicott in that words, like transitional objects, take on meaning in the intersubjective space between individuals:

Keeping in mind that signs are true mediators of two interpenetrating realities, the notion of words as transitional objects becomes quite conspicuous. [Leiman, 1992, p. 219]

Leiman (1994b) recasts projective identification from a dialogic perspective, where very early interactions between infant and carer are mediated by non-verbal signs. In Klein's account of projective identification, the boundaries between self and other are blurred but instead of seeing this as a normal way of being for a baby, she attributes this blurring to negative internal states and hence sees projective identification as defensive. Leiman does not see projective identification as primarily defensive and sees the bodily metaphors used by Klein as unnecessary, although he does see in these an implicit recognition of the materiality of mediating signs. In Leiman's dialogic account, projective identification is seen as an aspect of the integrated repertoire of "joint action sequences" that are a necessary precursor to, and become the signs that mediate, reciprocal actions. One of the clinical implications of this is that patient and therapist experiences of blurred boundaries during particularly creative or destructive moments in therapy can be understood as "joint action sequences" mediated by non-verbal signs. Leiman (1995) argues that understanding the processes of early development and how signs emerge is essential to the understanding of how symbolic tools are created in therapeutic discourse.

Stiles (1997) introduced the concept of "voices" into the evolving notion of projective identification in the context of sign-mediated activity being developed between Ryle and Leiman. He clarifies the implication of the Bakhtinian social understanding of consciousness, i.e. that the separate self-contained individual of traditional psychology is replaced by the individual conceived of as a community of voices, roles and objects and that psychological phenomena breach and transcend individual boundaries. The relationship between voices and signs is that signs carry meaning between voices (Stiles, 1992) and the dynamic nature of this process contradicts what Stiles (1997) refers to as the "cognitive fallacy", the notion that information is passive, that memories are "retrieved" or perceptions are "processed" in the manner of a computer or a library. Information is experience and:

> ... experience begins with feelings, values and motives, capable of action, having a voice. [Stiles, 1997, p. 154]

Stiles agrees with Ryle and Leiman that projective identification is a normal though primitive mode of communication whereby people induce their feelings and motivations in others through non-verbal signs outside of awareness. He suggests that a complementary way of thinking about projective identification is a means whereby voices use other people for their intentions. No conscious awareness of how this is done is needed. Other people are used as extensions of the self in the way that hands are used to alter the physical environment. Projective identification is then understood as a means of expression for suppressed voices, voices unable to express themselves in words because they were silenced or because of painful or traumatic events. In clinical terms, establishing empathic communication, the exchange of signs between active voices in therapist and client, is an essential part of allowing these suppressed voices to join the community of voices and confront other voices on equal terms.

According to Leiman the importance of Bakhtin for psychotherapy lies in his dialogical view of the human psyche:

> Our mental life is formed in a responsive environment that meets our rudimentary expressions by an interpretative, or evaluative position. Such a complex event, mediated by socially formed signs, is constitutive to our thinking and acting in the world. It accounts for the quite peculiar way of directing our acts and our thoughts to an addressee even when nobody is visibly there. [Leiman, 1997, p. 139]

Bakhtin's dialogical view of mental life is both compatible with Winnicott's intersubjective understanding of mental life and the implicit dialogical understanding in Kleinian and other Object

Relations theorists of the importance of the other and the other's voice in mental life. Leiman proposes that the dynamic interaction between "objects" could be conceptualised as a "dialogical pattern" with "dialogic position" referring to where a voice is speaking from and "dialogic sequence" referring to the interaction between them. "Dialogic patterns" may be internal or external. Leiman describes the dialogical pattern as a highly abstracted snap shot of a dynamic process in which the dialogical patterns are themselves mediating voices in on-going action sequences.

Dialogical sequence analysis (DSA) was devised as a micro-analytic tool for understanding interpersonal patterns in the supervision of psychotherapy, patterns that are enacted in the client's life and re-enacted in conversation with the therapist. It facilitates reformulation of the client's problematic experiences using the conceptual tools of position, counterposition, dialogical pattern and self-state (Leiman & Stiles, 2001). The concept of the dialogical sequence relies on Bakhtin's/Voloshinov's theory of utterance which Leiman (1992) states allows Bakhtin to develop his ideas about the word as a "living sign" that becomes infused with other voices and conversations or dialogues as it travels through time. Leiman (1992, 1994) acknowledges the complexity of Bakhtin/Voloshinov's theory of utterance but does not elucidate this to any great extent.

Although the utterance was pivotal to Bakhtin's philosophy, it was Voloshinov who first defined it (Hirschkop, 1999). For Voloshinov (1986), the utterance, as distinct from a grammatical entity, was the real unit in the stream of language-speech. It is defined by its boundaries or by its beginning and end rather than its grammatical or linguistic construction and by the social situation in which it is spoken or written. An utterance, which can range from a single word to a long novel, always has an addressee and is a response to previous utterances and is thus always part of a continual stream of verbal communication. How an utterance is understood does not lie in the word itself but is dialogic or dependent on the response of the listener or addressee. Verbal communication can only be understood in the context of a specific social situation. Voloshinov's concept of the utterance is dialectical, a synthesis of "abstract objectivism" i.e. Saussurean formalist linguistics and "subjective individualism", the view that speech is a product of the psyche. The utterance is a thoroughly social phenomenon that is wholly determined by the immediate social situation and the broader social context.

Bakhtin also stresses the responsiveness of the utterance, the beginning and end of which is defined by a change of speaking subjects:

> Any understanding of live speech, a live utterance, is inherently responsive ... Any understanding is imbued with response and necessarily elicits it in one form or another ... sooner or later what is heard and actively understood will find its response in the subsequent speech or behaviour of the listener. [Bakhtin, 1986, pp. 68–69]

> Each utterance must be regarded as primarily a response to previous utterances of the given sphere ... Each utterance refutes, affirms, supplements and relies upon the others, presupposes them to be known, and somehow takes them into account ... Therefore, each kind of utterance is filled with various kinds of responsive reactions to other utterances ... [Bakhtin, 1986, p. 91]

For Voloshinov (1986) and Bakhtin (1981), the utterance cannot just be described or defined in semiotic or linguistic terms. It is a social phenomenon and as such is also unique and unrepeatable. It has a sensuous dimension that is beyond scientific classification or understanding:

> Indeed, any concrete discourse (utterance) finds the object at which it was directed already as it were overlain with qualifications, open to dispute, charged with value, already enveloped in an obscuring mist—or on the contrary, by the light of alien words that have already been spoken about it. It is entangled, shot through with shared thoughts, points of view, alien value judgements and accents ... The living utterance, having taken meaning and shape at a particular historical moment in a socially specific environment, cannot fail to brush up against thousands of living dialogic threads, woven by socio-ideological consciousness around the given object of utterance ... [Bakhtin, 1981, p. 276]

Leiman suggests that the analysis of the dialogical sequence, the exchange of voices that can be inferred from the patient's speech and behaviour, should become the principal tool for assessment and therapy in a dialogically oriented practice. However an account by Leiman & Stiles (2001), in which DSA is applied to the transcripts of therapeutic material in some early sessions to make a tentative formulation of the client's "self states",[3] is limited by its failure to make links to the socio-cultural context in which the therapy takes place: the client is a 42-year-old married woman who presents with depression. Two "self states" are identified from the transcripts. One is characterised by a dialogical position of controlling/demanding to a counterposition of striving, which the client refers to as "The Superwoman" and a "depressed" "self-state" in which the dialogical positions of blaming/critical and rejecting have counterpositions of distressed and rejected. These "self-states" are derived from *dialogical positions* the client appears to take in her own speech and her responses to the interventions of the therapist. The client relates how she struggles to persuade her husband to do his share of the housework and rather than make an issue of it, as she sees this as "trivial" she does it all herself and then feels resentful while also dismissing her feelings as invalid.

The wider context in which women feel under pressure to be "superwoman" for social and economic reasons and in which men feel that they can shirk domestic responsibilities is not referred to either by the therapist or the authors. The social aspects of the client's apparent belief that her own concerns with domestic issues are not important are not related to a wider discursive culture in which traditionally male activities and concerns are accorded more importance. Subsequently, although the client's talk is seen as dialogical as she moves between different *dialogical positions*, there is no consideration of how these positions or voices came to be spoken by this particular client at this particular historical time and place. As a result, although the client's talk is understood as social and dialogic in that more than one voice is heard, her problematic "self-states" are not related to a wider community of contemporary and historical voices beyond her own individual psyche. The therapeutic dyad is isolated from the social context in which they meet. There is no attempt to relate her distress to what David Smail (1993) refers to as the "distal" as opposed to "proximal" causes of personal distress, the recognition of which has political as well as personal implications. An explicit acknowledgement of the distal causes of individual distress, that involve the dimensions of power and frequently money, can help free clients from the self-blame that often compounds depression. Used in this way DSA becomes another tool for assessment or reformulation within a developmental framework in which the client, assisted by the therapist, progresses through the various stages of assimilation necessary for enhanced psychosocial functioning. There is little sense of the vast complex tapestry of interacting and conflicting voices conveyed by Bakhtin.

A much fuller account of DSA is developed by Leiman (2004) in which Bakhtin's theory of the utterance is more fully elucidated and used as a framework for a structural analysis of the therapeutic dialogue. The meaning of the client's utterance is understood as being wholly determined by who is speaking and to whom it is addressed. As well as potentially having several different addressees, a single utterance could also be "multivoiced" or spoken by different people who are positioned differently. Thus the client or author of an utterance can be in two or more "semiotic" positions within the same utterance, both with regard to the therapist and other addressees and also in relation to the referential content of the utterance. The concept of the "addressivity" of the utterance is seen as equivalent to the Freudian concept of transference but is more complex because of its multiple connotations. Clients are also frequently understood as addressing different aspects of themselves in the utterance, as well as speaking from different positions. These "self-reflections", which are evaluative and frequently judgemental, can be understood as "double voiced", in that the voice of a significant other(s) is overlaid with that of the client's voice, as well as being spoken from different aspects of the self. A further connection is made here with psychoanalysis in that the dialogic nature of the utterance is seen as addressing different objects in the self and the Kleinian defence of projective identification can be conceived of when the client unconsciously induces the therapist to speak with his or her voice, a phenomenon Ryle (1997) has referred to as an identifying countertransference; in Bakhtinian terms, a form of responsive understanding.

Positioning and counter-positioning are crucial to the analysis of the therapeutic dialogue and the client's utterances in DSA, but are extended to include the referential object of the utterance. In this way the utterance positions the speaker in relation to the addressee, who is then counter-positioned and also positions the speaker in relation to the subject matter of the utterance. Charting this dynamic and complex interplay of position and counter-position is the essence of DSA, so that repeated, inflexible or problematic positioning or dialogical patterns can be identified. Leiman (2004) clarifies how Bakhtin's concept of the utterance is used for a structural analysis of psychotherapy, but there is a lack of clarity with regard to the dialogical and the semiotic position, terms which are used interchangeably. The non-prescriptive open-endedness of Bakhtin's dialogism is thus displaced by the focus on fixed and inflexible dialogical patterns. Although the social and historical context of the encounter is not explicitly referred to, it appears to be implied in the emphasis on the multi-voicedness of the utterance. Here dialogism is both a tool of descriptive analysis and a goal of successful therapy, as indicated by an ability to employ a greater and more flexible range of dialogical sequences. Signs are understood as acquiring meaning only as part of social practice, linguistic or otherwise, but the relationship between the sign and the utterance remains unclear. Although Leiman (2004) stresses the capacity of anything, as well as words, to be semiotic material, he retains a dualistic stance towards language and other forms of dialogic activity and so the embodied nature of dialogical interaction is not fully recognised.

Despite the varied and sometimes incompatible ways in which dialogism can be understood, Leiman and Ryle do not suggest a clear working definition despite the frequent use of the adverbs "dialogic" and "dialogical" by Leiman (1992, 1994, 1997) and Ryle (2001, 2002). This lack of clarity in cognitive analytic theory may reflect the lack of any precise or consistent definition, highlighted by Hirschkop (1999), in Bakhtin's writing. Fortunately Cheyne & Tarulli offer what, from a psychotherapy perspective, could be a useful working definition:

> Dialogism in the broad sense ... valorises difference and otherness. It is a way of thinking about ourselves and the world that always accepts non-coincidence of stance, understanding and consciousness. In dialogism, the subversion by

difference, of movements towards unity and the inevitable fracturing of univocality into multi-voicedness represents the fundamental human condition. [1999, p. 11]

There is also a lack of theoretical clarity about the way Voloshinov and Bakhtin are used in cognitive analytic theory and, although there is considerable overlap between them, their differences and the way these differences have been interpreted are not acknowledged. There is an assumption that Bakhtin and Voloshinov spoke with the same voice and while Voloshinov's concept of the sign is discussed in depth, there is no similar explication of dialogism. Leiman (1992) acknowledges the disputes about the authorship of Voloshinov's works and allows for the possibility that they might actually be the work of Voloshinov rather than Bakhtin, but then proceeds on the assumption that Voloshinov's concept of sign is not only shared by Bakhtin but is found throughout his writing. Leiman then makes a further assumption and claims that this concept of the sign is a direct expression of Bakhtin's religious interest in 4th century Russian Orthodox writing as discussed by Lock (1991). He argues that Voloshinov's emphasis on the role of signs as mediators is a result of religious influences that could not be openly acknowledged in the 1920s in the Soviet Union. This, of course, echoes Clark & Holquist's (1984) thesis that Voloshinov's works were essentially Christian writings by Bakhtin disguised in Marxist rhetoric. This position is refuted by Coates (1998) who, while arguing for a Christian interpretation of Bakhtin, maintains on the basis of her own intertextual analysis of Bakhtin and Voloshinov that they were two different writers and that the Marxism of Voloshinov was antithetical both to Bakhtin's Christianity and phenomenological method.

Lock makes no reference to Voloshinov in his paper and the Bakhtinian concept of sign he refers to is not clearly defined but it seems to differ from Voloshinov in the importance attached to the body. Like Voloshinov, Lock argues that Bakhtin's concept of sign is materialist but, unlike Voloshinov, he is not concerned with semiotics as such:

> What is matter and how is it represented? Bakhtin begins with the latter question, and inverts the semiotic axiom that every

figure needs a ground. Bakhtin's practice is to reduce the distinction, and to eliminate the hierarchical order, by grounding the sign in the material of its representation, and by grounding speech in the mouths and bodies of the speakers and auditors. This is not, as is often supposed, a development within semiotics, but a usage of semiotics in the advancement of what might unfashionably be called ontology. [Lock, 1991, p. 287]

Lock further argues that the constraints of censorship in the 1920s, which required Bakhtin to acknowledge Marxist-Leninism, also led to him reinscribing materialism in a Christian discourse, a manifestation of heteroglossia. In Orthodox theology the Incarnation made all matter potentially divine. The corollary of this for Bakhtin is that all words are potentially the Word.

In a dense and complex paper Leiman (2002) further develops the case for Voloshinov's concept of the sign to replace the utterance as the basic unit of analysis in psychotherapy. Influenced by Shotter's (1993a) concept of the "semiotic position", that is how people feel or experience themselves as "positioned" in relation to others around them in an "ethical" sense rather than causally,[4] Leiman nevertheless argues that Shotter's concept of the sign is still overly reliant on Vygotsky's instrumental or tool-like conception and that it should be replaced by Bakhtin/Voloshinov's conception of signs as "dialogical bridges". While Leiman acknowledges that, for Bakhtin, the utterance is the basic unit of analysis (as it is for Voloshinov), he argues that another unit of analysis is needed to analyse the utterance. For Leiman "semiotic positions" are mediated by utterances and the meaning of words is determined by the author and addressee rather than their relation to other words, as in a structural analysis.

However, the distinction Leiman makes between the utterance and the sign seems hard to sustain, resulting in apparent confusion between semiotic and dialogical positions and the difference between the terms remaining unclear. The reason Bakhtin chose the utterance as his basic unit of analysis is because in terms of his meta-linguistic analysis it includes extra-linguistic factors. The meaning of the utterance cannot be determined if these extra-linguistic factors are not taken into account. So many potential signs, linguistic and non-linguistic, operate in any given utterance so that meaning belongs to the utterance as a whole rather than the sign as such. Voloshinov and Bakhtin were quite clear about this. It seems clearer and more accurate to regard the utterance, rather than the sign, as "positioning" both the speaker and addressee and the dialogical position is a more useful concept than the semiotic position in that it implies a position in relation to someone or something else in dialogue or dialogic interaction.[5] Leiman (2002) elaborates further on the symptom as a sign, but like the word as sign it only has meaning in its particular dialogical context. If utterances and language are treated more as part of a continuum of dialogical interaction that includes other non-linguistic modes of communication and meaning, then the distinction between signs and their context in either speech and/or other activities disappears.[6]

According to Emerson (1991), Bakhtin rarely refers to signs in his untranslated work and, unlike Voloshinov, who attempted to find an objective explanation for inner experience through the sign, Bakhtin was not a semiotician. It was the utterance not the sign that was the main unit of analysis. In *Notes Made in 1970–71* Bakhtin writes:

> Only an utterance has a direct relationship to reality and to the living, speaking person (subject) . . . For here what matters is not elements (units) of the language system that have become elements of the text, but aspects of the utterance.
> The utterance as a semantic whole. [Bakhtin, 1986, p. 122]

and

> The utterance as a whole does not admit of definition in terms of linguistics (or semiotics). [Bakhtin, 1986, p. 136]

Perhaps Bakhtin does not write about signs because for him the meaning is in the utterance, which, as a semantic whole, cannot be broken into constituent parts. For Bakhtin, semiotics requires a system and therefore tends towards the monological and hierarchical and, as the range of possible meanings is infinite, it cannot be contained within any system. Leiman seems to be arguing that Bakhtin's background in Russian Orthodox theology lends credence to Voloshinov's materialist concept of the sign. This position can only be justified by reconciling Voloshinov's dialectical materialism with Bakhtin's phenomenology and open-ended dialogism.

The focus of phenomenology is the construction and nature of individual human consciousness. The focus of Marxism is the formation of human social relationships and how ideology plays a part in these. While individual human consciousness and social relationships are in psychological terms inseparable, for dialogically-oriented therapists Bakhtin's early phenomenology and later dialogism can be understood as open-ended and descriptive, whereas Voloshinov's Marxism, however nuanced, can be understood as deterministic.

Gerald Pirog (1987) argues that Voloshinov's determinism, in which he asserts that human mental life can be the object of scientific scrutiny within a Marxist dialectical framework and that therefore there are underlying laws governing human behaviour, is in apparent contradiction with Bakhtin's stress on unfinalisability and freedom. Although Voloshinov acknowledges a distinction between the natural sciences and human sciences such as psychology, Pirog argues that he does not follow this through and that his theories stay within an instrumentalist scientific framework. Social interaction, like material production, is determined by laws that can be established through the objective methods of dialectical materialism. As a result Voloshinov does not make the epistemological point that Bakhtin does, that the way a situation is structured in dialogue is the object of knowledge and that the facts of knowledge are constituted and have no independent existence outside of dialogue.[7] In defining mental life as a mirror image of public experience that is entirely sign-mediated, Pirog accuses Voloshinov of such a thorough-going socialisation of the psyche, a form of semiotically mediated determinism, that there is no room for any account of creativity or pathology, or even individual difference This orthodox Marxist position is spelt out by Voloshinov in *Freudianism*, underlined by a quotation from Marx:[8]

> Outside society and, consequently outside objective socio-economic conditions, there is no such thing as a human being ... Not a single action taken by a whole person, not a single concrete ideological formation (a thought, an artistic image, even the content of dreams) can be explained and understood

without reference to socioeconomic factors. . . . After all "the essence of man is not an abstraction inherent in each separate individual. In its reality it is the aggregate of social relationships." [Voloshinov, 1976, p. 15]

Voloshinov thus takes a very different position from Bakhtin on what Pirog defines as a central issue in Bakhtin's writing, namely whether the pervasive nature of intersubjectivity as the basis of all human existence rules out any possible individual experience outside it. The central issue here is freedom. For Bakhtin, dialogism allows for an endless multiplicity of unpredictable ideas and conjugations and the disclosure of self to another has therefore the potential for self-knowledge and liberation. Bakhtin's emphasis is on the indeterminacy and ultimate unknowability of each human soul. This crucial difference partly lies in Bakhtin's attention to embodied experience (discussed further in Chapter Seven) and how this allows for each human individual's experience to be both unique and intersubjective.

Bakhtin and Lacan

One of the advantages of dialogical thinking in psychotherapy is that it is not confined to a particular model of psychotherapy or psychoanalytic school and may therefore be less contaminated by the rivalries and allegiance to dogma that can restrict an open-minded appraisal of new ideas (see Eisold 1994; Young, 1999). Object Relations models and Lacanian psychoanalysis have traditionally been seen as rivals in the marketplace of psychoanalytic ideas, so the potential of dialogical thinking inspired by Bakhtin to inform both traditions is particularly interesting. Despite the apparent contradiction between Bakhtin's dialogism, with its emphasis on the diachronic, historical dimension of language and the ways in which language and its meanings change with human use, and Saussurrean structural linguistics, which informed Lacan,[9] in which language is an enclosed self-referential system, there are several concepts that are apparently close to each other in meaning. Lacan's insistence that an alienating identity is given to or imposed on us when we take our place in the Symbolic Order with the acquisition of language is comparable, if apparently less benign, than Bakhtin's concept of authoring, in which the self takes shape in dialogue with another and can only become known to itself, albeit partially, through the other's perspective by virtue of the other's outsideness. For Bakhtin, all speech is a response to previous utterances and pre-supposes the response of the other. Lacan (1977) similarly asserts that the purpose of speech is not to convey information, but to evoke a response. Both Bakhtin and Lacan draw attention to how the act of speaking positions the speaker in relation to the other who is being addressed and in relation to the referential content of the utterance. It is not possible to speak without both taking up a position that also positions the person we are addressing and revealing an attitude to what we are talking about. There is no such thing as neutral, value-free speech. Both Lacan and Bakhtin observed that all speech presupposes the existence of a "third" who is not present. For Bakhtin this is the superaddressee, whose responsive understanding or approval we assume or hope for. For Lacan, the "third" is the Other (*le grand Autre, 1977b (129)*) or Freud's ego ideal, part of the Symbolic Order, the hoped-for source of both narcissistic identification and recognition and in whose image we try unsuccessfully to create ourselves. There is even an uncanny resemblance in *Author and Hero* to Lacan's "mirror stage" in which the infant recognising herself in the mirror for the first time is granted an illusion of autonomy and self control in contrast to the uncoordinated and fragmented way in which she experiences herself. Bakhtin comments that the reflection we see of ourselves in the mirror is merely a reflection, which is both *spurious* and an alien image and emphatically not how others see us, from *outside* (1990, 32).

William Handley (1993), in a thoughtful and closely argued paper, distances himself from those theorists who claim that Bakhtin was unique among thinkers who define subjectivity as structured by language in his concern with responsibility and ethics. Handley attempts to show that Lacan shares a similar stance to that of Bakhtin. While both were influenced by Kant, both rejected transcendentalism. For Bakhtin, our perspective is constrained by how we are located in relation to others; we can see sideways but have no access to an overview. For Lacan (1977), there is no "metalanguage"; it is impossible to speak from a point external to language. Following from this, both reject any subordination of the particular to the general. For Bakhtin, this is conceptualised as the immediate and open-ended event of being while, for Lacan, it is the desire that is beyond categorisation and representation. There is nothing ontologically prior to human action and no one who is supposed to know for us. For both, there is therefore an insistence on the inescapability of individual responsibility without recourse to ethical systems or pre-existent rules and regulations. Interdependency is paramount for both Bakhtin and Lacan, due to the presence of the other in the self, the self's ultimate unknowability or unfinalisability and the need to negotiate identity and social relationships through dialogue. The activity of dialogue is therefore a profoundly ethical practice and, for Lacan, the capacity to sustain the analytic dialogue constitutes the purpose of psychoanalysis. For both, the importance of dialogue lies in its unique particularity in each dialogic encounter and therefore in the uniqueness of each individual. For Bakhtin, it is the unrepeatability of dialogue alongside the spatial and temporal aspects of embodiment that defines and shapes the singular aspects of each individual's experience, while in psychoanalysis how one is positioned in relation to others is as much a somatic as a psycholinguistic phenomenon. In Lacanian psychoanalysis, differentiation is a process of letting go of narcissistic but alienating identifications with the Symbolic Other and recognising the desires that have been excluded from symbolisation in a way that facilitates the accommodation of otherness in the self and difference in others (Bracher, 1993). Handley suggests that Bakhtin and Lacan would agree that "loving thy neighbour as thy self" is not a useful guide to genuine ethical action as we can neither presume to know what another wants or needs nor assume that the desire of another is the same as our own;[10] although both assert a subjectivity that is entirely social, both are also quite clear about the uniqueness and irreducibility of each individual.

Despite these similarities, there are also important differences between Bakhtin and Lacan, although these differences are matters of emphasis and not absolutes. There are differences in how they conceptualise language and the subject's relation to it. For Bakhtin, language is located between people and meaning can only be produced in this intersubjective space. His canvas is broader and his concerns are historical and social, as well as individual and subjective. For Lacan (1977b), the linguistic structure, while being exterior to those who are born into it, is also inscribed in the unconscious. Meaning is a product of intersubjectivity and is also determined by the structural relations of the language system. Alienation is unavoidable as, according to Lacan, *It is part of language itself* (1977, p. 212), as language while conferring identity prises us away from *Being*. Bakhtin's attitude to language is usually a far more optimistic one, viewing it as being the constitutive material of subjectivity that can be used creatively by human subjects to give shape to their experience and that of others; for Bakhtin subjectivity is both determined and determining. Although words themselves have inevitably been spoken before, they take on new meanings when spoken in a different context and from a different perspective and can become "our own words" if we assume full responsibility for what we say. For Lacan, words never become entirely "our own" as they are part of a pre-existing self-referential system of signification and there is, therefore, always a gap between what we intend to say and the meanings we convey.[11] For the human subject therefore, language is a source of alienation, part of the pre-existent Symbolic Order that from the moment we enter it, ensnares us in its unwritten rules. These "rules" constrain who we are, what we can say and what we can think although this does not absolve us of our total responsibility for our own conduct. For Lacan, the acquisition of language is the loss of the freedom and innocence of the imaginary world of infancy and its replacement by the laws and prohibitions of the adult world. However, for Bakhtin, the acquisition of language is a gain, not a loss, since only with language can we begin to express our intersubjectivity and fully enter the social world; prior to learning our native language all words are "foreign" words and our understanding of the world and our ability to exercise control and take responsibility for it is severely curtailed. It follows from this that unlike Bakhtin and Object Relations theory, Lacan holds out no hope, however remote, for a benign or fully satisfying relationship between subject and object and therefore that the damage caused by malign or deficient object relations can ever be repaired. As Sherry Turkle (1992) explains, the best that psychoanalysis can hope to achieve is to bring about an awareness of the self's fragmentation, discontinuities and inner contradictions, an awareness that does not lead to any escape from them. Unlike Lacan, for whom desire is the central concern, Bakhtin does not address how unconscious desire is revealed in dialogue or the importance of the other and the desire of the other in the genesis of desire.[12] Similarly Bakhtin does not posit the existence of an unconscious that, for Lacan, is both structured like a language and is the discourse of the Other in that it is a cultural phenomenon that transcends the individual. If there is an area of "unconscious" experience in Bakhtin's terms, it could be deemed to be those aspects of our selves that we cannot be aware of without the other's outside perspective, which allows others to see what we are unable to see for ourselves.

Eugenie Georgaca (2001, 2003) brings Bakhtinian and Lacanian concepts together in her analysis of psychoanalytic psychotherapy transcripts. She suggests that both Bakhtin and Lacan are consistent with a view of the self that is "plural", co-extensive with society and consisting of multiple voices, states and positions, in which language does not merely constitute subjectivity but is subjectivity. Traditional psychoanalysis, by contrast, is seen as reductive and individualistic, leading to hermeneutic closure rather than to an opening out of multiple possible meanings that can lead to greater dialogical flexibility and reflexivity. While acknowledging the differences between Bakhtin's dialogic approach to language and Lacan's theory of subjectivity derived from structural linguistics, she suggests that their similar stance with regard to subjectivity and language is justification for using them jointly in psychotherapy.

Like Leiman and Stiles, Georgaca reframes psychoanalytic concepts in linguistic terms: drawing on Kristeva (1980), she proposes that introjection and projection can be understood as intertextuality, in which the psyche, social world and interpersonal interactions are viewed as mutually influencing and interlinked semiotic systems. Intertextuality means that words must be understood as carrying multiple meanings, both in their general social usage and with regard to significant interactions in the analysand's personal history. Each voice or dialogical position will have its own language and mode of expression, together with different subject and addressee positions, which can only be discerned by a micro analytic attention to the therapeutic dialogue.

Likewise, transference can be seen as having a similar structure to the utterance: the analysand speaks from a specific position, positioning the analyst as the counterpart of that position, thus re-enacting dialogical interactions from the past with the analyst. Transference is not seen as an inflexible position but as interchangeable with other reflexive positions.

Georgaca also draws attention to the conflictual aspect of dialogism that Bakhtin referred to as heteroglossia, or the struggle between different social languages. In therapy, this could be understood as the struggle between the official language of the therapist and the everyday language of the client's life. However, both client and therapist can move in and out of official and unofficial languages and the positions associated with them so that authorship of the therapeutic dialogue becomes a shared project with jointly created signs and metaphors. It is incumbent on the therapist not to collude with the transferential position she is placed in but to respond from a "third" or Other position that the client does not expect, thereby unsettling the transference and encouraging reflection on it. Georgaca sees this as cutting through the client's frame by use of what Bakhtin refers to as the penetrative word.

The aim of dialogically oriented therapy is generally seen as facilitating the expression of the different voices of the self, particularly those that have been suppressed or silenced, as well as reducing disassociation between them. Developing reflexivity is also seen as important, although Georgaca (2001) cautions against a reflexive position that dominates other voices to the extent that it becomes an overarching monological observer, suggesting that a fluent and complex interplay between reflexive and other voices is a better outcome. Although she does not explicitly refer to it as such, Georgaca seems to make use of Bakhtin's concept of internally persuasive discourse, a term that could be used to refer to a cluster of therapist interventions that avoid authoritative finalising responses but encourage reflexive working through by disentangling intertextuality and creating fresh meanings. Implicit in Georgaca's account is an ethical aspect to the use by the therapist of different dialogical interventions, although the distinctions between them are subtle, complex and dependant on intonation and other contextual factors that are specific to each therapeutic pairing. It follows from this that the therapist's task is a particularly demanding one that requires what could be described as "polyvalent" attention to the different voices, positions, social and transferential meanings that emerge in each utterance. Moreover the creation of shared meanings is a finely balanced art that, if practised too early in therapy or without sufficient sensitivity, could be experienced as controlling or even abusive if the therapist distorts the client's words to serve her own purposes (Finlay & Robertson, 1990).

Despite the Lacanian component, Georgaca's account seems to be more Bakhtinian than Leiman's, employing a broader range of Bakhtin's concepts both as analytic tools and therapeutic interventions. In her emphasis on the multiple social as well as the interpersonal and intrapsychic meanings of words, Georgaca allows for this excess social meaning and its effect on the client's subjectivity to be explored in the therapy. The accounts of Leiman and Stiles and Leiman are constrained by the repetitive nature of object relations, leading to dialogical or semiotic positions that are relatively static. Georgaca's account brings out the mobility of the different "I" positions in the dialogical self that are less constrained by fixed relational schema. A weakness in her account is her failure to draw out the full implications of Bakhtin's concept of heteroglossia, thereby reducing the coming together of different voices or discourses to intertextuality, a linguistic term that fails to convey the force and energy of the opposing discourses. Her account is also limited by its failure to open up the differences between Bakhtin and Lacan and so fails to test the limits of their compatibility, particularly when it comes to the question of desire and the role of the unconscious. An obvious but important difference is that Bakhtin was not a psychoanalyst, and his ideas about subjectivity were atheoretical. In a rather scathing attack on Bakhtin (whom he conflates with Voloshinov), Harold Baker (1995) nevertheless argues correctly that compared to Lacan, Bakhtin does not develop a coherent theory of the subject. This limitation is reflected in Bakhtin's exclusive focus on authoring, how consciousness is revealed in the text, and his neglect of the responses evoked in the reader. However, from a psychotherapy perspective, this could be seen as a strength as well as a weakness since Bakhtin neither prescribes nor describes development. Bakhtin's position could rather be understood as anti-developmental, insofar as he speaks with approval of Dostoevsky's antagonism towards psychology:

> He saw in it (psychology) a degrading reification of a person's soul, a discounting of its freedom and its unfinalisability, and of that peculiar indeterminacy and indefiniteness which in

Dostoevsky constitute the main object of representation for in fact Dostoevsky always represents a person on the threshold of a final decision, at a moment of crisis, at an unfinalisable and unpredeterminable turning point for his soul (stress in original). [1984, p. 61]

Lacan's position on development, like Freud's, was ambiguous, sometimes appearing to endorse developmental arguments and other times distancing himself from them (Morss, 1996). Despite the various reworkings of Lacan in the light of post-structuralist and feminist critiques, the extent to which he relies on the systematic structure of the Symbolic Order, which does not seem to allow for changes (Dews, 1995), could be seen as a constraint on possible meanings.

Dialogical psychotherapy and other discursive approaches to psychotherapy

Despite the radical potential of the explicit recognition in dialogical self theory of the thoroughly social nature of subjectivity, most accounts stay within a normative, developmental framework in which the role of psychotherapy in contemporary culture remains unchallenged and the various models or approaches do not theorise or account for their own existence. While dialogically influenced psychotherapy often eschews diagnostic labelling, when specific "disorders" are mentioned, neither the constitutive nature of diagnostic categories (Parker, 1999) nor the power accorded to the therapist to define the subjective experience of another person are acknowledged. Similarly the social identities of therapist and client in terms of class, gender, race, age, sexuality, and so forth, and how these mutually interact, remain largely unexplored. One of the themes that will be explored in the following chapters is how dialogical psychotherapy has failed so far to draw out some of the more radical implications of Bakhtin's thinking for psychotherapy practice and has, therefore, been outflanked on the "left" by more radical approaches influenced by Michel Foucault and Jacques Derrida. These "deconstructive" approaches attempt to combine a deep respect for the client's subjective experience with an intensely critical stance towards the practices of psychotherapy that involves a willingness to recognise not only how we are positioned but how also how we came to stand there (Parker, 1999).

One of the pitfalls of social psychology, which applies equally to psychotherapy, is the separation of individual distress from its socio-historical context and its resituation in a professionally created social reality (Shotter, 1990) that usually involves a theory of development. Despite indeterminacy and unfinalisability being essential characteristics of Bakhtin's dialogism, dialogical accounts of psychotherapy seem unable to escape developmental assumptions, whether the normative assumptions of Object Relations theory in Cognitive Analytic Therapy, the desirability of a progressive increase in the ability to assimilate problematic experiences (Stiles, 2002, Stiles et al, 2004), or the pathological implications of a deficit in "metarepresentative skills" (Semerari et al, 2004). While radical and critical psychologists have attempted, with some considerable qualifications and caveats, to use Freud and Lacan to undermine traditional psychology's prescriptive developmentalism,[13] Bakhtin's potential in this respect is relatively unexplored. However, this does not imply that Bakhtin's phenomenology and dialogism should be applied uncritically. Although Bakhtin's focus is wide ranging in some respects, as dialogic relations can be seemingly read into all aspects of human history and culture, it is narrow in others. The limitations of a dialogic approach and the subsequent requirement to bring Bakhtin into a dialogic relation with other discourses, outside of psychoanalysis, is discussed in the following chapter. What I intend to explore is the possibility of a radical Bakhtinian psychotherapy that is neither dependant on the normative assumptions of (some) psychoanalytic models nor the anti-humanism of poststructuralism.

Notes

1 The historical origins of the modern novel can be traced back to Socratic dialogue, Mennipean satire and the carnivalesque discussed further in Chapter 7.
2 The concept of outsideness is discussed further in the last Chapters 7 and 8.
3 A self-state is a term used in cognitive analytic theory to refer to a partly disassociated aspect of the self characterised by a particular

relational configuration associated with particular feelings, thoughts and behaviours.

4 Ethical here refers to the moral implications of the "position" in terms of allowable action or behaviour. Shotter (1995) explains that people involved in shared activity experience themselves as having a particular moral obligation towards those they are sharing the activity with which is different to that they feel towards others outside of it. This takes on a multi-dimensional aspect if dialogic conversation is understood as a historical phenomenon and that our participation both creates and limits future possibilities beyond the immediate situation.

5 Speech as part of a continuum of dialogic interaction rather than a separate ability is discussed further in Chapter 6.

6 Leiman (2002) gives two case examples of "signs" as mediators of positions in therapy. The first concerns a man who feels humiliated when his psychiatrist gives him a prescription. Leiman suggests that the prescription is the sign that positions him as humiliated but the prescription itself acquires meaning only in the dialogical interaction; the meaning lies in the *activity* of the psychiatrist giving him a prescription. The second concerns a man who is reminded of his carefree youth by walking through autumn leaves and kicking them around. Leiman suggests that it is the leaves that are the sign that repositions him as a happy young man rather than the sensual *activity* of kicking the leaves.

7 Shotter (1995) amplifies this point by highlighting the illusion of conversation being about something that already exists, for example concepts such as society, the individual, mental states and so forth. These concepts only have meaning or make sense as they are developed or constructed in dialogue and have no independent existence. Their significance lies in how they open up or close down conversational possibilities and how they position speakers in relation to each other. This of course raises serious methodological problems as well as ethical questions about how such things as mental states, emotions and various psychiatric diagnosis can be measured or evaluated in the process of researching psychotherapy.

8 Sixth Thesis on Feuerbach, London: The Marxist Leninist Library, 1942, 17, 198.

9 Lacan (1977a, 676) notes that European structuralism had its origins in Russian Formalism. This was the dominant current in cultural criticism at the time Bakhtin and Voloshinov were writing. Roman

Jakobson whose elaboration of metaphor and metonymy profoundly influenced Lacan was, himself, influenced by Voloshinov's Marxism and the Philosophy of Language.

10 As referred to previously, desire in Lacanian terms is quite distinct from need or a demand (1977a, 681) and is a continuous force that unlike a need can never be satisfied (Evans, 1996). In this respect it is similar to the Girardian concept of desire discussed in the next two chapters.

11 Lacan (1977b) makes a distinction between making a statement i.e. using someone else's words and an enunciation when we reveal an aspect of ourselves when we speak, but this does not entirely eliminate the gap between intention and meaning.

12 Handley (1993) notes Bakhtin's failure to examine the machinations of human desire in his polyphonic reading of Dostoevsky, a theme that will be pursued further in the next chapter from a Girardian perspective.

13 For a comprehensive discussion of these issues see Henriques et al (1984) now regarded as a classic critique of traditional psychology and Morss' (1996) discussion of some of the issues they raise.

CHAPTER FOUR

Some Limitations of Dialogism as a Model for Psychotherapy

Bakhtin's dialogic conception of self and consciousness, in the context of the growing influence of discursive approaches in psychotherapy, apparently offers an optimistic alternative to post-structuralist accounts in proposing a less alienated account of human self-hood that, as Gardener (1998) argues, while being socially determined also possesses a degree of agency and free will. Rather than focus on the ways in which we are constrained and determined by language, Bakhtin seems to celebrate discourse in a way that suggests that the self has at its disposal the endless creative potential of language. His concepts of polyphony and dialogism apparently complement and inform contemporary progressive agendas of acknowledging, respecting and valuing human cultural difference and diversity.

As well as stressing the diversity of social and cultural life, Bakhtin and Voloshinov emphasise communication as a fundamental and defining feature of the human self and, by implication, the healing potential of dialogue, the intersubjective process of talking, listening, and creating meaning.

> To be means to communicate dialogically. When dialogue ends everything ends . . . Two voices is the minimum for life, the minimum for existence. [Bakhtin, 1984, p. 252]

Unlike most psychological theories, the dialogical model, despite its theoretical complexity, has the potential to be a non-pathological model. Even if it has not yet managed to elude normative assumptions, it could still become a significant challenge to medical models that seek to measure and quantify. However, the healing potential of dialogue on its own can be overestimated, as dialogue itself is morally neutral and can therefore be harmful or beneficial and the rationale for dialogic discourse as a model for psychotherapeutic practice is questionable, depending on whether Bakhtin is considered a social theorist (Aronowitz, 1994) describing an ethics of dialogue, or a cultural theorist concerned primarily with aesthetics. For Bakhtin, the creation of meaning is an intersubjective process but accounting for the desires and emotions that make meaning *meaningful* is not part of his remit. This omission has consequences for a dialogical analysis of psychotherapy, in terms of its ability to describe and understand meaning positions. This chapter therefore considers some of the limitations of dialogism from the perspective of some of Bakhtin's critics, with particular attention to Natalia Reed's critique that comes from a Girardian perspective. Girard's approach to Dostoevsky focuses on the desires and motivations of Dostoevsky's characters and is entirely different to that of Bakhtin. From a psychotherapy perspective, it will be argued that a Girardian analysis is complementary to a Bakhtinian dialogical analysis as it gives substance to the human desires that are expressed in sometimes complex ways in dialogic discourse.

Can the benevolent role of dialogue be overestimated?

Such has been the output of the "Bakhtin industry" in recent years that some long established Bakhtin scholars are beginning to sound rather jaded and cynical, particularly with regard to the appropriations of Bakhtin's ideas in a piecemeal fashion without apparent regard to their overall context. This overall context keeps changing as new texts and translations of them are brought to light. It is therefore particularly difficult for psychotherapists to evaluate Bakhtinian contributions to theory as Bakhtin's position in relation to language changed over time and when Bakhtin scholars themselves disagree strongly as to which ideas to prioritise. As noted in the last chapter, one of the main inspirations for the concept of the "dialogical self" is Bakhtin's "discovery" of polyphony and dialogism in Dostoevsky's novels as the vehicle for human consciousness. The apparently benign refusal of Dostoevsky to adopt a controlling or superior position with regard to his characters' speech and thoughts has become a metaphor for a decentred self, consisting of voices that enter into dialogue with one another on equal terms creating an endless chain of unrepeatable utterances. Shotter and Billig (1998) present the case for a new social psychology based on Bakhtin's and Voloshinov's dialogical analysis of language in use, emphasising both the uniqueness and the indeterminacy of each utterance and the significance of "small" differences in the way we express ourselves in revealing our "inner" lives. They quote:

> An utterance is never just a reflection or an expression of something already existing and outside it that is given and final. It always creates something that never existed before, something absolutely new and unrepeatable, and, moreover, it always has some relation to value (the true, the good, the beautiful, and so forth). [Bakhtin, 1986, pp. 119–120]

However this particular interpretation of Bakhtin's analysis of Dostoevsky has been questioned for its over-optimistic view of dialogue and, by implication, of what goes on in human consciousness. This interpretation of Dostoevsky has also been criticised by American scholars (e.g. Emerson 1997, Fogel 1985, 1989, Bernstein, 1989) as altogether too innocent and as failing to see the magnitude of the tensions between individuals and their social environments and, if polyphony really was Bakhtin's only big idea, then they have a valid point. Holquist (1990), comparing Sartre's pessimistic view of the other with Bakhtin's more benevolent view, writes that Bakhtin, in his earlier works at least, fails to consider issues of conflict and power relations between self and other, particularly with regard to gender and class. In addition Emerson (1997) argues that, from an ethical point of view, there are problems with Bakhtin's notion of dialogue as unfinalisable, as it can never then be judged. To this it could be added that the boundlessness of possible interpretations that may be a source of liberation in literary criticism (Bernard-Donals, 1994) may be a source of confusion in psychotherapy. And meaning itself can only be arrived at when a dialogue is closed down: an endless stream of dialogue avoids submitting itself for evaluation:

> ... dialogism must be tested not merely lauded ... dialogism itself is not always just clement or life enhancing, and the resonance of multiple voices may be a catastrophic threat as much as a sustaining chorale. [Bernstein, 1989, p. 199]

The assumption that dialogue and the valorisation of multiple perspectives always leads to a beneficial outcome is questionable. Seeing a situation from different viewpoints can be a way of avoiding taking a moral position that can also herald a dangerous slide into post-modern relativism in which truth becomes a matter of "choice" or even indifference. If all points of view embody a truth, it is difficult to justify and sustain a moral position. The rich diversity of discourses that Bakhtin saw in the polyphonic novel does not fully account for the unequal and often disharmonious relationships between them. The "polyphonic" Bakhtin does not take full account of the sometimes violent nature of verbal interaction and of dialogic breakdown and failure. Not all diverse voices are tolerant of diversity. As Slavoj Žižek (2003) points out, the advocates for diversity are often people for whom religious and political beliefs and practices are either disavowed or lived at a distance, as an aspect of culture: they therefore have little invested in adherence to religious and political institutions. Bakhtin's polyphonic dialogism does not necessarily bridge the gap between diverse voices that do not or cannot tolerate each others' convictions and beliefs. For a conversation to become dialogic in a way that allows new, jointly created intersubjective meanings to emerge there has to be some agreement about truth between the respective viewpoints (Kop, 2000).

Dialogue and truth

A superficial reading of Bakhtin can give a misleading impression of the power of words as a force for good or of dialogue as a means to truth. Dialogic discourse can also be endlessly evasive and entangling (Emerson, 1999). Bakhtin himself draws attention to the ambiguous relationship of words and truth in his analysis of Rabelais:

but the truth does not seek words, she is afraid to entangle herself in the word, to soil herself in verbal pathos. [Bakhtin, 1981, p. 309]

"Truth" in Rabelaisian terms is embodied only in what is "official" and authoritative, seeking to dominate and control. All words are spoken in some relation to the truth but it is rare for words to express it directly. In Bakhtin's analysis of Dostoevsky, the exception is penetrative discourse, monologic discourse that is spoken

"... without a sideward glance, without a loophole, without internal polemic." [Bakthin, 1984, p. 249]

Such words are spoken with love that enables the listener to realise some truth about themselves. In his later work Bakhtin (1981, 1986) expresses increasing scepticism about the capacity of words to express the truth and the possibility of any straightforward discourse that is not false.

It seems that Bakhtin is questioning the assumption that truth and morality necessarily coincide. For Bakhtin's generation of intellectuals, disguising the truth of intended meanings in discourse was sometimes a means of survival and subverting censorship, while offering those who wished to understand the opportunity to read or hear differently. The extent to which Bakhtin and Voloshinov used "Aesopian" or allegorical language (Emerson, 1996) to disguise their intentions has been the subject of considerable debate among later scholars. Even apparently straightforward monologic discourse dealing with "facts" can, on close examination, be found to be internally dialogised double-voiced or double-directed discourse, in which the intended meaning is disguised.

The neutral property of words or linguistic signs that Voloshinov (1986) describes that enables them to be used for different purposes in different contexts can also apply to whole discourses, or in Bakhtin's terms, social languages. So, as Malik (2003) wrote in the *Guardian* newspaper, even the fascist BNP now employs the discourse of diversity and many politicians are adept at using the discourse of peace while pursuing agendas of domination and exploitation. Both are examples of what Parker (1992) identifies as the capacity of radical discourses to become entangled with the discourses of oppression and control:

> The Dostoevskian word is not only double-voiced (in Bakhtin's innocent altogether too hopeful formulation) this word ... can also be insecure, unreliable, mean spirited, sickeningly dishonest; and by its very essence as a narrated word, inadequate to transmit an honest authorial intent. [Emerson, 1994, p. 172]

Coerced dialogue

Aaron Fogel (1985, 1989) argues that Bakhtin had a utopian view of dialogue as free, spontaneous and natural and therefore underestimated the extent to which dialogue is coerced, when it is not in someone's interests to speak and words are forced out of them. An example is the public enquiry, which attempts to establish the "truth" by compelling people to speak, often against their own interests. Joseph Conrad angrily denounced such an inquiry into the sinking of the Titanic, which he saw as a reflection of the disproportionate attention paid to the deaths of the upper class passengers and the disproportionate blame heaped on the labourers who built the ship, a disproportion that is

> Dialogical but virtually physical in its misapplied force—a useless scene of disproportionate coercion to speak. [Fogel, 1985, p. 5]

Public enquiries are not the only forums where there is coercion to speak: there are also courts, prisons, police stations, immigration halls, families, schools, hospitals, and, in its most extreme form, coercion to speak through torture.

Fogel argues that dialogue that is spontaneous and free in a way that allows people to reach deeper levels of creative intellectual understanding and emotional intimacy is the exception, enjoyed only by an educated and privileged elite. In Conrad's novels, force rather than sympathy is what makes dialogue cohesive. A forced dialogue can take the form of compelling the other to speak or compelling the other to listen. Many dialogical interactions are asymmetrical, involving people with differing amounts of social power which, as Hermans (1996) points out, is an important dimension often missing from analysis of the dialogical self. People do not have equal access to the power of words. Linguistic capital, the ability to influence others and control the self by the use of words, is unequally distributed. For Conrad, dialogue and communication, rather than the lack of it, is the problem.

Michael Bernstein (1989) paints an even more disturbing picture of dialogical discourse not as liberation, but entrapment. He argues that Bakhtin's notion of dialogue is so abstract and idealised that it is unlikely to be found anywhere outside a work of art. Bakhtin fails to take account of the prevalence of pain and suffering in human experience and the existence of multiple voices or dialogues as inner torment, rather than as vibrant exchange. Rather than words offering the possibility of endless creative potential, most people are doomed to repetition, parody and pastiche, unable to find a voice of their own, even in extremes of suffering, and thus condemned to an existence that has already been scripted.

Dostoevsky's (1972) *Underground Man* suffers from *ressentiment*, that is an awareness of his utter lack of singularity and a total inability to take action, in his case to take revenge against those others whom he perceives as the source of his humiliation. His inner dialogues only serve as an endless repetition of shame and humiliation. His awareness of the "fictional" nature of his pain, that he can only conceive of himself in the words of others, thus compounds his distress. Bernstein suggests that the terrifying unleashing of *ressentiment* on a mass scale leads to fascism, that all its rage, racism and hatred are attempts to quell

> ... the intolerable babble of other voices both outside of and within consciousness. [Bernstein, 1989, p. 221]

Some of Bakhtin's ideas about consciousness and the self are derived from or perhaps justified by his reading of Dostoevsky. Bakhtin extrapolates directly from the dialogic relationships he finds in Dostoevsky to real life:

> ... dialogic relationships are a much broader phenomenon than mere rejoinders in dialogue, laid out compositionally in the text; they are an almost universal phenomenon, permeating all human speech and all relationships and manifestations of human life—in general, everything that has meaning and significance. [Bakhtin 1984, p. 40]

It is questionable to what extent novels—even Dostoevsky's novels—represent real life or life as it is lived outside the pages of a book. As Terry Eagleton (2003) points out, what constitutes realism in the novel is a matter of opinion: one person's realism is another person's fantasy. All works of art edit and manipulate raw material and the novel's commitments to both representation and form are ultimately incompatible. There is always a gap between the book and the world (Lodge, 2006).

Not everyone who reads Dostoevsky finds polyphony and unfinalisability and the limited attention Bakhtin pays to Dostoevsky's convoluted gothic plots and the human frailty, wickedness and suffering of his "heroes" could be seen as quite perverse. Polyphony itself, the ability that Bakhtin bestows on Dostoevsky's heroes to enter into dialogue with the author on equal terms, can only be a fictional illusion. Bakhtin was himself unable to resolve the problem of authorial control in the polyphonic novel. Eagleton (2003) implies that the realism that Bakhtin saw in Dostoevsky is the depiction of the lives of ordinary people granting them psychological complexity but Bakhtin, for the most part, declines to investigate the psychology of Dostoevsky's characters or what they actually say or think. Bakhtin focuses on form rather than content and is primarily interested in how the internal and external dialogues of the characters in Dostoevsky are arranged compositionally in the text. Bakhtin (1981) goes so far as to say that form and content in discourse are identical with the implication that all that matters in life is not what we say but the form in which it is expressed.

Some questions regarding Bakhtin's interpretation of Dostoevsky from a Girardian perspective

What if Bakhtin misread Dostoevsky and the real "hero" of Dostoevsky's novels is not human consciousness in all its dialogic complexity but the human capacity for self-deception? What if, as Emerson (1997) asks, all the convoluted conversations and internal dialogues are designed not so much to provide the heroes with open-ended options but to make their search for truth more difficult?

> ... there is a tension between Bakhtin's benevolent and domesticated image of Dostoevsky and the much darker,

more perverse and alarming Dostoevsky himself. [Emerson, 1996, p. 169]

Bakhtin does not address the meaning or function of scenes in Dostoevsky's novels where there is no dialogue but which are nevertheless charged with meaning, and neither does he refer to the predicament of characters, often children, who are tortured or silenced. Bakhtin does not allow for the possibility that the outcome of a dialogue might be to make things worse (Emerson, 1997). Dostoevsky was aware of the failures of language to connect directly to consciousness, its capacity to corrupt human communication and human relationships and its consequent association with individual and social disintegration (Jackson, 1993).[1]

> This corruption of language, this short circuiting of the sign and the signified, is the concomitant in the linguistic realm of the breakdown of those moral and social "connections" which distinguish the functioning social organism from an arbitrary collection of disconnected happenings. [1993, p. 234]

An alternative view is that Bakhtin's focus on the polyphonic construction of Dostoevsky's novels overlooks Dostoevsky's moral purpose: that the moral function of a character can only be understood in the context of a whole scene, not the minutiae of dialogue and in the endings of the novels, an aspect Bakhtin avoids paying attention to; that Dostoevsky's moral purpose is to demonstrate the process of developing self-awareness as the layers of self-deception are peeled off (Emerson, 1996). Bakhtin ignores the prevalence of suicides, murders and cruelty in Dostoevsky's fiction, as if the deeds of his characters had no significance, and therefore does not acknowledge that part of his moral purpose is the depiction of violence, not out of gratuitous voyeurism but because we have a moral duty not to avert our gaze from the violence in the world and to acknowledge our own propensity for violence and evil as well as suffering (Jackson, 1993).

Natalia Reed (1994, 1999) goes even further in her critique of Bakhtin and raises serious questions about Bakhtin's dialogical conception of consciousness. She suggests that Bakhtin substitutes his own theory of polyphony for the actual content of Dostoevsky's novels. She argues that this substitution is a "violent" one as it ignores the meaning of Dostoevsky's novels as he intended them to be understood. Bakhtin's dialogue is not with Dostoevsky but a proxy of his own making. Not only does Bakhtin pay no attention to the rivalrous and self-deluded dialogue of Dostoevsky's characters but, Reed argues, his own theory of polyphony was formulated in rivalrous opposition to and is a systematic mimetic inversion of the principles of monologic writers. Reed considers that Bakhtin's purpose in seeking to establish the superiority of participative dialogic consciousness over non-participative monologic consciousness was to establish his own originality and difference. In his theory of polyphonic consciousness, Bakhtin avoids any discussion of

> the content of ideas; a real, genuinely other person; conflict with that real genuine other person; acts of violence against real other people; death; the compulsive and rivalrous disposition of the human consciousness that manifests itself as envy, jealousy, hatred and scapegoating . . . [Reed, 1999, p. 122]

as to do so would undermine his thesis of the benevolent nature of the polyphonic dialogic consciousness as opposed to the finalising monologic consciousness. Bakhtin's very refusal to recognise and take account of actual violence creates the conditions for it to flourish, creating a moral vacuum in his analysis of Dostoevsky.

As Reed (1994) observes, Bakhtin's analysis of discourse all takes place inside the consciousness of Dostoevsky and he treats internal dialogue within a single consciousness as identical to dialogue with a real other person since all dialogue anticipates a response, whether internal or external. Dialogue with other people is, however, qualitatively different from internal dialogue, which can be merely an unfinalised

> . . . perverse, self-perpetuating, negative, run away bickering with other points of view. [Reed, 1994, p. 304]

as is the case with Dostoevsky's *Underground Man*, or it can be a leisurely "conversation" with a fantasised other who says whatever we want them to say as opposed to an interaction with a real and unpredictable other. An internal dialogue is selfish in that it involves no responsibility towards or interaction with another person. Polyphony absorbs everything into its own consciousness and its unfinalisable dialogues avoid facing up to the consequences of authentic living in the world (Emerson, 1997):

> Thus Bakhtin's is a philosophy that has no place for a real personal other and therefore for a theory of obligation suitable for discussion of interpersonal relations or, for that matter, verbal communication between genuinely independent and separate consciousnesses. [Reed, 1999, pp. 138–9]

As Reed (1994) points out, the principle of unfinalisability in polyphony guarantees the equality of all points of view, liberating them from the author's finalising judgement. Polyphony can also represent a refusal to take a moral position since it demands the author's detachment from all points of view. As Bakhtin blurs the distinction between internal and external dialogues, treating them as the same phenomenon, he apparently overlooks the fact that external dialogues between people are conclusive. For Bakhtin the "living utterance" travels endlessly without ever being pinned down by meaning:

> The internal dialogism of authentic prose discourse, which grows organically out of a stratified and heteroglot language, cannot fundamentally be dramatised or dramatically resolved (brought to an authentic end). [Bakhtin, 1981, p. 326]

Determining meaning involves making a finalising judgement but the polyphonic author leaves characters "free" from such finalising judgements about themselves. Reed questions whether this is any more liberating than the freedom to choose to receive a "final truth" about oneself:

> Thus instead of illuminating the meaning of Dostoevsky's narratives, Bakhtin's commentary is more instructive in that it reveals the critic's own romantic cult of the autonomous consciousness which he finds embodied by Dostoevsky's polyphonic vision, capable of operating ideological forms and remaining divinely indifferent to meaning. [Reed, 1994, p. 355]

In his analysis of dialogue, Bakhtin attributes desire to words rather than the people who use them. Utterances strive to express themselves but as Reed (1994) observes, Bakhtin does account for the source of the human impulse for self-expression. This is essentially an anthropomorphic account of language endowed with a romantic desire for original self-expression, in which human existence is made subordinate to the life of language. Human beings merely become the containers for the utterance and its ideology. Reed further argues that Bakhtin confuses ideological beliefs with human desire, thus implying that ideology is the motivation for action without accounting for why people adopt particular ideas and beliefs. Bakhtin advances a theory of human consciousness and communication without any account of motivation and desire. Reed is sceptical. She argues that Bakhtin's statement

> . . . to be is to communicate. . . . Should be replaced with: to be a novelist means to write down "conversations" among ideas in one's own mind. [Reed, 1994, p. 313]

In failing to take account of human motivation or desire, Bakhtin also fails to recognise or take account of violence. In failing to take account of the real other Bakhtin also fails to take account of the most powerful and most destructive emotions that occur between people. Polyphonic or dialogical consciousness, a consciousness fragmented into different unfinalised voices, is neither free nor autonomous, but is rather enslaved by its desire to imitate other people and is prone to violence. Far from withholding his "final word", Dostoevsky submits his characters to his own negative evaluation:

> While Bakhtin links the polyphonic consciousness with freedom and autonomy of the self, Dostoevsky associates the fragmented self with violence and imitation of human models. [Reed, 1994, p. 361]

So, Bakhtin's polyphonic interpretation of Dostoevsky amounts to an inversion of Dostoevsky's own monologic Christian convictions, drawing very different conclusions about his moral purpose as an author from that he intended. Reed (1994, 1999) concludes that polyphony is no less controlling than monologism, leaving characters doomed to *perverse inconclusiveness* (1994, p. 368) and argues convincingly that Bakhtin's concept of polyphony is not supported by Dostoevsky's actual texts but is a mimetic inversion of the principles of monologic writers.

Polyphony or heteroglossia?

Despite these arguments, Reed and other critics of polyphony have underestimated Bakhtin's appreciation of disharmony and discord in dialogue (Wall, 1998a) and this could well be because they have overestimated the importance of polyphony in Bakhtin's overall literary stylistics, an observation that also applies to some theorists of the Dialogical Self. Furthermore, the polyphonic metaphor for the self ignores the fact that the orchestra has a conductor, the music a composer, and the book an author, which seems to weaken the proposition that the different "voices" of the self are equal, independent, and autonomous. As Hirschkop (2001) suggests, Bakhtin's early account of dialogism failed due to its over-reliance on the fiction that an author can create characters out of "bits and bobs of discourse" who have an existence independent of their creator. Polyphony represents Bakhtin's transition from phenomenology to sociology and was superseded by heteroglossia, a multi-languagedness that is dynamic, embodying historical change and social conflict.

Heteroglossia, which is often confused with polyphony, is what Holquist (1981) describes as the "master trope" that is central to Bakhtin's thinking and to which all his other categories are subordinate. Although polyphony and heteroglossia are closely related and dialogism in the novel requires both, the distinction between them is important. As Sue Vice (1997) points out, polyphony refers to many voices while heteroglossia refers to the many "languages" within a culture or a society that represent competing ideas and interests as well as the different and opposing languages within a single utterance. Language, in this context, refers both to different national languages and local dialects and to the innumerable discourses or social genres that are particular to different social groups. Heteroglossia could be said to be the manifestation in language of the tensions, conflicts and struggles that are endemic in the class-ridden societies typical of capitalism where some languages are more powerful than others. Heteroglossia is the turbulent life of language in the social world, with the clash of genres ideologically opposed to one another and the conflicts and contradictions that language continually throws up. Heteroglossia is the intersection between the centripetal authoritative languages that seek to dominate, unify, and control, and the centrifugal languages that pull us towards disunity, diversity and fragmentation. From a psychotherapy perspective, heteroglossia forces us to look beyond the duality of client and therapist to the immense plurality of languages, points of view and sectional interests in society as a whole and to think about how they are reflected and refracted in the therapeutic space, in the speech of therapist and client. It potentially widens our responsibilities as therapists to move beyond what we do with our individual clients and as Hirschkop suggests means

> ... jumping into the fray, not allowing historical change to function as a mere backdrop to one's private life or story. [2001, p. 33]

In heteroglossia the emphasis shifts from how individual subjectivity is a reflection of wider social discourses to how these social discourses affect the individuals who live them and must negotiate their path through life whether subjugated to them, in conflict with them or in apparent harmony with them. Heteroglossia recognises how politics insinuates its way into our psychic life, how the dominant discourses are reflected in our speech and how we think about ourselves as well as emphasising that what Bakhtin had to say about the novel transcended narrow linguistic analysis. Karine Zbinden (1999) argues that missing heteroglossia is to read Bakhtin from a logocentric perspective thereby reducing dialogism to "intertextuality" and, by reducing dialogism to intertextuality, misrepresenting Bakhtin as a semiotician whose only concerns were related to language.

> Thus dialogism is no longer the constitutive interaction of the self with other consciousnesses and objects but the fragmentation of the self into texts. [1999, p. 48]

The "heteroglossic self" is both a better metaphor for the differing degrees of power accruing to the discourses that constitute the psyche and the social world and also for the conflict and struggle between them. As Bakhtin describes it:

> True, even in the novel heteroglossia is by and large always personified, incarnated in individual human figures, with the disagreements and oppositions individualised. But such oppositions of individual wills and minds are submerged in social heteroglossia, they are reconceptualised through it. Oppositions between individuals are only surface upheavals of the untamed elements of social heteroglossia, surface manifestations of those elements that play on such individual oppositions, make them contradictory, saturate their consciousness and discourses with a more fundamental speech diversity. [Bakhtin 1981, p. 326]

However, even the transition from polyphony to heteroglossia does not solve the problem that Bakhtin's focus was the novel and however well an author might create a rich, multi-layered conglomeration of conflicting discourses, they are still created and are qualitatively different from the ways in which we use and encounter language in our everyday lives. Hirschkop (1998b) argues that the discursive world, compared to discourse in the novel, is "unevenly structured" and is not just a series of dialogic exchanges between speaking subjects. We encounter language in many different forms: newspapers, books, television, radio, and electronic media of various kinds, in lectures and legislation, in varied kinds of music and other performance arts to give but a few examples. Some kinds of utterance are more durable and unresponsive than others, while other less durable forms may be more flexible and more responsive. Of all the differing forms that language can take, conversations between individuals are just one. Hirschkop holds Bakhtin responsible for mistakenly seeing all the diversity of language as existing on the same plane, representing specific and different points of view.

Another valid criticism is that heteroglossia is not merely a description of language; Bakhtin regards dialogism as always superior to monologism and heteroglossia as always superior to monoglossia and sees the development of language through history as a progressive development from unity to diversity and plurality, thus loading language with social and political values. As Tony Crowley (1996) notes, plurality and diversity in language may be progressive in some political circumstances, for example in resistance to colonial rule, but also a means whereby a disunified population may be exploited by the cultural hegemony of a ruling class in others. Although Bakhtin's heteroglossic vision of language and consciousness gives due weight to conflict and struggle, it cannot account for why human beings are so often in conflict with other human beings and what it is that they are fighting for or against. Language is not the only medium through which struggle is expressed and conflicts waged: if it were then the world would be a much safer place. Bakhtin expects too much of language; it cannot account for all aspects of human consciousness, social life and experience.

The Girardian self and mimetic desire

While Reed's critique of Bakhtin underestimates his understanding of the centrality of conflict in human life, her preferred interpretation of Dostoevsky, according to the French literary critic René Girard, is still compelling: Girard proposed that the human self is constituted by desire and is dynamically shaped by its external relationships with other people in a way that involves conflict and violence. For Dostoevsky, this was a fundamental fact of human life, the source of human creativity as well as tragedy. Far from being free, Dostoevsky's characters are caught in the most advanced stages of metaphysical desire or ontological sickness and to demonstrate this was, according to Girard (1966), his fundamental concern as a novelist. Polyphony and dialogicality do not represent freedom but the attempts of people to grapple with the multiple, often conflicting, desires provoked by different people in a complex and bewildering social world. When Dostoevsky allows his characters dialogical freedom without imposing his final word it is because he wishes to demonstrate the banality of human desire, particularly the desire for originality or difference. It is for the reader rather than the author to judge (Girard, 1966) and to see how this destructive energy can be transformed into creative energy if people model themselves on Christ rather than each other (Reed, 1999). In contrast Bakhtin seems to dismiss Dostoevsky's avowed Christianity as being unimportant:

... the important thing for us is not Dostoevsky's Christian declaration of faith in itself, but those living forms of his artistic and ideological thinking. . . . [Bakhtin, 1984, p. 98][2]

Unlike Bakhtin, Girard sees violence at the heart of human nature and human relations. Unlike Bakhtin, Girard does not emphasise a linguistically dialogical account of consciousness but rather a self driven by an unconscious desire to imitate others that leads to rivalry, conflict, and violence. Because this desire is unconscious it is also non-representational and precedes language. Desire is always triangular in that it is mediated by another: it is therefore social.

Mimetic desire is a dynamic process that always involves a subject, a rival and an object. We desire the object (whether success, respect, goodness or the latest designer trainers) because the other desires it, which can lead to rivalry and conflict (Girard, 1977). Our desires arise because of what we perceive to be a lack in ourselves that the other possesses:

> To understand desire is to understand that its self-centredness is indistinguishable from its other-centredness. [Girard, 1996, p. 8]

> ... interior life is already social and social life is always a reflection of individual desire. [Girard, 1966, p. 222]

By desiring what the other desires we compensate for the perceived lack in our selves. The other then becomes both a rival and an obstacle but also remains a model for the subject who, because he both encourages and discourages the imitation of the subject, places him in a double bind so that the subject becomes fascinated with the rival, both admiring and enviously hating him. As the conflict intensifies, the subject and rival become violent "doubles" of each other, forgetting the object which they both desired. This can lead to injury or death or, more usually, they direct their violent impulses towards a third person who becomes the "scapegoat". This is the origin of the religious practice of sacrifice and human culture is itself a mechanism for containing and drawing off the contagious violence generated by mimetic desire. Girard takes banal aspects of human behaviour and endows them with immense significance: it is commonplace in everyday life for people to copy each other, worry about how they are seen by others and get angry and resentful over apparently trivial concerns and this is reflected in and exploited by advertising that plays on peoples' insecurities, the fascination with "celebrity" and in television dramas, films and literature (Taylor, 2002). As adults our pride conflicts with our desires, once we become aware of their imitative nature, and we experience more conflict and get caught up in what Girard (1966) calls the "dialectic of indifference" or negative imitation. Primarily we desire autonomy, self-sufficiency, freedom from desire and to establish our originality, independence and difference from others around us. We feign indifference to the desires and opinions of others and our dialogues with them are designed not to further the truth but to deceive others and ourselves as to the real nature of our own desires.

In intellectual and cultural life, the dynamic process of mimetic desire is reflected or played out between different ideas. The world of ideas is similar to people insofar as

> It has fighting for territory, cut-throat competition, struggles for prestige and recognition, jealousy, fear, and mutual fascination . . . The transition from violence to critical reason was an evolutionary step forward . . . made possible by the emergence of a descriptive and argumentative language. [Dupuy, 1995, p. 1]

Eric Gans (2000) argues that not only does language permit the transition from violence to reason but it originated as a way of deferring and containing violence through representation, making the sign into a sacred mediator, which allowed the first human communities to come into existence. But ironically language, while functioning as a safeguard against internal violence between members of a community, also permitted the development of increasingly complex and dangerous means of perpetrating external violence in the form of weapons or legislation.

Can Bakhtin and Girard be reconciled?

Despite Reed's attempt to set up an opposition between them, there are similarities between Bakhtin and Girard and their differing interpretations of Dostoevsky's understanding of human consciousness could be seen as complementary. Bakhtin describes how language as a social phenomenon is constitutive of consciousness, while Girard describes the social nature of the desires that animate language and motivate human communication. Both are concerned with the relationship between self and other and have a thoroughly social conception of the self. Girard uses the term "interdividual" to refer to the centrality of the other in his conception of self. Bakhtin seems to be not too distant from Girard's position when he states:

> In Dostoevsky, consciousness never gravitates towards itself but is always found in intense relationship with another consciousness. Every experience, every thought of a character is internally dialogic, adorned with polemic, filled with struggle, or is on the contrary open to inspiration from outside itself—but is not in any case concentrated simply on its own object; it is accompanied by a continual sideways glance at another person. [1984, p. 32]

In his *Draft Exercise Books*,[3] Bakhtin (1992) refers to the violence in knowledge and artistic form that is proportional to falsehood and that accounts for the human motivation that animates words in a way that seems to be entirely compatible with Girard's thesis:

> This word violence (and lie) is linked up with thousands of personal motives in the creator, muddying the purity of his thirst for success, influence, recognition (not of the word but of the creator) with the striving to become an oppressing and consuming force. [cited in Coates, 1998, p. 153]

Both thinkers have a religious, specifically Christian, outlook which is reflected in different ways in their work. Both saw Dostoevsky's novels as representing the most advanced development of their ideas and both have a historical perspective that reaches back to the ancient Greeks. Both derived some of their ideas about the human self and consciousness from literature and both are critical of "scientific" or psychological attempts to define subjectivity and consciousness. The significance of both thinkers is illustrated by the interest their ideas have generated not only in literature studies but also throughout the humanities and human sciences. At another level, the Girardian perception that Western civilisation is founded on the perpetual struggle and conflict between different ideas[4] (Ranieri, 2002), is compatible with a Bakhtinian understanding of the unfinalisability of dialogue.

Bakhtin and Girard's respective analysis of Dostoevsky's novel *Notes from Underground* are comparable, although they approach the work from very different perspectives. For Bakhtin, the *Underground Man* represents

> . . . extreme and acute dialogisation: there is literally not a single monologically firm undissociated word . . . [1984, p. 227]

and

> The work does not contain a single word gravitating exclusively towards itself and its referential object, that is there is not a single monologic word . . . [1984, p. 228]

Every word the *Underground Man* utters in his internal dialogue is directed towards the anticipated response of another. His discourse is riddled with "sideways glances" and "loopholes" to the extent that he can never reach a final word about him self and is caught up in a vicious circle from which there is no escape.

For Girard (1987), *Notes from Underground* is the first of Dostoevsky's novels to reveal mimetic desire and its paradoxes. Girard (1966) regards the "Underground" consciousness as a disintegration of individual and collective being that was historically specific. He quotes a passage from a speech by Prince Myshkin in Dostoevsky's *The Idiot* to illustrate how this came about and that could be a description of dialogical consciousness:

> People of long ago . . . were very different from people of our own time: they were like another kind of human species . . . In those days man had, as it were, one idea only; our own contemporaries are more nervous, further developed, more sensitive, capable of following two or three ideas at the same time. Modern man is broader and it is this, I would say, which prevents him from being a single unified being as in past centuries. [cited in Girard, 1966, p. 94]

For Girard, however, this is not a progressive development but a phase in the dynamic evolution of mimetic desire that has led to the

> ... underground man, a human rag soaked in shame and servitude, a ridiculous weather-vane placed atop the ruins of "Western humanism." [Girard, 1996, p. 94]

While Bakhtin is primarily concerned with the formal structural aspects of the *Underground Man's* discourse, he does not seem to be as unaware as Reed implies of the meaning behind it, of what motivates him and of his utter dependence on the consciousness of the other coupled with his extreme hostility towards it. His descriptions are consistent with a Girardian perspective, if not quite so damning:

> This final word must express the hero's full independence from the views and words of the other person, his complete indifference to the other's opinion and the other's evaluation. What he fears most of all is asking someone's forgiveness, that he is reconciling himself to someone else's judgement or evaluation, that his self-affirmation is somehow in need of affirmation and recognition by another ... He fears that the other might think he fears that other's opinion. But through this fear he immediately demonstrates his own dependence on the other's consciousness. [1984, p. 229]

Neither Girard nor Bakhtin are concerned with pathology but with illuminating the human condition in different ways. To think of dialogical discourse as animated by mimetic desire and by the powerful and potentially disturbing emotions that it can give rise to could be one solution to the "content" that Reed (1994, 1999) finds missing in Bakhtin. Girard's theory of desire also goes some way towards accounting for the intolerance of difference between different theories and schools of thought, particularly in psychotherapy, as well as accounting for the creation of new theories, something the theories themselves are not able to explain. As Girard would predict, the smaller the difference between existing theories, the more intense their rivalry can become. However, in the battle of ideas (Dupuy, 2000) desires and rivalries are often revealed and concealed in subtle and convoluted ways, by employing double-voiced discourse with "sideways glances" that purport to say one thing while saying something else entirely.

When it comes to attempts by the two increasingly powerful discourses of science and professionalisation to subjugate the diversity of other discourses in psychotherapy, the violence and scapegoating that result from the clash of rival desires is not always so subtly concealed. This is illustrated by Emmy Van Deurzen, a former chair of the UKCP, who used the metaphor of the overgrown garden to describe the burgeoning field of therapy:

> Sprawling plants obscure each other's light and deprive each other of nutrients. It is then necessary to cut the plants back quite drastically and carefully select the ones that one wishes to encourage and make room for, at the same time as uprooting those plants considered to be weeds. [1996, cited in Postle, 1997, p. 153]

As Samuels (1997) observes, the conflict and rivalry between different schools and theories may say far more about the human psyche than any of the theories themselves.

Regardless of their differences, most discourses of psychotherapy are predicated on the idea that mental distress can be ameliorated by an increase in awareness, particularly self-awareness, and that this can be acquired through dialogue with another in a way that leads to increased autonomy or self-responsibility. However, the contextual background of contemporary psychotherapy discourses is one in which rising levels of mental distress is correlated with increasing inequality despite overall rising levels of material wealth, an issue that is discussed further in the final chapter. Far from challenging the institutional structures and mechanisms that promote and maintain inequality, psychotherapy and the wider field of mental health often reflects them and the values associated with them. Psychotherapy, in its allegiance to professionalisation, is following a path already well trodden by psychiatry, which, as Peter Good (2001) observes has, by attaching itself to scientific medicine, solidified its commitment to conservative social goals. From a Bakhtinian perspective, Good notes how the pre-occupation with description, prescription, and measurement and the consequent need to apply systems of logical control to messy non-linear human problems reinforces the social standing of professionals, drawing them into a unified centrepetal language that seeks to dominate the centrifugal languages that surround it. This bears comparison with Girard's warning against attempts to diagnose and categorise people:

> Let us note that contradictions which in reality are the very basis of our psychic life always appear as "differences" between Others and ourselves. The connections established by internal mediation vitiate many would-be "scientific" observations. We dehumanise every desire whose harmful consequences we perceive in order not to recognise the image, or caricature, of our own desires. Dostoevsky accurately observes that by having our neighbor confined to a mental institution we convince ourselves of our own sanity. [Girard, 1966, p. 183]

Similarly Bakhtin (1984, 1993) warned against attempts to impose unitary theories and against the devaluing reification of people that denies their indeterminacy, internal freedom and threshold possibilities, and advocates instead a descriptive rather than a prescriptive philosophy that allows for something irreducible in people and resists systematisation.

Conclusion

For Bakhtin, the dialogic nature of human life and human consciousness was paramount:

> The dialogic nature of human consciousness, the dialogic nature of human life itself. The single adequate form for verbally expressing authentic human life is the open-ended dialogue. Life by its very nature is dialogic. To live means to participate in dialogue: to ask questions, to heed, to respond, to agree and so forth. In this dialogue a person participates wholly and throughout his whole life: with his eyes, lips, hands, soul, spirit, with his whole body and deeds. [1984, p. 293]

Dialogical discourse, however, is morally neutral and can perform many different functions, benevolent or otherwise. To describe consciousness purely in dialogic terms does not account for human desire and could be seen as an evasion of our moral responsibilities as language users. The mere fact of engaging in dialogue is no guarantee of a beneficial outcome. A dialogical or semiotic position (Leiman, 2002) needs to be understood in terms of the desires it reveals or attempts to conceal as well as its antecedents.

A troubling aspect of Bakhtin's analysis is its resistance to closure or finalisation so that meaning is never pinned down (Emerson, 1984, Reed, 1999) in a way that allows increased self-understanding, including understanding the mimetic nature of desire. Many people who seek psychotherapy are seeking understanding and closure and may even be harmed by an opening up of an array of possible meanings. As Emerson suggests in relation to Dostoevsky's tortured heroes, people in distress do not

> ... thirst after any fancy double-voiced dialogism, which can create for them only more doubts and confounding options. From within their own unhappy, unstable worlds, they simply want to believe in something; they want to be understood; and they want to be loved. [Emerson, 1997, p. 136]

The dialogic conception of consciousness needs to be supplemented with an understanding that dialogue is driven by desires, intentions, and attempts to convey meaning in complex and contradictory ways, a theme that is discussed in more detail in the following chapter.

Notes

1. Jackson gives the example of how Ivan and Smerdyakov communicate their mutual intentions to aid and abet a murder in the Brothers Karamazov by linguistic signs designed to obfuscate their actual thoughts.
2. Bakhtin (1986) in the 1970–71 notebooks makes several references to Dostoevsky's Christian beliefs. Towards the end of his life Bakhtin apparently said to one of his executors, Bochorov (1999), that he was forced to avoid any discussion of the religious and philosophical content of Dostoevsky because of Stalin's raids on the intelligentsia.
3. Untranslated, cited in Coates (1998).
4. That between the Judeo-Christian tradition of obedience to God and the Athenian tradition of freedom and love of knowledge.

CHAPTER FIVE

Interdividual Psychology and the Dialogical Self

In the last chapter I discussed some of the limitations of a Bakhtin-inspired dialogical model of consciousness for the theory and practice of psychotherapy. It was argued that a dialogical model is far from an exhaustive explanation for human consciousness and is therefore inadequate on its own as a model of psychotherapy. I argued that Girard's theory of mimetic desire offers an alternative account of consciousness that, while it sometimes contradicts, can also complement and supplement the dialogical account.

The dialogical approach is a discursive structural analysis of both external dialogue between people and inner dialogue. Bakhtin's later account of dialogism suggests that human speech cannot be other than dialogic and that even apparently monologic discourse is animated by a concealed or hidden dialogism: as Bakhtin (1981) said, ever since the first word was spoken, words cannot help but be interrelated to other words. However, just as Bakhtin's dialogical analysis of Dostoevsky's novels does not fully convey the complexity, depth or moral purpose of his writing, an analysis of dialogue in psychotherapy does not fully take account of the desires and the moral dilemmas with which the patient and therapist are struggling. What the patient communicates is always more than language alone can convey. In looking only at discourse, the dialogical approach tends to find binary oppositions rather than triangular relationships and significations of difference, rather than sameness. Bakhtin, like most literary critics, used non-literary disciplines as analytical tools to deepen his understanding of Dostoevsky. Girard, however, approached the novels themselves as a source of knowledge. He found that while Dostoevsky wrote about the same issues in his earlier works, his understanding of the motives and meanings involved in his characters' behaviour deepened in the later works; this could be read as a critical commentary of his early work that reflects his own development as a writer (Douchemel, 1988).

Where Bakhtin saw double-voiced discourse in Dostoevsky's novels, Girard sees the anguish of characters that are entangled in the web of mimetic desire. The inner dialogues of the *Underground Man* are a classic example: he is consumed with what Girard calls *metaphysical desire,* the most extreme and intense form of mimetic desire, a desire born out of a painful awareness of what he experiences as lacking in himself and which he fantasises the other possesses. The object of the *Underground Man's* fantasy, or model, is an officer with whom he is scarcely acquainted with but whom he imagines as having the social standing, self sufficiency, autonomy, and indifference to others that he desires for himself. He despises himself for stepping aside for the officer while promenading on the Nevsky Prospect in Saint Petersburg, and is determined to assert himself as his social equal:

> Suddenly, three paces away from my adversary, I unexpectedly made up my mind, scowled fiercely, and ... our shoulders came squarely into collision! I did not yield an inch, but walked past on an equal footing! He did not even glance round, and pretended he had not noticed; but he was only pretending. I am certain of that. I am certain of it to this day! Of course I was the greater sufferer, since he was the stronger but that was not the point. [Dostoevsky, 1972, p. 58]

The stranger in the street becomes for the narrator a fascinating obstacle, simultaneously a model and a rival. In Girard's terms fascination means the peculiar intensity and ambivalence of feelings towards someone whom we wish to emulate but whose very possession of the "object" we desire prevents us from obtaining it. Part of the significance of this from a Girardian viewpoint is that anyone can be a model for anyone else. The *Underground Man's* selection of this particular officer arose solely because he had felt slighted by him on a previous occasion.

A more complex example of mimetic desire is illustrated in the following example from the *The Brothers Karamazov*. Kolya, a precocious 13-year-old, takes the saintly Aleksy Karamazov as a model whom he both admires and wishes to emulate. He also wants to win the admiration of Aleksy but wishes to conceal both his admiration and his desire for it to be returned, so he can appear indifferent and self-sufficient. Dostoevsky uses the stylistic device that Bakhtin refers to as free indirect discourse, where the authorial voice is intermingled with Kolya's own voice, to represent Kolya's consciousness:

> Thus the present moment was an important one; for one thing, he must not be found wanting, must demonstrate his independence: "Or else he will think I am thirteen and take me for one of those junior boys. And what are those junior boys to him? I shall ask him when I meet him. It's a pity I'm so small though. Tuzikov is younger than me, but he's half a head taller. However, I have an intelligent face; I'm not good looking, I know my face is rotten to look at, but it's an intelligent one. I must also not talk too much, or else we'll start off with embraces straight away, and he'll think ... Pah, what a horrible thing it will be if he thinks that! ... [Dostoevsky, 2003, p. 680]

The present chapter will describe Girard's ideas, insofar as they are relevant to psychotherapy, in more detail. I will present a brief outline of Girard's critique of the Freudian Oedipus Complex and narcissism in order to illustrate, from a Girardian perspective, the "myth" of original spontaneous desire and the real mimetic nature of desire. This will be followed by a discussion of the ways in which Girard's mimetic psychology could inform ideas about self and consciousness. Finally, the general relevance of Girard's ideas for psychotherapy will be considered, including some possible drawbacks and limitations.

The violent origins of human civilisations, the "scapegoat mechanism" and the genesis of language

As previously mentioned, these aspects of Girard's thought are frequently contentious (Webb, 1993). The primary role Girard assigns to violence in human culture and its relationship to desire can be profoundly disturbing.[1] It seems important to note here that while Girard considers it is important to recognise and acknowledge our capacity for violence, both on an individual and a societal level, he does not advocate violence in any shape or form. On the contrary, he sees the renunciation of violence as the only hope of ensuring the long-term survival of the human community (Girard, 1987). Girard's (1977) analysis is wide, encompassing early religion, Christian and Jewish theology, Greek tragedy and research in social anthropology. A brief overview of Girard's position will be given here as a context for those aspects of his thinking of more immediate relevance to psychotherapy.

Fundamental to human psychology is the propensity to imitate others, particularly the desires of others. Objects are desired primarily because they are desired by others. It is the desire of the other that endows any given object with value (Ouzgane, 2001). If this mimetic[2] desire is unrestrained, it will inevitably lead to rivalry, conflict, and violence. Girard (2001) asserts that this wisdom was enshrined in the last of the Old Testament Ten Commandments, the only one to forbid not an act but a desire: in prohibiting "coveting" the neighbour's wife or worldly goods there was an implicit recognition that these things were desirable not in themselves but because they belonged to the neighbour and that to seek to deprive him of them would lead to violence. Girard surmises that, prior to the first human communities, such mimetic violence was generalised and self-perpetuating, ultimately reaching a "mimetic crisis" that was only resolved when the collective violence was directed towards a third party who became the universal victim, or scapegoat. The mimetic principle ensures that once a few direct their violence towards a common target, others will follow and their violence is then deflected from each other onto the victim (Webb, 1993), which leads to the warring parties becoming reconciled. The victim or scapegoat is seen as wholly responsible for the violence and his or her death brings about peace between those previously at war with each other.[3] The apparently miraculous peace that then ensues after the murder of the victim is posthumously attributed to the powers of the victim, who is then worshipped as a god. In fact there is nothing "special" about the victim and the violence is entirely random (Alison, 2001). Despite this, the original murder is ritually re-enacted to maintain peace in the community. In this way violence and the religious practice of sacrifice are inextricably linked. Girard (1987) maintains that all myths contain a murder followed by a collective reconciliation. The resolution of violence and conflict through murder or victimisation is known as the scapegoat mechanism. The tendency towards scapegoating is prevalent in contemporary societies where it takes the form of sexism, racism and the oppressions of minorities such as refugees, political dissidents, homosexuals or the mentally ill. In each case there is a collective act of demonisation against a fantasised other, often fuelled by the popular media (Kearney, 1995). As Webb (1933) points out, the Nazis' selection of the Jews and other minorities as the scapegoat "resolved" the "sacrificial crisis" brought about by the collapse of the old social order in Germany after the First World War as mimetic violence was then deflected onto a common victim.

Among Christian theologians, Girard (1987) is noted for his controversial non-sacrificial interpretation of the gospels; his position is that Christ was not "sacrificed" to atone for the sins of humankind but was crucified because he preached against violence and sacrificial ethics of all kinds. This was a culmination of revelation throughout the Old Testament of a non-vengeful God who desires mercy, not sacrifice. Girard (1987) further argues that when, as believed by the followers of sacrificial religion, violence is divine and an aid to salvation, such violence is not a source of terror. However when the "founding mechanism" or collective murder is exposed for what it is, it loses its power to put an end to violence and the human rather than divine origin of violence can no longer be concealed. Moreover, once people become aware of the true nature of violence, they are burdened with the responsibility to renounce it, as the former myths and rituals have lost their power to bring about and maintain peace and reconciliation. Girard (1987), refers to the collective guilt that humankind carries for the founding murder, the knowledge of which is unbearable and leads to the blame for violence always being attributed to other people. Girard argues that historical Christianity became a persecutory religion because of its sacrificial reading of the Passion and the Redemption:

> The very fact that the deity is re-infused with violence has consequences for the entire system, since it partially absolves mankind from a responsibility that ought to be equal and identical for all. [Girard, 1987, p. 225]

The cycle of violence can only broken by people individually and collectively acknowledging and taking responsibility for their own capacity for violence.

As well as seeing the origins of society in the scapegoat mechanism, Girard sees it as the source of signification and language, or hominisation (Webb, 1993). The peace that follows the murder of a sacrificial victim allows for what Girard (1987) refers to as a *new kind of attention* (99), which is non-instinctual and is focused on the cadaver of the victim. The victim becomes the signifier or the first sign, the source of all cultural meaning (Webb, 1993). As the community wishes to maintain this state of peace and reconciliation, the sign is reproduced through ritual in which new "victims" are substituted for the original victim:

> Driven by sacred terror and wishing to continue life under the sign of the reconciliatory victim, men attempt to reproduce and represent this sign; this attempt consists first of all in the search for victims who seem capable of bringing about the primordial epiphany, and it is there that we find the first signifying activity that can always be defined, if one insists in terms of language or writing. The moment arrives when the original victim, rather than being signified by new victims, will be signified by a variety of things that continue to signify the victim while at the same time progressively masking, disguising, and failing to recognise it. [Girard, 1987, p. 103]

Representation is therefore the deferral of mimetic desire and violence. Girard's account is radically different from structuralism as he looks outside signifying systems to actual events and insists on the underlying historical reality of the violent events described in myth and re-enacted in ritual:

I suggest that the symbolic order is born of the scapegoat mechanism, that is, of collective violence that is always at the mercy of reciprocal violence. [Girard, 1978, p. 111]

For Lacan it was Oedipisation, the passage from the imaginary to the symbolic, that marked the transition from pre-social to social humankind. Thereafter there is no distinction between the individual and society, as man becomes a social being with the appropriation of language and it is language itself that constitutes the human subject (Turkle, 1992). By contrast, for Girard, the origins of language and the transition from the pre-social to the social lie in universal mimesis and the concrete reality of human relationships in history. In French thought this is a radical break with the idealist approach to psychology with its origins in Cartesian philosophy, which subordinates contingent reality to abstract meaning constituted by the linguistic structure of consciousness. For structuralists such as Lacan and Levi-Strauss it was mental structures that determined the shape of myths, while for Girard these myths were shaped by historical events of a violent nature (Webb, 1993).

Girard (1978, 1987) is highly critical of the structuralist approach to understanding cultural phenomena in terms of self-referential symbolic systems that take no account of the role of violence in the production of meaning. One set of significations is reduced to another set of hidden significations and it is always difference that is signified. He provocatively argues that in only focusing on differential meanings, structuralism misses the point of some of the great works of literature. In Dostoevsky's works this is the sameness of "doubles" that signifies "nothing". He argues that man both creates symbolic forms and confuses them with reality rather than recognising that particular sets of symbolic forms are used to interpret reality in particular ways.

Interdividual psychology

A Girardian understanding of the self is consistent with dialogical models insofar as both are social. Whereas language defines and constitutes the dialogical self, for Girard, it is desire that brings the self into existence, a desire that precedes language and symbolic systems. Since desire is mimetic, it can only arise in the social sphere as a product of social interaction. The concept of mimetic desire as the foundation of both the self and society is the basis of interdividual psychology, a psychology that is purely social. As in dialogical self theory, the individual can only be conceived of in social and relational terms but the role of the other in the psyche is conceived of somewhat differently.

Jean-Michel Oughourlian (1991), a psychiatrist and a Girardian, argues that mimesis is as fundamental to human psychology as gravity is to the physical universe; the capacity for imitation is what makes us human. He conceives of mimesis as the force that attracts individuals to each other, a force that is proportional to mass. Mass in this sense can refer to the physical mass of the adult in relation to a child but, more importantly, to the capacity that each individual has to attract or influence another. In groups or crowds the mass would correlate with the number of people, thus accounting for the powerful mimetic forces involved when large numbers of people congregate. Oughourlian (1984) succinctly describes the paradox of mimesis: it both repels and attracts. Imitation can lead to conformity and uniformity, but when it comes to *gestures of appropriation (72)* it can drive individuals apart, as two or more desires converge on the same object. It can also do both of these things simultaneously, which leads to people both agreeing and disagreeing with each other at the same time. So mimesis, like gravity, is the force that both brings people together and keeps them separate from each other (Webb, 1993).

Mimesis is so integral to our humanity that it is taken for granted and rarely evokes comment. Studies of early infancy have demonstrated that the capacity to imitate is present in the infant from only a few days after birth.[4] Learning and development are driven by the child's natural urge to imitate firstly her parents and subsequently an ever expanding range of other people. Without it there would be no civilisation or culture:

> ... this remarkable force that attracts human beings to one another, that unites them, that enables children to model themselves on adults, that makes possible their full ontogenesis and, as I just said, their acquisition of language—if this force did not exist, there would be no mankind. [Oughourlian, 1991, p. 2]

Without mimesis there can be neither human intelligence nor cultural transmission. Mimesis is the essential force of cultural integration. [Oughourlian, 1987, in Girard 1987, p. 17]

Recent research in neuroscience also supports the idea that imitation is crucial to human learning and social cognition. The discovery of the mirror neurons system (MNS) has led to a radical reconsideration of mental functions and their relation to consciousness (Stamenov & Gallese, 2002). The MNS was first observed in monkeys when it was noted that particular neurons became active when the monkey makes a particular action and when it observes another monkey or human perform a similar action (Gallese et al, 1996, Rizolatti et al, 1996). Further research on human subjects supported the hypothesis that the MNS functions in a similar way (Buccino et al, 2001), leading to the conclusion that the motor functions of the nervous system not only provide the means to control and execute actions but also to make internal representations of them (Fogassi & Gallese 2002). From this, Rizolatti et al (2002) suggest that the MNS also has the function of action understanding, i.e. the facility to predict the consequences of the actions of another as well as one's own, an essential pre-condition and the main ingredient in mediating imitation (Wohlschlager & Bekkering, 2002). Billard & Arbib define imitation as being more than the mere ability to reproduce the actions of others:

> ... it is the ability to replicate and learn skills which are not part of the animal's usual repertoire simply by the observation of those performed by others. [Billard & Arbib, 2002, p. 344]

They suggest that learning by imitation is fundamental to social cognition and to the ability to interpret the behaviour of others and to deceive or manipulate another's state of mind.

It follows from this that human mirror systems may also be involved in social goals as well as object-directed actions (Morrison, 2002). Mimetic desire is a social goal in the sense that it is motivated by something beyond the satisfaction of a physical need. Just as the child naturally imitates the expressions and behaviour of those around her, she also imitates what she perceives to be their desires or goals. An example of primitive acquisitive mimesis is often observed when a number of young children are placed in a room with a number of identical toys; the first toy to be selected will attract the interest of all the other children and quarrels will ensue (Bertoneau, 1987). Girard and Oughourlian make a crucial distinction between desires and needs. The latter refer to the physical requirements for life[5] such as food, drink, and shelter (Webb, 1993),[6] whereas desires are only directed towards goods or objects with symbolic meaning and are shaped and learnt by imitating the desires of others. Desire is therefore always triangular in that it is mediated by another, the triangle consisting of the subject who desires, the object of desire, and the model whose own desire designates the object as desirable. As Girard (1966) points out, children's play is always triangular, an imitation of adults, with toys that are endowed with symbolic meaning by adult activity. Rather than being an alternative explanation for play to the internalisation and re-enactment of object relations, mimesis precedes internalisation and is its essential pre-condition. As noted by Mikkel Borch-Jacobson (1988), who was influenced both by Girard and Lacan, mimesis also precedes desire. The child first identifies with the parents in play and in doing so desires to be grown up.

Internally and externally mediated desire

Another crucial distinction Girard makes is between externally and internally mediated desires. An external mediator, such as a parent or teacher, can be an appropriate model for a child to imitate and the distance in power and status guarantees that they will not come into competition or conflict over pursuit of the same objects. However, if the external mediator is insecure or has not resolved their own mimetic conflicts, they may perceive the child's entirely innocent imitation as a threat and place her in "double bind", a term which Girard borrows from Bateson (1972), that says both "imitate me and don't imitate me", a potential source of later neurosis discussed further below. External mediation is essential for human learning and is non-conflictual. In the psychologically healthy individual, desires are continually shaped by external mediation throughout life. Adults and children model themselves and their desires on colleagues, relatives, teachers or friends as well as more distant models. The role of external mediation in shaping the desires and the behaviour of adults has implications for psychotherapy and the training of psychotherapists. Of particular importance is the transition from external to internal mediation, for example when the therapist or teacher becomes an obstacle to the patient's recovery or the student's development.

External mediation becomes internal mediation when the subject and model have overlapping spheres of interest and thus pursuit of the same object leads to rivalry and conflict which, if uncontrolled, can lead to violence. Cultural prohibitions, laws and socially agreed codes of conduct arose in order to prevent and contain the unrestrained pursuit of mimetic desire and rivalry. Girard (1966) traces the evolution of mimetic desire from Cervantes' Don Quixote, whose external mediator is the imaginary knight Amadis of Gaul, through the works of Stendhal, Flaubert, and Proust to Dostoevsky, whose characters are mostly driven by internally mediated desires. This evolution is parallel to changes in society from relatively stable hierarchical and differentiated forms of social organisation to the less stable, more fluid, undifferentiated forms that obtained under early capitalism, the period when Dostoevsky was writing. As social differences between people are eroded, internal mediation and the triangular emotions associated with it—envy, jealousy and rage—become more pervasive.[7] In internal mediation, the model is also a rival and an obstacle standing between the subject and the desired object. This double bind serves only to intensify the desire and make the model into even more of an object of fascination for the subject. People become models, rivals and obstacles for each other, a phenomenon Girard refers to as double mediation. The more intense the rivalry, the more the difference between them is eroded so that they become "doubles"[8] of each other. This raises interesting issues for the conceptualisation of object relationships in psychotherapy, which are conceived of as vertical relationships in which one part, frequently derived from a parental relationship, is more powerful. Internal and double mediation suggests that object relations could also be conceived of as horizontal relationships with a more equal balance of power: in Girard's terms this would be a relationship between "doubles", each being a model and an obstacle for the other.

The subtle transition between external and internal mediation could also be understood as a reflection of the greater mobility of voices in the dialogical self. However, such horizontal relationships may be more difficult to acknowledge and formulate, particularly as they occur within the therapeutic relationship, because of our propensity to deceive ourselves about internally mediated mimetic desire.

Whereas external mediation is characterised by open respect or admiration for the model, internal mediation is characterised by denial, deceit and dissimulation. Cultures that value individualism, originality, and autonomy find it hard to give up what Girard (1966) refers to as *the lie of spontaneous desire (16)*. Desire has become a private experience and the former social mechanisms of catharsis and expulsion, as well as some of the protective prohibitions arising from religion and rigid social divisions, are no longer available. Rather than shoring up the illusion of the autonomous and independent subject, interdividual psychology draws uncomfortable attention to our interpersonal dependency and to how the objects of desire are pursued not because of their intrinsic worth but because of an experienced deficit or lack in our selves that we perceive or imagine the other possesses. There are obvious parallels here with Lacan, who also asserts that we are not the originators of our desire but that desire is nevertheless fundamental to our human subjectivity. In some respects, Girard's account is remarkably similar to Lacan's in its emphasis on lack, the role of the other and the other's desire and its insistence on the differentiation of desire from need. For Lacan, desire can only become known to the subject insofar as it can be articulated in speech (Evans, 1996), but for Girard it is our enslavement to the desire of the other that limits the extent to which we can bear to become aware of our desire. Imitation is so hard to perceive because the more fervent it is, the greater the extent to which it is denied. At its most extreme, mimetic desire becomes "metaphysical desire", a desire for the very being of the other who is perceived as self-sufficient, independent, indifferent, and immune to desire or as embodying "absolute difference". When desire reaches this pitch of unreality, Girard (1987) suggests that it is has crossed the threshold of psychopathology, although it is entirely continuous or even identical with what passes as normal because it is socially sanctioned as professional or intellectual ambition, a craving for adventure, a determination to win or poetic angst.

Girard's critique of Freud

Like Lacan, Girard is critical of biological interpretations of Freud and the notion of instincts or drives. Although Freud's positing of the unconscious implied a radical decentring of the autonomous self, desires were still regarded as emanating from the individual rather than arising in the context of relationships with other people. Oughourlian (1991) suggests that the early Freud came very close to dismantling the illusion of the autonomy of individual desire in his studies of hysteria and hypnosis but shied away from the implications of this, and instead "invented" the unconscious as a way of explaining neurotic symptoms outside voluntary control. In this way individual ownership of desire is preserved without the individual having responsibility for its effects and the person can instead be treated as suffering with symptoms of an illness. Central to Girard's critique is his differing interpretation of two myths of enduring significance in psychoanalytic thinking, that of Oedipus and Narcissus. Violence, envy, rivalry, and thwarted desire are pervasive aspects of both these myths.

The Oedipus complex

Girard's critique of the Freudian Oedipus complex is a provocative one for psychoanalytic purists, as he accuses Freud of failing to see its most significant aspects.[9] For Freud there is a straight line between desire and its object and although the idea of identification with the father in the Oedipus complex has mimetic elements to it, Freud never followed these through (Girard, 1977). The child's erotic desire for the mother exists independently of and completely separate from his[10] identification with the father in Freud's account. Central to Girard's critique is his reinterpretation of the triangular relationships that can re-occur throughout life that structure the plots of many works of literature and that Freud attributed to the Oedipus conflict. A weakness in some Object Relations accounts is that the role of the father in psychic life is under-theorised, the focus being on dyadic relationships, with an emphasis on the mother. Girard (1977, 1978, 1987, 2004) accounts for the father in the psychic life of the child but does not attribute to the child the destructiveness of incestuous desires, rivalry, and revenge. The child is seen as innocent and vulnerable in relation to the power of adults. For the child, the father is a model and his imitation is entirely innocent. His desires are directed towards the objects of his father's desire, only because his father designates them as desirable. The child does not see the father as a rival and has no wish to usurp him. The child is bewildered, even traumatised, if he is then chastised for his imitation and finds himself placed in a double bind:

> The model-disciple relationship precludes by its very nature the sense of equality that would permit the disciple to see himself as a possible rival to the model ... the disciple fails to grasp that he can indeed enter into competition with his model and even become a menace to him. If this is true for adults, how much truer it must be for the child experiencing his first encounter with mimetic desire!
> ... The incest wish, the patricide wish, do not belong to the child but spring from the mind of the adult, the model. In the Oedipus myth it is the oracle that puts such ideas into Laius's head, long before Oedipus was capable of entertaining any ideas at all. [Girard, 1977, pp. 174–175]

The fault therefore lies entirely with the parents, a conclusion that Freud turned his back on when he abandoned the seduction theory.[11] However, unlike Freud, Girard does not see family relationships as playing the central role in the pathology of desire. Identification with the father is normal but imitation and rivalry are restrained in a functional family and the father does not serve as a model for sexual desire. This restraint prepares the child for the mimetic pressures in the wider social world. Pathological desire is mimetic, not Oedipal. The family, rather than being the crucible of pathology, is a protection against the less restrained rivalries of the wider society and its social institutions. In dysfunctional families such desire is not canalised and restrained and the child is subject to what Girard (1987) refers to as *indifference* or *morbid attention* (p. 354), which can be understood as neglect or abuse. In the *Brothers Karamazov*, as Girard (1987) points out, the destructive rivalry between the father and two of his sons arose because of his failure as a father and not because of any prior Oedipal wish to destroy him on the part of his sons.

Despite Freud's biased reading of Oedipus, the Oedipus complex has enjoyed widespread popularity as an explanation for neurosis, a popularity that could be accounted for by its exoneration of parents while simultaneously relieving the child of blame by attributing his rivalrous and murderous feelings to the unconscious. A more careful reading of the Oedipus myth would have reinforced Freud's original thesis regarding the abuse of children by parents or the seduction theory (Webb, 1993). The most vociferous critics of Freud, often feminists, have centred on classical psychoanalysis' denial of the reality of child abuse and neglect as well as what Alice Miller (1983) refers to as ordinary cruelty disguised as "child rearing". Girard is, however, quite clear about the innocence and vulnerability of children in a way that accords with recognition of how abuse and trauma in childhood is often a constituent factor in mental distress in later life:

> If there is a stage of human existence at which reciprocity is not yet in operation and at which reprisals are impossible, that stage is surely early childhood. That is why children are so vulnerable. The adult is quick to sense a violent situation and answer violence with violence; the child on the other hand, never having been exposed to violence, reaches out for his model's objects with unsuspecting innocence. Only an adult could interpret the child's actions in terms of usurpation. Such a usurpation comes from the depths of a cultural system to which the child does not yet belong based on cultural concepts of which the child has not the remotest notion. [Girard, 1977, p. 174][12]

While Freud has to posit the death instinct to account for the damaging repetition of triangular rivalries in later life, Girard's description of the dynamics of mimetic desire allows for an explanation of rivalry without reference to either myth or the nuclear family and also accounts for the unlimited repetition of these triangular relationships:

> The object of desire is indeed forbidden. But it is not the "law" that forbids it, as Freud believes—it is the person who designates the object to us as desirable by desiring it himself.

The non-legal prohibition brought about through rivalry has the greatest capacity to wound and traumatise. This structure of rivalry is not a static configuration of elements. Instead the elements of the system react upon one another; the prestige of the model, the resistance he puts up, the value of the object, and the strength of the desire it arouses all reinforce each other, setting up a process of positive feedback. [Girard, 1987, p. 296]

Rather than the Oedipus myth accounting for mimetic rivalry, Girard (1978) suggests that mimetic rivalry gave rise to Freud's account of it by directing attention away from the rivalries between himself and his followers towards *some ludicrous fable* (p. 62).

Narcissism

Girard (1987) also brings the mimetic principle to bear on the subject of narcissism. Freud and Lacan derive the concept from the myth of the nymph Echo and her unrequited love for Narcissus. He spurned Echo, who was captivated by his beauty and aloofness, only to be captivated in turn by his own reflection which eventually led to his death. There is no unified account of narcissism in psychoanalysis: the details of Freud's account changed in his different writings about the subject and it has been elaborated in various ways by different psychoanalytic writers. All accounts are, however, consistent in the distinction drawn between narcissistic love for the self and anaclitic love, love for another. However it is conceived in psychoanalytic terms, narcissism is also regarded as immature compared with object love. Developmentally it is associated with a stage in infancy where the sense of self is unclear and the boundaries between self and other are not yet in place: narcissistic "disorders" in contemporary Object Relations-based psychoanalysis are understood as originating in childhood relationships where achievement and appearances are overvalued or where a child compensates for emotional deprivation or abuse in the family by seeking attention elsewhere. Common features of narcissism are an idealised self and sense of entitlement, coupled with a denial of emotional dependency on others. The self is nevertheless experienced as fragile and acutely vulnerable to perceived slights or criticism and is therefore prone to feelings of despair and rage against which it defends itself by attributing its own weaknesses and failings to others. Narcissistic disorders are seen as exacerbated by contemporary post-modern culture with its "inflation" of the detached self (Ryle & Kerr, 2002). Bernadette Waterman Ward describes this bleak social world from a Girardian perspective, in which metaphysical desire is pervasive and narcissistic vulnerability is intensified:

> General, aimless rivalry dominates a social world of fragile undefined selves in which anyone can be a model of imitation, and therefore anyone can be a threat to one's sense of self. What an imitator actually seeks to have is whatever is desirable: most desirable of all, perhaps, is the ability to know what is desirable, a mysterious quality that is constantly attributed to others; Girard calls this quality "being".... As human desire has no real single object, it has no closure; envy and revenge threaten others in a widening net of destruction. [Waterman Ward, 2000, p. 19]

Whereas Freud distinguishes between object-related desire and narcissistic desire, Girard (1987) asserts that all desire is mimetic. Object desire is attracted to narcissistic desire because it is also mimetic. The apparently "intact narcissism" of the other that gives the impression of complete self-sufficiency attracts the desire of others. Girard refers to Freud's account in which narcissism is seen as being particularly applicable to beautiful women, suggesting that what Freud was attracted to in these women was not so much their beauty as their indifference. Girard redefines narcissism, not as an essence but as a strategy: as desire attracts desire, to desire oneself as an object is to draw the desire of the other to oneself. The successful narcissist creates an illusion of self-love and self-sufficiency that actually depends on the desire of the other to sustain it. Metaphysical desire, in which the self is experienced as insufficient or inadequate in relation to the other, is humiliating and painful: a way of avoiding this is by imposing it on others:

> The strategy of desire consists in setting up the dazzling illusion of a self-sufficiency that we shall believe in a little ourselves if we succeed in convincing the other person of it.

> In a world that is utterly devoid of objective criteria, desires are entirely devoted to mimetism.... So each person must feign the most impressive narcissism, must advertise as subtly as he can the desire that he experiences for himself, so that he can compel others to imitate this appetising desire. [Girard, 1987, p. 371]

Such narcissistic strategies are widely reflected in advertising in which the symbolic rather than the use value of goods is the selling point, and in numerous self-help books that promote success in business, social life or what passes for love. Successful narcissists may not in fact be perceived as such but rather seen as having high self-esteem or as possessing confidence and leadership qualities. However, such strategies also lead to diminishing returns:

> The narcissistic libido feeds on the desire that it directs toward itself, but quickly enough this food comes to seem a delusion. The very fact that others' desires are directed toward it causes them to become devalued and lose their identity. [Girard, 1987, p. 373]

Narcissistic disorders could be understood as the eventual failure of this strategy to win the desire and admiration of the other. In societies where narcissism is both encouraged and is, to a certain extent, necessary for psychological survival, failed narcissism may be partly a reflection of the social and economic inequalities that deprive many people of the means to acquire self-esteem and social recognition. Girard (1987) implies that increased social instability in contemporary societies means that it is easier now than it was for Freud to see that there is no essential difference between what Freud perceived as mature, object-directed desire and immature, narcissistic self-directed desire, insofar as both are mimetic. Nevertheless, Girard credits Proust with a deeper understanding of desire including his own desire, than Freud:

> He never makes the mistake of supposing that, besides object-directed desire—which causes an impoverishment of the libido—there exists a narcissistic desire that is directed toward **the same** and not toward absolute otherness, aiming at what

most resembles the narcissistic subject himself. Proust knows very well that there is no desire except for absolute difference and that the subject always lacks this difference absolutely. [Girard, 1987, p. 389]

Proust writes about the aristocracy in early 20th century France, describing a world in which all needs had been satisfied and people had become increasingly alienated from each other, despite the lack of concrete differences between them. Girard argues that this form of alienation has subsequently become prevalent throughout societies where people are free from want. It is distinct from Marxist class alienation in that the other is indistinguishable from the self in material terms, the only differences being abstract and symbolic. These residual differences assume huge significance as people struggle to both differentiate themselves from and deny their dependency on the other. Girard suggests that Proust's account of mimetic desire and double mediation in the small, enclosed world of the Faubourg Saint-German keenly anticipated the global abstract conflicts of the 20th century where ideology is merely a pretext for *ferocious oppositions that are secretly in agreement (1966, 225).*

Freud's condemnation of narcissism was, according to Girard's mimetic principle, motivated by the resentment that narcissism can provoke by being both the model for desire and the obstacle that stands in its way. Unlike Proust, Freud was only partially aware of the nature of his own desires. Girard sees the post-modern trend towards the deconstruction or demystification of any ideas that have the appearance of stability in avant-garde academic research as yet another example of the fascination and resentment inspired by the other's apparent self-sufficiency. Both Girard's critique of Freud and Reed's critique of Bakhtin can be seen in this light, as can my attempts in the last chapter to qualify the overall usefulness of Bakhtin's dialogism for psychotherapy. The conflict of ideas is in Girardian terms an evolutionary development that in civilised societies replaces physical violence. Jean Dupuy (1995) cites Lakatos who states that

> ... a theory can become a hero only through murder. A theory becomes testworthy on presenting a threat to some extant theory.[13] [p. 2]

However, Dupuy warns against the devaluing of such critiques on this basis, pointing out that the fascination and resentment is mutual and extends in both directions. Drawing on Derrida's notion of undecidability, he suggests that any idea or theory that affirms its own self-sufficiency or completeness needs the affirmation of the other as well, and is therefore similarly fascinated with the other who threatens to destroy its autonomy.

The Girardian self

A dialogical account of self side-steps the issue of mimesis and mimetic desire, in the same way that Freud did by placing the Oedipus complex at the origin of the subject and giving primacy to object desire. According to Mikkel Borch-Jacobson (1988), Freud wished to preserve the myth of the autonomous individual subject at all costs. He argues that Freud preferred to admit to unconscious homosexual attraction to, rather than acknowledge his rivalry with, his colleagues, as this would have revealed the extent of his personal ambition that the theory of psychoanalysis both satisfied and disguised. Anthony Ryle, a dialogically-oriented theorist, is by contrast open when it comes to acknowledging his own fascination with psychoanalysis when he states:

> On the one hand I owe to it (psychoanalysis) my most profound insights into the psychotherapeutic process: on the other hand I am impatient with many aspects of its practices and with the complacency, conservatism and self-absorption of its institutions. [Ryle, 1990, p. 221]

In this passage, which can be read as self-deconstruction (Dupuy, 1995), Ryle seems to acknowledge both his dependency on and admiration for psychoanalysis and the resentment this "self-sufficiency" inspires, and his consequent desire to both demystify psychoanalysis and differentiate himself from it. However, he does not follow this self-insight through in his theorisation of cognitive analytic therapy. It is possible that cognitive analytic theory fails to take account of desire in its account of the self because the term is itself laden with the traditional psychoanalytic overtones from that Ryle wishes to distance himself from.

For Girard and Oughourlian, mimesis is prior to consciousness and representation and by its actions brings the self into being. Oughourlian (1984) emphasises that learning is always mimetic and that children have an extraordinary capacity to reproduce parental behaviour. In the infant a temporal dimension quickly supplements the initial spatial dimension of mimesis so that the repetition of a gesture or sound is separated by a period of time. This is the basis of memory and allows for the acquisition of language. It is also the dimension of mimesis that is makes us human. Without a temporal dimension to mimesis, there would be no memory to guarantee the continuity of the self over time (Oughourlian, 1991). For Oughourlian and Girard, mimesis comes first and is the precondition for language that allows for the formation of a self and an identity. If desire is understood as the dynamic force that animates consciousness (Oughourlian, 1996), the question of desire is then the central to the understanding of self and consciousness.

When it comes to his critique of Freudian unconscious, Girard (1987) asserts that if there is any use for a concept of the unconscious it is the existence of non-representational mimesis. In this respect it is a negative unconscious consisting only of what we are unaware, because it has become habitual. There is no particular mystery attached to it. As referred to above, Oughourlian (1991) argues that Freud invented the unconscious to account for human neurosis and irrationality, while still preserving the notion of the autonomous individual as the originator of spontaneous desire. Like Girard, Oughourlian is sceptical about the use of the term unconscious but if it does have a use it refers, with echoes of Lacan, to a mythic representation of the Other who is the unrecognised source of desire. He goes on to say in a way that bears an uncanny resemblance to Ryle's subsequent (1994)[14] critique of the Freudian unconscious:

> ... the Freudian unconscious, that mythic hypostasis peopled with all sorts of occult mythic forces in conflict with one another, and to whose quarrels we have to submit as inevitably as bad weather, simply does not exist!
>
> The Freudian unconscious does not truly exist any more than did the Demon that it succeeded as the mask of the Other. The Id, the Superego, Eros, Thanatos, and the rest have neither more nor less actual existence than Asmodeus, Beelzebub,

Leviathan, and the various other demons. [Oughourlian, 1991, p. 152]

From this it can be understood that both Oughourlian and Ryle give priority to consciousness and that if the unconscious can be said to exist at all, it is the repository of those aspects of ourselves outside our present awareness which can, if we choose, be brought into conscious awareness. For Ryle and other theorists of the dialogical self, it is suppressed or silenced voices that lie outside conscious awareness, for Oughourlian it is the other who is the source of the desire that we imagine to belong to ourselves. By "inventing" the unconscious to account for the failure of his patients to remember the psychic traumas that gave rise to their symptoms, Freud moved further away from recognising the mimetic nature of desire and the interdividual relationship (Oughourlian, 1991).

Following from the above discussion, it can be seen that a further area of agreement between theorists of the dialogical self and theorists of interdividual psychology is their disavowal of Cartesian dualism, the idea of the autonomous individual or monad, which, from a Girardian perspective, Freud is understood as having perpetuated. Both conceive of the self as embedded in a social matrix of consciousness arising in relation to the other and of consciousness itself as occupying the area between the psyche and others or being "interdividual". Girardian thought is characterised by

> ... a common rejection of any psychology oriented toward radical individualism, just as they also reject what they refer to as "subject psychology", that is a quasi-Cartesian conception of the person as characterised by a consciousness intrinsically rational and self-transparent as well as monadically unitary. [Webb, 1993, p. 208]

Some of the social implications of interdividual psychology

Girard's theory of mimetic desire arose from a study of literature and culture in which the social and political aspects of the phenomenon are indistinguishable from its interdividual psychological aspects. He began writing at a time when Thorstein Veblen's concept of conspicuous consumption was beginning to gain currency, which

Girard (1966) refers to as an example of triangular desire. This was illustrated in Vance Packard's (1965) classic study of corporate life in the USA in which he observed how the prestige afforded to business executives in 1950s North America led to houses being marketed as "executive homes" that were designed to reflect the "success" of the owner and how the pursuit of "success" had become a lifelong obsession for those in business:

> They devote their adult lives to assaulting the slippery, crevice-ridden slopes of the pyramids in the hope of arriving at the peak or at least a ledge near the peak. . . . Their desire is to be touched by Success, the goddess who stands guard on the mist-covered peaks. Success permits only a few select climbers to enter her cloud clubs. [Packard, 1965, p. 13]

All the ingredients of triangular desire are contained in the above passage. The disciple (the pyramid climbers); the model (those who have arrived at the peak); the desired object (the goddess, success); the obstacle (the slippery crevice-ridden slopes), and the exclusivity of the select few who are seen as possessing the desired object. Above a certain level of income and wealth, inequalities between people matter, not because of the material effects of such inequalities, but because of what those inequalities signify. Thus, material goods such as clothes, cars, houses, holidays, gardens, education, and even food acquire symbolic value way beyond their use value. This is widely reflected in the media, fashion and lifestyle magazines and is exploited ruthlessly in advertising. As people get used to their wealth, mimetic rivalry finds other ways of expressing itself. Conspicuous non-consumption replaces conspicuous consumption. Rivalry can take on many forms including rivalries of non-acquisition and renunciation:

> The more wealthy we are, in other words, the less grossly materialistic we can afford to be in a hierarchy of competitive games that become more and more rarefied as the escalation continues. Ultimately this process may turn into a complete rejection of competition, which is not always but may be the most intense competition of all. [Girard, 1996, p. 11]

Mimetic desire is therefore relevant to understanding economic behaviour. Orlean (1988) argues that economic decisions are characterised by the same *radical incompleteness* (p. 102) as behaviour in other spheres of life. The speculator in the market is driven by a desire for wealth, self-sufficiency or completeness. Unlike traditional economists, who define value in terms of utility or labour, in Girardian terms there is no objective criteria for exchange value, which is determined only by the conflicting desires of individuals for wealth. That wealth is defined by money, a sign, is entirely arbitrary, as money has no intrinsic value other than that conferred by a convergence of mimetic desires. The identification of wealth with money saves it from indeterminacy and the markets are characterised by relative stability but once doubt, itself propelled by mimesis, about this relationships sets in, chaotic undifferentiation returns as each speculator looks at the other and finds only more unpredictability. Mimesis and speculative behaviour go hand in hand and as people's expectations of the market are usually self-fulfilling, mimesis in this context is not irrational.

When desire is directed towards abstract objects such as success, prestige, admiration, respect, goodness, influence or power it becomes more intense and is likely to lead to conflict. Societies in which traditional rigid class divisions have been eroded and which have become both more individualistic and supposedly more meritocratic are particularly prone to extremes of triangular desire both at the individual and at the group level. Where social and economic privilege is "earned" rather than conferred by an accident of birth, the subjective experience of being unsuccessful is all the more painful. As mimetic theory predicts, individuals and groups who possess or are perceived as possessing these abstract objects will react ruthlessly against other individuals or groups in pursuit of the same objects, but this conflict and rivalry will be fiercely denied and concealed. This leads to a corresponding increase in feelings of anger and resentment alongside feelings of envy, shame, and humiliation among those deprived of these objects, arising out of negative comparison of self with the other.

Girard (1966) predicted that the increased wealth and material well-being of the late 20th and early 21st centuries would lead to even greater spiritual suffering and that the insidious affects of double mediation would intensify as it becomes a global phenomenon. As technical progress eliminates some of the differences between people, the awareness of the remaining differences becomes more painfully acute. There are few people in the world now who, through the global media or mass tourism, are unaware of the relative privilege that most Westerners enjoy. The Turkish novelist Orhan Pamuk comments on the effect of "self-righteous Western nationalism" on less privileged populations, drawing a parallel with Dostoevsky's *Underground Man*:

> Today, an ordinary citizen of a poor undemocratic Muslim country ... is aware of how insubstantial is his share of the world's wealth. At the same time however, he senses in a corner of his mind that his poverty is to some considerable degree the fault of his own folly and inadequacy ... This is the grim, troubled private sphere ... And it is while living in this private sphere that most people in the world today are afflicted by spiritual misery. [cited by Taylor, 2004, p. 31]

This is also an illustration of the political effects of global heteroglossia: how the self has become inescapably plural, infected by alien discourses and alien values and how this plurality disproportionately oppresses people living outside the dominant discourses. For Girard, it was the scapegoat mechanism and religion, with its rituals and prohibitions, that served to contain and limit the violent consequences of acquisitive mimesis in human culture. This does not hold out much hope for the future if, as Girard suggests, the only hope for humankind lies in the renunciation of all violence. A possible side effect of prohibitions against violence, coupled with the decline in religious observance in some contemporary Western societies, is the increase in self-scapegoating, violence directed against the self in the form of depression, self-harm, and eating disorders. The higher incidence of this among girls and young women may reflect their limited access to socially approved violent activities. It is also itself a mimetic phenomenon.

Girard's thesis, that the social order arose out of disorder by the resolution of collective violence through the scapegoat mechanism and has been maintained since by religious and cultural mechanisms that produce and maintain difference, suggests that the revelation of mimetic desire is potentially dangerous. Oughourlian (1991) argues that it is only since Western culture has become sufficiently desacralised and the nature of violence so obviously profane and even more dangerous that it is both safe and necessary to talk about mimetic desire and its shameful secrets. However, Western society in the 21st century seems to be further from desacralisation than it was in 1991 with the rise of Christian fundamentalism and its growing influence in neo-conservatives politics in North America, which is matched by a corresponding and opposing rise in Islamic fundamentalism in other parts of the world. Some on both sides believe violence is justified in pursuit of their identical aims. A disenchanted Republican politician, speaking about George W. Bush's lack of rational analysis in his attitude towards Al-Qaeda, said:

> He believes you have to kill them all. They can't be persuaded, they're extremists, driven by a dark vision. He understands them, because he's just like them . . .[15]

In Girardian terms they are doubles, formerly united in their opposition to the Soviet invasion of Afghanistan and now united in their mindless pursuit of violence against each other. They represent the unreflective mimesis that, if unchecked, leads inexorably to the unleashing of violence. Desire and violence go together in that the most violently defended objects are the most desired. Violence, like desire, is mimetic and generates yet more violence until or unless it is directed towards a common victim.

Interdividual psychology and psychotherapy

Psychotherapy and its associated professions cannot avoid engaging with domestic and even international politics and, as discussed in the last chapter, psychotherapists are also engaged in their own political struggles for power and influence and while physical violence is eschewed, policies of exclusion and expulsion are ruthlessly pursued. Psychotherapy, in common with other professional groups in their formative stages, could be understood as going through a mimetic or sacrificial crisis, which can only be resolved by the institutionalisation of difference, maintained by hierarchies, enshrined in training institutes, prohibitions governing who is and who is not allowed to practice, enshrined in registration bodies, and guarded by taboos enshrined in codes of ethics. Psychotherapy is also an economic activity; psychotherapists are in competition with each other for wealth in the form of jobs, patients, and trainees. Dupuy (1984, 1995) invokes Adam Smith's metaphor of the invisible hand that ensures that social benefits come from the operation of the market, even though it is driven by the selfish economic decisions of individuals acting in their own interests. The invisible hand both contains the numerous individual selfish decisions motivated by envy, greed, pride or vanity and is also contaminated by them. The analogy here would be that those that seek to control and regulate psychotherapy, which may result in some social benefit, are no less contaminated by selfish motives than those they seek to control. We are all, to varying degrees, seekers after wealth not only because of its intrinsic value but also because of what it signifies. From this perspective wealth is created by foolishness for which we pay a moral price (Dupuy, 1995).

This moral price could well be "madness", which Oughourlian (1991) defines as the opposite not of health but of wisdom. At first sight this may seem a retrogressive definition that either ignores the social and economic deprivations that are correlated with mental distress or blames sufferers for their deprivation. A different interpretation would be that the economy and the social order that it is built on are fuelled and maintained by foolishness but wealth is itself a protection against the slide into madness, which therefore disproportionately affects disadvantaged, less powerful groups. It is not imitation, or even mimetic desire, that lead to "madness" as both are essential to our humanity, but the thwarted desire that comes from rivalry that can be expressed in various symptoms (Ougherlian 1991). "Madness" is not an illness but a form of folly that arises from a failure to recognise the origin of desire in the other:

> Rivalry is recurrent, it repeats itself. The repetition syndrome identified by psychoanalysis is mimetic for two reasons: 1) because it is always the clinical expression of a rivalry and that rivalry is always mimetic; 2) because it reproduces itself, duplicates itself, imitating the circumstances of the first rivalry and always looking for an impossible victory. That victory is impossible, since it stems from a situation which mimics the circumstances of defeat. But those circumstances are the only ones of interest, since the only battle worth winning is the one that has every chance to be lost (Oughourlian, 1996, 43).

As discussed above in Girard's critique of the Oedipus complex, rivalry does not emanate from the child but from the parent, who being the stronger would always win. Oughourlian suggests that for people who have suffered abuse in childhood, the violence against which they cannot retaliate is "stored up" for later use and that the greater the humiliation, which stems from vulnerability, the greater the "stored up" energy which, if it finds no satisfactory outlet, results in clinical symptoms in later life.

All psychotherapies deliberately employ mimetic techniques such as mirroring, reflection, and empathy in establishing a therapeutic relationship and fostering change. Body language that mirrors that of the patient is understood as reflecting a congruent emotional response on the part of the therapist. In showing respect or even love to their patients, therapists encourage patients, through identification, to respect and love themselves. The therapist is also a model from whom the client can learn the skills of self-reflection and self-management. The difficulty often encountered with "narcissistic" patients is that the therapist is often no longer an external mediator but an internal mediator or rival who, while being a model, is also from the patient's perspective an obstacle to their recovery. This involves acknowledgement of feelings such as envy, jealousy, and rivalry which are associated with a deep sense of shame as they reflect the self's awareness of its own inadequacy. Perhaps even harder is when the patient becomes the obstacle for the therapist, thwarting their desire to be regarded as an effective therapist as opposed to merely being one. Therapies that fail or reach an impasse may be a result of both parties' inability to recognise and acknowledge these feelings in the context of the therapeutic relationship. This is why it is so important that therapists acknowledge the source of their own desires in the other if they are to enable their patients to do the same. As Webb (1993) points out, it is only when we realise that our desires are neither spontaneous nor our own, that we can begin to let go of them.

Some limitations of interdividual psychology for psychotherapy

No discussion of Girardian ideas would be complete without acknowledgement of some of Girard's critics and the difficulties in using Girardian ideas in psychotherapy. The first is the apparent circularity of some of his arguments. For example, the assertion that psychological theories seldom acknowledge the importance of mimesis, mimetic desire, and the violence that can be a consequence of it, because of their prevalence and the discomfort with ideas that challenge the romantic illusion of the spontaneity of desire and individual autonomy. In other words, the lack of acknowledgement of these ideas is proof of their existence. The alternative argument to this is that psychology does not elaborate on these themes because neither mimesis nor mimetic desires are significant aspects of human social and psychological life. Any theory that seeks to account for itself only in terms of itself without reference to any external evidence is undecidable in logical terms (Goodchild, 2000). Nevertheless, Girard has inspired research across several disciplines, including language acquisition, philosophy, theology, and psychology as summarised by Fleming (2004).

Another stumbling block is Girard's claim for universalism, particularly when coupled with the aforementioned lack of analytical rigour. In the battle of ideas, Girard, unlike Bakhtin, apparently stakes a claim to a final explanation of human history and goes against the grain of the post-modern trend towards shifting and incommensurable paradigms (Kuhn, 1970). Oughourlian (1991) anticipates criticisms of universalism by making an unfashionable distinction between truth and reality. Truth, he acknowledges, is always relative and is a mimetic cultural phenomenon, while maintaining that the psychological reality that underlies belief is universal. He aims to demonstrate the same "scientific" basis for interdividual psychology as for physiological medicine by identifying the universal mechanisms that operate in producing cultural differences. Establishing and preserving difference has always been the primary function of religion and culture, in the form of hierarchies, prohibitions, and taboos because undifferentiation is a potential source of violence and disorder. Culture therefore has a vested interest in denying or hiding the mimetic nature of desire and preserving difference. At an individual level, revealing the workings of mimetic desire is discordant with our view of ourselves as autonomous self-directed or self-actualising individuals that we frequently make strenuous attempts to suppress any knowledge of it (Webb, 1991).

Girard, like Bakhtin, is a supremely gifted and original thinker whose work has required the critical attention[16] and clarification of later scholars in order to be better appreciated. From a psychotherapy perspective his work lacks a systematic theory but is rather a collection of general insights and hypotheses (Livingstone, 1992). His religious and eschatological themes are off-putting for many people, as is his insistence on Christianity being the only religion to reveal mimetic violence. He also seems to considerably underestimate the human capacity for mutuality and co-operation. Colin Davies (2000) argues that Girard fails to acknowledge the ethical truth that is constructed in relationships of mutuality, in which mimetic desire is displaced by intersubjectivity and the location of subjectivity in narrative discourse, that mimesis can lead to trust as well as violence. On the other hand, Pamela Anderson (2000) argues correctly that Girard bypasses sexual difference in his account of mimetic desire and sacrificial violence and, by implication, he oversimplifies the formation of subjectivity as well as overlooking the truth of sexually specific violence against women. She also sees consequences that are beyond violence in mimetic desire and suggests its reconfiguration as an ethic of love unconstrained by patriarchy.

The "Bakhtinian" themes that Davies and Anderson find missing in Girard constitute a challenge to the totalising ambition of his ideas and suggest that, like Bakhtin, his concepts require further clarification and modification to be useful to psychotherapists.

Conclusion

The last chapter argued that the dialogical model is a useful but not a sufficient metaphor for human consciousness and self-hood and that Girardian theory could supply the missing dimensions of mimesis and desire. This chapter has attempted to elucidate further how interdividual psychology could enlarge the understanding of self and consciousness that is both explicit and implicit in dialogical self theory.

However, although Oughourlian (1991, 1996) has written about how it can be used in clinical practice, there is no generally recognised school of psychotherapy based solely on interdividual psychology. This could be because on its own, like the dialogical approach, it is an insufficient basis for a model of psychotherapy. Despite the universal social and psychological reality that is claimed for mimetic theory and despite the diverse and widespread human behaviours that appear to lend support to those claims, it is not sufficiently inclusive of other aspects of human experience to justify being the sole basis of a school of psychotherapy. Mimesis and mimetic desire are fundamental to human consciousness, self-hood and culture but they are not the whole story. While for human beings language is primary when it comes to pursuing, expressing or concealing desires, it does not encompass all communication and humanity cannot be defined entirely by the symbolic. Human beings are also flesh and blood so consciousness cannot be defined solely by the symbolic realm of desire and language, while disregarding biological needs. Bakhtin recognised the importance of embodiment in consciousness, which he explored in his earlier phenomenological writings and in his later work on the chronotope and the carnival, aspects of his thinking that have received less attention from dialogical self theorists.

A criticism of Bakhtin's ideas about consciousness is that he fails to take enough account of the more disturbing and violent aspects of human experience. The reverse could be said about Girard; that he paints a peculiarly bleak and pessimistic picture of humanity in which the human capacities for disinterested rationality, unselfish love, kindness, and mutual respect rather than envious rivalry are underestimated. Neither the dialogical, nor the interdividual, have much to say about creativity, humour, and laughter and the emotions associated with them which may be crucial aspects of psychological health. Chapter Seven will attempt to bring the dialogical and the interdividual together with Bakhtin's thinking about the chronotope and the carnival to suggest a broader basis from which ideas about human consciousness that inform psychotherapy can be further developed, while the next chapter will briefly examine some recent research in the field of developmental psychology, cognitive neuroscience, and linguistics that seem to offer convergent support for mimetic psychology as well as its integration with dialogical models.

Notes

1 That is between the Judeo-Christian tradition of obedience to God and the Athenian tradition of freedom and the love of knowledge.
2 This capacity for violence was acknowledged by Freud (1994) who maintained that aggression was instinctual and that "Civilised society is perpetually menaced with disintegration through this primary hostility of men towards one another" (p. 40).
3 The term mimesis originated in Plato's *Republic* where it referred to the relationship between art and reality. It has been interpreted in many different ways since then and its precise meaning is therefore difficult to define. It can refer to imitation, mirroring, representation, miming, mimicking and yet is more than all these terms and is perhaps best described as a *thematic complex* (Potolsky, 2006).
4 Again Freud (1994) describes a similar process: *It is always possible to unite considerable numbers of men in love towards one another, so long as there are still some remaining as objects for aggressive manifestations* (p. 42). He also refers to the murder of the primal father at the dawn of civilisation, a victim who was reviled and subsequently became a deity after his death by violence.
5 Oughourlian cites the work of Meltzoff & Moore (1977) "Imitation of Facial and Manual Gestures by Human Neonates", *Science*, 198 (7): 75–78. There have been considerable advancements since in research regarding imitation in infancy, which are discussed in the next chapter.
6 Attachment needs would also fall into this category.
7 In societies where needs are already met, those basic items satisfying those needs usually acquire symbolic value as well.
8 Girard here differs from the Kleinian thesis of innate envy, greed and hatred in which the child can be destructively envious of the parent and the patient of the therapist (Polledri, 2003). Instead these feelings arise in the context of desire and thwarted desire and children and patients are no more vulnerable to them than parents and therapists.
9 The term doubles can cause some confusion as rivals are obviously also different from each other. Girard's intention is to demonstrate that the structural equivalence between people with identical desires outweighs the differences between them (Anspach, 2004).
10 For a more detailed discussion than space allows here see Girard (2004), Oedipus Unbound, Selected writings on rivalry and desire and Girard (1987) Chapter Four, Psychoanalytic Mythology, 352–392.

11 Girard's use of the masculine pronoun is followed here, but the argument applies equally to mothers, fathers, daughters and sons and the relationships between them.
12 As Marie Balmary (1986) (cited in Webb, 1993) points out Oedipus tried to avoid his fate by leaving the people he believed were his parents and could not have known that the stranger he killed was his father or that the woman he married was his mother. Freud abandoned the evidence of his clinical work that child sexual abuse was widespread, in favour of a misapplied myth in which the child was deemed to be at fault.
13 Some similarity might be perceived here with Lacan's imaginary phase but Girard does not see the cultural system that follows it in symbolic terms, determined by language, but as arising out of the necessity to contain violence through the expulsion of a victim. It could also be argued that there is nothing progressive in the child's loss of innocence when she learns about the rivalry of competing desires and that Girard's model of the self is therefore anti developmental.
14 Lakatos, I. (1968) Problems of Inductive Logic. Amsterdam: North Holland:

> there is no need to postulate a parallel mental world, peopled by partly savage inhabitants and partly by subversive exiles, banished from the rational conscious world. The personification of innate, opposed drives as quasi-autonomous internal objects and the meaningless concept of unconscious gratification as ways of describing humans as governed by an army of unconscious "ghosts in the machine (p. 122).

15 Bruce Bartlett, former treasury official, quoted by Ron Suskind in the Observor Newspaper, 31st October 2004.
16 The majority of Girardian scholars are based in the France. He has attracted relatively little attention in the UK outside theological circles. Cultural Values, (2000) 4, 2 is a collection of papers critiquing Girard from different perspectives, arsing out of a conference at the University of Lancaster.

CHAPTER SIX

Towards a Further Integration of Interdividual Psychology and Dialogical Consciousness via Developmental Psychology, Cognitive Neuroscience, and Linguistics

In the last chapter I discussed in greater detail how Girard's interdividual psychology could contribute to dialogical self theory, while acknowledging that a theory of desire on its own is not a sufficient or adequate basis on which to construct a model of human functioning that could usefully inform psychotherapy. I further argued that while the dialogical model and the interdividual model are complementary accounts that together have the potential for a greater understanding of human functioning and that although both are necessary, neither on their own nor in combination are sufficient. The linguistic turn in psychotherapy that conceives of the self as dialogical is reductive in that it offers a structural analysis of consciousness without adequately accounting for desire or motivation. The scope of interdividual psychology encompasses an apparently exhaustive range of human behaviour and subjective experience but is still inadequate in either accounting for or describing those aspects of human behaviour that are not governed by imitation, rivalry and, competition. In largely confining themselves to the symbolic realm of experience, both models could be said to perpetuate dualistic ways of thinking in that they do not take enough account of the fact all that human experience is embodied experience and therefore of human physiology.

In describing some recent research in the fields of developmental psychology, cognitive science, and of linguistics that appear to lend support to the concept of a dialogical self that is also a mimetic self and an embodied self, I want to emphasise what I consider to be the importance of approaching the question of the self in psychotherapy from different perspectives. These brief accounts are not intended in any way to be exhaustive of such vast fields of study and it seems important to keep in mind Paul Broks" (2003) caution that scientific research can neither locate the self in the biological structures of the brain nor explain how consciousness arises from matter:

> . . . phenomenal consciousness—the raw feel of experience—is invisible to conventional scientific scrutiny and will forever remain so. It is by definition subjective . . . Science can study the neural activity, the bodily states, the environmental conditions, and the outward behaviour . . . but the quality of—the feel—of our experiences remain forever private and therefore out of bounds to scientific analysis. [Broks, 2003, p. 140]

Nevertheless I think it is significant that social psychology, developmental psychology, and cognitive neuroscience seem to have reached a convergence in their understandings of the self. This self is both a social self, similar to others and dependent on them and also a unique self. Successful social interactions depend both on understanding that others are similar to ourselves and also different and separate from us. Mutual imitation has emerged as central to the development of a sense of self and intersubjectivity. The apparently natural and innate tendency to imitate that developmental psychologists observed in infants is supported by the neuroscientists' discovery of the Mirror Neurons System referred to in the last chapter. The self that emerges from these different areas of research is at the same time unique, social, and shared (Decety & Somerville, 2003).

Since some theorists of the dialogical self invoke Voloshinov under the rubric of Bakhtin and there is in any case considerable overlap between them, I have considered some of Voloshinov's thinking in the light of recent developments in neurolinguistics, which also brings to light important differences between Voloshinov and Bakhtin.

Imitation and psycho-social development

Despite a considerable volume of research into human imitation in the past decade there has been little attempt by Girardian scholars to integrate these findings with mimetic theory. An exception is Garrels (2004) who, having surveyed the recent research into imitation and the MNS, argues that:

> Convergent evidence across the modern disciplines of developmental psychology and cognitive neuroscience demonstrate that imitation based on mirrored neural activity and reciprocal interpersonal behaviour are what guide and scaffold human development. Not only does imitation function powerfully in the mother-infant dyad to bring about experience-dependant neurocognitive development, but it continues to thrive in adulthood as perhaps the most organising characteristic of human relations, significantly affecting mental representation, empathy, language, and intersubjective experience. [2004, p. 3]

Contrary to Piaget's (1969) thesis that the capacity to imitate is a developmental acquisition, research into imitation in infancy suggests that it is present from birth and reveals the mind of the newborn infant to be far closer to the adult mind than previously thought:

> The modern empirical findings establish a rich innate foundation for human development. Infants are not blank slates waiting to be written on. They are born with predispositions, perceptual biases, and representational capacities. The research on infant imitation reveals three important aspects of the pre-verbal mind: cross-modal co-ordination, memory, and intersubjectivity. [Meltzoff, 2002, p. 34]

In a seminal study, Meltzoff & Moore (1977) demonstrated that three-week-old infants could imitate facial gestures, distinguishing between different parts of the face, and could also reproduce these gestures over short and longer periods of time. Further studies showed the same results for newborn infants (Meltzoff and Moore, 1983, 1989). Numerous studies since have confirmed these results. These are reviewed in Meltzoff and Moore (1997), and Nadel and Butterworth (1999) give a comprehensive historical overview of imitation research. The fact that infants can imitate facial gestures, having never seen their own faces, is particularly significant. These studies showed that infants can imitate prior to any learning experience, which indicates an innate mapping between observation/ perception and execution (Melzoff, 2002) and that imitation precedes representation and symbolic functions.

Meltzoff and Moore (1997) describe a model of the mechanism underlying such imitation, which accounts for the apparent unity of self-other experience observed. They refer to this as *active intermodal mapping* or AIM:

> The crux of the AIM hypothesis is that infant imitation involves a goal-directed matching process. The goal or behavioural target is specified visually. Infants' self-produced movements provide proprioceptive feedback that can be compared to the representation of the observed act. AIM proposes that such comparison is possible because the observation and execution of human acts are coded within a common framework. We call it "supramodel act space". . . . Metaphorically, we can say that exteroception (perception of others) and proprioception (perception of self) speak the same language: there is no need for associating the two through prolonged learning because they are intimately bound at birth. [Meltzoff, 2002, pp. 24–25]

The discovery of the innate link[1] between observed and performed actions that goes along with the ability to imitate has implications for attachment, suggesting what Meltzoff (2002) refers to as a primordial connection between infant and caretaker, with further implications for emotional learning and intersubjectivity. Two people imitating each other share similar representations of the action as well as information specific to their own point of view. Mimetic reciprocity is an essential part of parent and child interaction that promotes both attachment and self-other differentiation (Meltzoff & Decety, 2003). Infants are not only aware of imitating others but also of other people imitating them and therefore initiating imitative behaviour can be a pre-verbal way of checking out another's identity i.e. is this the person that does this with me? (Meltzoff, 2002). In the young infant the prefrontal lobes are not fully developed, which means that their behaviour is characterised by a lack of inhibition and restraint. Imitation is therefore unrestrained although intentional. Kinsbourne (2002) suggests that imitation could be the preverbal infant's way of perceiving what others do and repetition a form of remembering.[2] However, AIM does not account for goal-directed imitation that requires achievement of a goal rather than a direct matching of motor actions. This requires both an awareness of self as agent and an ability to infer the mental states of others or a theory of mind (ToM).

Meltzoff (2002) proposes a model in which motor imitation is the basis for the subsequent development of empathy and a ToM, which is the capacity to infer the goals, intentions, desires, and mental states of others that indicates an understanding of other minds as separate. It develops from early imitative behaviour in which the infant learns that others are "like me" but also "separate from me". Meltzoff (1995) found that toddlers aged 18 months could imitate at a more sophisticated level, being able to infer the goals of the experimenter when he "accidentally" failed to achieve it and were able to match the experimenter's goal rather than merely copy his actions. He suggests that this is one of the building blocks of an early ToM, which develops from the innate ability to recognise equivalence between perceived and executed acts. Meanwhile Rochat (2002) proposes that self-imitation, the repetition of one's own body movements, is also a way of establishing self-identity. His research found that infants at two months old respond to audio-feedback that reflects the intensity of their own sucking on a pacifier in a way that newborn infants do not. He argues that this self-imitation or the ability to reproduce their own actions leads to the sense of self as an agent separate from other entities and is the origin of the capacity for self-reflection or self-contemplation. Kinsbourne (2002) suggests that rhythmic and repetitive movement of the limbs is the infant's way of feeling ownership of its body parts.[3] In the process of self-imitation, the infant maps the relation between mental states and bodily movements. S/he experiences the fulfilment and frustration of desires and needs, feelings of various kinds and the facial expressions, bodily gestures and vocalisations that accompany them. In this way infants come to associate different states of mind or feelings with different modes of behaviour. Consequently when they see others behaving in similar ways, they infer mental experiences with which they are already familiar (Meltzoff & Decety, 2003).

Meltzoff makes an implicit connection between imitation, ToM, and the beginnings of dialogical interaction:

> The crux of the developmental theory offered here is that imitation sets children on a trajectory for learning about the other's mind. The "like me-ness" of others, first manifest in imitation, is a foundation for more mature forms of social cognition that depend on the self-equivalence between self and other. The Golden Rule, "Treat thy neighbour as thy self" at first occurs in action through imitation. Without an imitative mind we might not develop this moral mind. Imitation is the bud and empathy and moral sentiments are the ripened fruit—born from years of interaction with other people already recognised to be "like me". To the human infant, another person is not an alien, but a kindred spirit—not an "It" but an embryonic "Thou." [Meltzoff, 2002, p. 36]

The recognition of the other as another "I," rather than a she or an it, that is that the other has a separate existence and viewpoint independent of self, is a necessary part of the development of a fully formed dialogical self (Hermans, 2004). This recognition, in which knowledge of the other goes hand in hand with an awareness of self, would not be possible without the empathic capacity that is allowed for by imitation. Empathy is the extension of the ability to imitate bodily movements into the realm of the emotions, to feel as someone else feels (Lakoff & Johnson, 1999). Mimetic desire in Girardian terms could also be understood as a form of empathy, desiring what the other desires.

The Mirror Neurons System, language, and dialogic interaction

The discovery of the mirror neurons system (MNS), referred to briefly in the last chapter, seems to lend substantial support to the observations regarding imitation in general and more particularly the AIM theory from the discipline of neuroscience (Wohlschlager & Bekkering, 2002). From a psychotherapy perspective, the most interesting aspect of the MNS is the discovery of a cognitive function that is entirely devoted to processing social information (Knoblich & Jordan, 2002) at a very basic level of involuntary and unconscious brain function and that may also be instrumental in the evolution of the human language capacity (Rizzolatti & Arbib, 1998). Part of the importance of the discovery of a neurological basis for the social nature of human consciousness is that it arguably depoliticises the idea of consciousness as a social phenomenon to which we can choose whether or not to subscribe, and exposes the fallacy of the psychological monad:

> The peculiar (first to third person) "intersubjective character" of the performance of mirror neurons and their surprising complementarity to the functioning of the strategic (intentional conscious) communicative face-to-face (first to second person) may help shed light from a different perspective on the functional architecture of the conscious v unconscious mental processes ... And they may help to rearrange, at least to a certain degree, some aspects of the puzzle of the emergence of the language facility, the relation of the latter to other specifically human capacities like social intelligence and tool use, and their neural implication. [Stamenov & Gallese, 2002, p. 2]

From a linguistic perspective, Edda Weigand (2002b) argues that the MNS demonstrates the original fundamental social orientation of human beings, specifically that human beings are, from birth, oriented towards other human beings purposefully, interactively, cognitively, and dialogically. What is highly interesting from a dialogical perspective is the consistency of Weigand's ideas with those of Bakhtin and Voloshinov, despite the fact that they analyze language from very different standpoints.

Weigand (2002a, 2002b) insists that the only relevant object of study for contemporary linguistics is language in use, and that this is a complex phenomenon that must be studied as a whole. Her emphasis in the conceptualisation of this complex phenomenon is different but complementary to that of Voloshinov and the later Bakhtin. They were primarily concerned with language as a sociological phenomenon whereas Weigand's interest is its neurobiological origins but with an explicit acknowledgement that language is also thoroughly social. She also stresses the importance of emotions in dialogue and that a scientific analysis of language as a natural phenomenon must address its irrational aspects and its limitless possibilities (Weigand, 1996). Weigand's approach to language starts from the premise that human beings are complex adaptive systems, living and acting in a complex environment by mediating between order and disorder and that dialogical discourse is an inherently unstable system. This means that language in use cannot be understood from within the narrow confines of any particular disciplinary boundary. It also means, as Weigand (1996) argues, that scientific analysis cannot be limited to the rational and conventional and has to take account of the irrational and undecidable, which includes the emotional. Emotions cannot be hived off into a separate area of study, as all communication has an affective component, and emotions in dialogue should therefore be an integral part of the subject matter of linguistics. This necessarily requires abandoning the "language myth"; that language is a system of fixed codes or signs through which autonomous independent monads transfer ideas from the mind of one person to another (Harris, 2002). The notion of the transference of ideas is misleading as the idea still stays in the mind of the person sending it and the notion that language is used to communicate ideas is circular as nothing else could be conveyed. The sign conveys an idea only if the recipient knows the idea that the sign conveys. Thus the concept of semiotic or sign mediation depends on the assumption that there are two discrete individuals and, as Harris points out, has no purchase otherwise. Like Cartesian dualism, the language and communication myth is so pervasive and so much of Western intellectual and cultural tradition depends on it that it is hard to challenge. Harris suggests that:

> The theory of natural mimesis is the only serious competitor the theory of the fixed code has ever had in Western aesthetics. [2002, p. 22]

The language myth treats language as a fixed self-enclosed system of signs that exists independently of human beings. Weigand (2002a, 2002b) argues instead that language should be seen not as a sign system but as a complex multi-faceted phenomenon that is characterised by uncertainty, indeterminacy, and open-endedness. What Harris and Weigand refer to as the "language myth", Voloshinov (1986) refers to as "abstract objectivism". The idea that language has an independent existence as a system of incontestable and immutable norms is, for Voloshinov, hugely mistaken. His view of language as something that is always changing, evolving and in the constant process of becoming seems to coincide with Weigand's premise that language is inherently unstable. What matters for the individual speaker is not the form of language but the meaning it acquires in the context in which it is used:

> ... what is important for the speaker about a linguistic form is not that it is a stable and always self-equivalent signal, but that it is an always changeable and adaptable sign. [Voloshinov, 1986, p. 68]

Voloshinov's object of study is the dynamics of speech rather than the isolated word or sign, which can acquire a multiplicity of meanings and accents. The meaning of a word is determined entirely by its context and contexts are infinitely variable. Language in use is characterised by an inner generative process rather than being a ready-made system handed on from one generation to the next. Voloshinov quotes the Russian linguist, Vossler, to illustrate the futility of a study of language based on "abstract objectivism":

> Roughly speaking, the history of language, as it is given to us by historical grammar, is the same sort of thing that a history of clothing would be, which does not take the concept of fashion or the taste of the time as its point of departure, but provides a chronologically and geographically arranged list of buttons, clasps, stockings, hats, and ribbons. [1986, p. 79][4]

To study the complex means taking a holistic or integral view that does not separate language from the human beings who use it or separate language from other forms of dialogical action or human activity. From an evolutionary perspective, neuroscientists argue that language developed over time from the adaptation of non-linguistic behavioural patterns or gestures and that the mirror neurons could be the simple minimal integral complexes that discharge in response to a perceptual phenomenon (Fadiga & Gallese, 1997, Rizzoletti & Arbib, 1998). They are complexes in the sense that they combine perceptual phenomena and mental abilities with a biological function. Weigand (2002b) asserts that the firing of the mirror neurons signals from the outset a dialogical gesture. By dialogical gesture she means any action, whether linguistic or not, that is intentional and communicative.

However, the evolutionary account does not explain what is going on in human dialogic interaction and this is where the limitations of neuro-linguistics must give way to a multidisciplinary approach. Weigand argues that the minimal unit for an analysis of the complex phenomenon of language in use is what she terms the "Dialogic Action Game" in which speaking is understood as a form of action that requires a correlation of purposes and means. Communicative action is distinguished from other forms of activity by its dialogical orientation. There is no such thing as autonomous communicative action (Weigand, 1990). Her theory of dialogic interaction could be understood as a refinement of Bakhtin's much looser definition of "dialogism". Her starting point is to question why human beings behave in certain ways and her answer is it that human beings are social creatures with needs and desires. Communication is purposeful and therefore any theory of dialogic interaction must have meaning as its basic minimal component, an aspect that biological science has so far been unable to address. Weigand defines these purposes as either claims to truth or claims to volition.

Weigand (2002a) defines her assumptions about the nature of dialogical interaction with greater precision than Bakhtin. These are necessarily assumptions, because if there is an external reality, we are constrained by our abilities to recognise it and truth as such is a claim by human beings to understand reality from their own point of view. As a complex phenomenon, language in use involves not just verbal texts, words or "signs" but the integrated human abilities of perceiving, speaking, and thinking. The minimal unit in which all these abilities are present is the "Dialogic Action Game", which is defined by and delimited by human beings and their communicative and interactive purposes. It is these communicative purposes or meanings that, according to Weigand, must be the focus of analysis. These integrated abilities that are needed to communicate—speaking, thinking, and perceiving—are dialogic in that they operate in relation to both interlocutors. When we speak, we assume that there will be a corresponding understanding, perceiving requires producing the means to be perceived, and when we make assumptions or draw inferences we assume that others will do the same. The mirror neurons that fire when an action is performed or perceived confirm this dialogic or double face (Wiegand, 2002b). As Bakhtin emphasises the individual's spatial and temporal situation, Weigand draws attention to the differences between the individuals in a dialogic interaction, differences of experience, ability, and perspective. The "Dialogic Action Game" brings the differences between the interlocutors into relationship with each other and, consequently, meaning is not defined but is indeterminate and subject to negotiation. The general communicative social purpose of this minimal unit of dialogic interaction could be understood as an attempt to clarify or negotiate meanings and positions. This necessarily involves perceptual and cognitive abilities as well as speaking, as not all meaning is or can be explicitly expressed verbally. Hence linguistics is limited in its ability to analyze dialogic interaction.

Weigand's approach bears comparison to Bakhtin's emphasis on the indeterminacy and endless meaning possibilities of dialogical interaction. An unlimited depth of contextual and historical meaning is potentially embedded in the utterance or speech act and meanings can never be finalised (Leiman, 1998):

> Summarising these assumptions, the conclusion has to be drawn that our object of study does not represent a closed system of rules presupposing understanding but an open system integrally combining order and disorder, determinacy and indeterminacy, and interactively accepting problems of understanding. Human beings as complex adaptive systems address the complex by trying to find regularities but being in principle different human beings and unable to join the other on the level of fixed codes, they have to tackle the problems of individuality, probability, particular situations and even chance. [Weigand, 2002a, p. 65]

Uncertainty or indeterminacy is therefore an important and inevitable property of the "Dialogic Action Game", which Weigand suggests is comparable to the uncertainty principle in quantum physics. Human beings deal with this uncertainty in dialogic interaction by applying principles of probability. Again she seems to be in agreement with Voloshinov (1986), who points out that the other side of the dialogic equation, the addressee, who has the task of understanding the utterance, does not do so by relying on the linguistic form but on the form used in a particular context. The linguistic form or sign is changeable and adaptable and what matters in understanding is not its self-identity but its novelty or unpredictability.[5] Weigand takes this further by arguing that misunderstanding, far from being the exception in dialogical interaction, is in fact the norm. This is due to the differences between human beings in terms of their abilities cognitively, physically, and emotionally, and differences of experience. It is also due to the complexity of the world and, crucially, the fact that not everything that is meant is said—inferences have to be drawn.

Weigand (1999) outlines the ways in which misunderstandings commonly occur in dialogue: they can be due to variables in linguistic and gestural performance and competence; to cognitions based on presumptions that lead to erroneous inferences; to ambiguity as the language act or utterance may function in a way that is not linguistically expressed; and to lack of clarity with regard to referential function because of the infinity of knowledge. Nevertheless, most misunderstandings are clarified in the normal course of dialogue.

Weigand (2002a, 2002b) suggests a number of principles that must be brought to bear when defining the "Dialogic Action Game", the minimal unit in which all the complexity of language in use is present.

These are that:

1. Speech is a form of action that requires a correlation of purposes and means.
2. Speech acts are purposeful mostly two main ways, being either claims to truth or claims to volition that correspond to mental states of belief and desire.

3. Speech acts are always dialogic, being orientated towards the response of another, and that there is an interdependence of action and reaction.
4. Coherence cannot be found at the level of the text or the words used unless it is related to situation or context. Weigand calls this the coherence principle and it confirms that an integration of verbal, perceptual, and cognitive abilities are needed on the part of the interlocutors in an attempt to achieve understanding particularly as what is meant is often not explicitly expressed.

Weigand (2002a) further describes a set of corollary principles, which are also involved in the minimal dialogic action game. In negotiating meaning and understanding, people bring their ability to reason to bear, applying a principle of rationality. There are also principles of politeness or convention that apply in certain contexts: principles of supposition without which conversations cannot proceed; the principle of emotion that relates to the varying emotions that accompany any dialogue; and the ways in which these are expressed and understood; and the principle of rhetoric, the other face of the coherence principle, which is the attempt by the interlocutors to negotiate their own positions or pursue their own desires, by direct or indirect means. Weigand deals with real dialogue between people who are using the minimal exchanges to illustrate the complexity in terms of human abilities and context, to illustrate the extent of possible meaning in the utterance, and dialogic exchange and the inevitability of misunderstanding given the extent to which meaning depends on assumptions, inferences and contextual factors and is not explicitly stated. An example Weigand gives is the simple statement made by a mother to her child: "You are playing the piano again"—depending on the context and the mother's feelings, this brief utterance could have a variety of possible meanings including a reproach, a neutral statement of fact, an indication of approval or an implicit demand to be quiet or do something else. The words alone do not convey the meaning that is intended by the speaker or that is understood by the addressee. Another example could be a spouse's telephone call to say "I will be home in 10 minutes" and the response "I"ll send the children to bed", in which again the meaning of either utterance is not conveyed by the words used and much is left to emotion, inference, context, and probability.

Embodied dialogical consciousness

Voloshinov (1986) approaches the study of language from a sociological perspective, insisting that the only possible objective definition of consciousness is a social, cultural, and historical one, a consciousness that develops only through semiotic material, by far the most important part of which is language. For Voloshinov, ideological signs have an objective reality and consciousness itself is merely

> a tenant lodging in the social edifice of ideological signs (1986, p. 13).

Despite his insistence on the materiality of signs, Voloshinov dismisses the biological sciences as being irrelevant to the study of objective psychology or language, which in his view are purely socio-ideological phenomena. By contrast, Weigand argues that the complexity of human dialogical interaction is such that a multidisciplinary approach is needed to begin to analyze it. She also argues that as human beings we have no access to any objective reality. Her view is consistent with that of second generation cognitive science, which regards all mental functions as embodied and therefore constrained by physiology.[6] The world can only be perceived through the senses and interpreted through embodied conceptual systems. There is no such thing as disembodied pure reason that has direct access to an objective reality. Embodied truth gives rise to many varied and equally valid versions of reality, none of which is uniquely correct. What is accepted as real is ultimately a practical matter of what is needed to function, survive or achieve certain ends (Lakoff & Johnson 1999). However, insofar as they are both attempting to arrive at descriptions of language that further our understanding of how language functions in use by human beings, Voloshinov and Weigand could be said to reflect different aspects of embodied truth.

Voloshinov argues that all the individual needs, desires, and emotions that motivate communication take on an ideological form wholly determined by social context. He insists that:

> The immediate social situation and the broader social milieu wholly determine—and determine from within, so to speak—the structure of an utterance. [1986, p. 86]

In contrast Weigand draws attention to the individual human differences that come together in dialogical interaction and is not concerned with how these are refracted through ideology. Dialogical interaction is defined by human beings negotiating their positions with other human beings, asserting their needs and desires, and their versions of truth. She takes it for granted that consciousness and the language ability are embodied and that the experience of embodiment is inextricably bound up with consciousness. The individual experience of embodiment is marked by both its similarities to others, which allows for imitation and empathy, and its difference: all bodies are distinctive and different from other bodies and are also physically separate from them. There is therefore no contradiction in stating that consciousness is both a shared, social, interdividual phenomenon and a distinctive or unique individual experience, delimited by birth and death.

In contrast to Weigand, who draws attention to the prominence of non-linguistic elements in dialogical communication, Voloshinov places far more emphasis on the role of words. While acknowledging that other things such as religious ritual, material objects, and gestures, also function as signs, he maintains that they can only do so when accompanied by speech (1986, p. 15). Weigand pays more attention to the cognitive processes that accompany any dialogical interaction that take place outside conscious awareness. These are too numerous and transitory to be classified as semiotic material and yet they also shape and structure experience. Hence, Weigand's (1990) definition of the utterance is broader than Voloshinov's in that it gives more prominence to non-linguistic elements, particularly situational factors such as material objects, facial expressions, gestures, and institutional conditions. Furthermore, Weigand (2002a) draws attention to individual processes of thinking, perceiving, and intention which can be claims to volition or claims to truth. These claims are also part of the situational context of the utterance but are not immediately observable. Thus, in dialogical interaction, not everything is explicitly expressed: the most significant meanings can be left unsaid and many different forms of utterance can communicate the same purpose. Hence the integration of different means or abilities is required in any dialogical interaction (Weigand, 2002a).

For Weigand, language is on a continuum of dialogical communicative action and is not a special case that can be separated from other human abilities:

> The thesis of the symbolising character of language has to be relativised in the light of the integration of means. Language has evolved not as a separate verbal ability of mastering symbols but as an integral part of a complex interactive ability. [Weigand, 2002b, p. 241]

Dialogical interaction is embodied interaction involving complex human abilities that cannot be separated from biological functions. Weigand argues that the scientific study of human beings has to address the issue of integration of different abilities rather than continuing to think in separate categories:

> It is biology-in-function which relates the cell to the world and intentionally orientates human beings towards other human beings and the world . . . Human beings behave from the very beginning as dialogically purposeful beings, manifesting themselves primarily as the dialogic not the symbolic species. [Weigand, 2002b, p. 246]

From this it can be seen that Weigand and Voloshinov's positions are less easily reconcilable when it comes to the emphasis that Voloshinov places on the sign. For Voloshinov, consciousness is a semiotic and ideological phenomenon and the word is the purest form of the sign as it has no other function. It is also the principle unit of behavioural communication. Despite his critique of abstract objectivism, Voloshinov still makes a Cartesian distinction between the psyche that

> . . . can only be understood and interpreted as a sign (1986, p. 26)

and the physiological processes within the organism. For Weigand (1990, 2002a) human beings are primarily dialogic in their orientation towards each other rather than symbolic. Signs as such can only function in the context of the complex human abilities needed for dialogical interaction and to isolate the sign from this and use it as the basic unit of analysis is an over-simplification of the complex process of integrating purposes and means. Weigand (2002b) argues that this process is set off by the simultaneous firing of the mirror neurons in both interlocutors. This would suggest that the concept of semiotic mediation is both inaccurate and unnecessary, as consciousness is already connected in a more direct and immediate way. Much of what is spoken would make no sense in semiotic theory, as meaning is indeterminate. So much of interactive meaning is based on individual evaluations, suppositions, and expectations, which in turn depend on how the interlocutors are feeling and thinking, aspects of dialogue that are not observable to a third party. Fundamental to dialogic interaction is what Weigand (2002b) refers to as the "principle of meaning uncertainty", a complex mix of order and disorder:

> ... In language use, there are no signs and symbols having meaning independent of the speaker. As Wittgenstein told us, words in ordinary language use "have meaning only in the stream of life." [Weigand, 2002b, p. 237]

Despite the flexibility of Voloshinov's (1986) concept of sign, he insists that meaning is entirely dependent on the sign and cannot exist without it. However, when it comes to contextual meaning, Voloshinov gives priority to the utterance. He makes a distinction that Weigand does not make between contextual meaning, which is infinitely variable, and fixed meaning, which is relatively stable over time and in different contexts. The meaning in any given situation belongs to the utterance as a whole and this meaning is determined not just by words, syntax, and intonation but also by extraverbal situational factors that, for Voloshinov, are the concrete historical circumstances that give rise to the utterance. These extraverbal factors could include the embodied nature of any dialogical interaction. Voloshinov (1986, p. 100) refers to this enlarged sense of meaning, which is unique and unreproducable, as the theme of the utterance and distinguishes it from meaning that is reproducible and self-identical. The former is dependent on the latter, which he refers to as the technical apparatus for producing theme. Meaning as theme must base itself on some degree of self-identical meaning otherwise it could not relate to previous or future utterances. Weigand does not appear to give sufficient weight to the relative stability of meaning that is essential for any communication to take place at all. Nevertheless, these two distinct types of meaning could be understood as analogous to Weigand's notion of order and disorder in dialogical interaction.

From the way they use the term, it is apparent that Weigand and Voloshinov understand meaning differently, though in ways that could be seen as complementary. For Weigand it is human beings who mean something as a form of intention. Weigand's view of language appears to be of a flexible, user-friendly means of communication that human beings have adapted to their needs to interact dialogically. There is no sense here of language as an alien system by which human beings are constrained and determined. The emphasis is not so much on language shaping consciousness but on the human propensity for dialogical interaction evolving into spoken language. There are no meanings independent of human beings who mean something, and meaning is therefore dependent on individuals, their purposes, and their abilities. There are always ambiguous points in dialogue, where meaning has to be negotiated, so misunderstanding is a constituent feature of dialogic interaction because words themselves alone cannot convey meaning, because so much is contextual and because of the differences between individual interlocutors (2002b). She says that in the end only the speaker knows what he or she means.

For Voloshinov, meaning as theme can only arise from responsive understanding in the process of dialogic interaction. It belongs neither to the sign nor to the intention of the speaker. Voloshinov's description is similar to Weigand's account of open or indeterminate points in dialogue and also could be said to anticipate the role of the mirror neurons:

> For each word of the utterance that we are in the process of understanding, we, as it were, lay down a set of our own answering words ... Any true understanding is dialogic in nature. Understanding is to the utterance as one line of dialogue is to the next. Understanding strives to match the speaker's word with a counter word ... In essence, meaning is realised only in the process of active, responsive under-

standing. Meaning does not reside in the word or in the soul of the speaker or in the soul of the listener. Meaning is the effect of interaction between speaker and listener produced via the material of a particular sound complex. **It is like an electric spark that occurs only when two different terminals are hooked together** (present author's emphasis). [MPL, pp. 102–103]

This passage suggests that Voloshinov's understanding of how meaning is produced is more direct and immediate than sign mediation. The sign is not an intermediary between people but a part of the complex, multi-faceted phenomenon of dialogical interaction. Voloshinov and Weigand are in agreement that there is no fixed relationship between utterances and specific situations. The same words can function in completely different ways and different words can accomplish the same communicative function. However, whereas Weigand's emphasis is on different human beings negotiating their positions in particular situations, Voloshinov's is on the wider past and present socio/historical context.

Bakhtin's (1981, 1986) understanding of meaning, like that of Voloshinov and Weigand, is contextual and multifaceted. Although Bakhtin can be interpreted in different ways, his later writings appear to argue against semiotics as the only or even principal determining factor in meaning, as dialogical interaction involves far more than mere words or text. Intentions count for far more than linguistic markers which are merely:

> ... signs left behind on the path of the real living project of an intention ... these external markers, linguistically observable and fixable, cannot in themselves be understood or studied without understanding the specific conceptualisation they have been given by an intention (Bakhtin, 1981, 292)
>
> A code presupposes content to be somehow ready-made and presupposes the realisation of a choice among various given codes. The utterance (speech product) as a whole enters into an entirely new sphere of communication ... which does not admit of description or definition in the terms and methods of linguistics or more broadly semiotics. [Bakhtin, 1986, p. 136]

Whereas Weigand's focus is on individual human beings negotiating their positions in particular situations, Bakhtin's canvas is broader, giving less priority to the individual interlocutor and more to the relationships between utterances, that is the position of the utterance in the stream of utterances that preceded it and will come after it. Weigand describes how consciousness is connected at the biological/neurological level, while Bakhtin describes the contextual depth in the utterance that, by definition, is infused with innumerable other "voices". This historical depth in the utterance means that the individual speaker, whatever their purposes, has to grapple with

> ... a dialogically agitated and tension-filled environment of alien words, value judgements and accents ... (Bakhtin, 1981, p. 276)

For Bakhtin, words and utterances cannot escape from past uses and associations or their encounters with other words and other utterances. Their meaning is both changed and enriched by the contexts in which they have been used previously and the individual speaker cannot erase the influence of other voices speaking in other contexts. Bakhtin (1981) writes that the word is half someone else's; that we take our words not from dictionaries but from the mouths of other people and have to adapt them to our own purposes. While Weigand acknowledges that meaning is indeterminate and has to be negotiated, she locates meaning as a form of intention in the speaker. For Bakhtin, meaning cannot be defined by the intentions of the speaker alone but is shaped and, to an extent determined by, the previous contexts in which the words and utterances have been spoken. Not that Bakhtin (1981) discounts individual intention; he states that words have no meaning without the impulse that gives rise to them but that they are already contaminated by the intentions and evaluations of others. There are no neutral words or utterances. This adds a further dimension of complexity to Weigand's account: that whatever the intentions, desires or purposes of the interlocutors, the words in which they choose to express these will inevitably change, shape or distort their meaning, which therefore cannot be entirely determined by the intention of the speaker.

It is therefore clear that even the single word can be, in Bakhtin's terms, dialogical or internally dialogised in itself, because of the contexts in which it arose and has been previously used and because every word is profoundly influenced by who it is addressed to and the anticipation of a response. Words and utterances can be double-voiced, that is they contain a clash of two or more "voices". There can be two or more addressees who can "respond" to each other within a single utterance. Often the addressee is an absent, imagined or internalised other, whose identity is not obvious but who nevertheless influences and partly determines the meaning of the utterance and the course of the dialogical interaction. The existence of other voices, other points of view or other semantic positions within the utterance, and that these can be addressed to multiple others, not necessarily other people, adds further complexity to Weigand's concept of meaning uncertainty and to the potential for misunderstanding.

For Bakhtin and Voloshinov, dialogical consciousness is social consciousness because, when we speak and think, by definition, we use the words and utterances of other people. Our words and thoughts are filled, whether we like it or not, with the voices of other people who have spoken before us and with their intentions and evaluations. Furthermore, the more highly developed and differentiated a society is, the more other people's utterances become the main topic of concern, conversation, and impassioned debate (Bakhtin, 1981), and individuals in such a society will correspondingly experience a more complex and vivid inner or mental life (Voloshnov, 1986).

For Bakhtin and Voloshinov, the inner world, as in thought or inner speech, is as much a social phenomenon as outward speech. This adds a further level of complexity to Weigand's account of dialogical interaction, which is concerned solely with utterances addressed to an external other. For Voloshinov (1986) and Bakhtin (1984), inner speech is the mirror image of outer speech and is also dialogic in structure and without it inner life would wither away. The question of inner speech therefore raises the question of the internal other, or the internal interlocutor whose presence is also reflected in the, only partly observable, internal dialogisation of the external utterance: hence Bakhtin's concept of multiple addressees, the other or others who are addressed in the utterance and who are not necessarily either present, or the audience to whom it is directed. Each utterance thus contains not only the possibility of multiple voices but multiple addressees. Bakhtin describes the complexity of this property of dialogical interaction in his analysis of the discourse of Devushkin, the hero of Dostoevsky's early novel Poor Folk, which reflects Devushkin's uneasiness with his social surroundings in relation to his own poverty:

> ... the hero's self-awareness was penetrated by someone else's consciousness of him, the hero's own self-utterance was injected with someone else's consciousness and the other's words then give rise to specific phenomena that determine the thematic development of Devushkin's self-awareness, its breaking points, its loopholes, and protests on the one hand, and on the other the hero's speech with its accentual interruptions, syntactic breaking points, repetitions, reservations, and long-windedness . . . .
> ... let us imagine two rejoinders of the most intense dialogue—a discourse and a counter-discourse—which instead of following one after the other and being uttered by two different mouths, are superimposed one after the other and merge into a single utterance issuing from a single mouth. [1984, p. 209]

The above passage, according to Bakhtin, reflects the existence of internal interlocutors whose existence is reflected in the "loopholes", hesitations and reversals of his external discourse. These can be conceptualised as different "selves" or different "voices". The dialogical self is understood in terms of dialogically related separate voices or selves who "speak" to each other and co-define one another (Angus & Mcleod, 2004). In this sense embodied dialogical interaction with an external other becomes metaphorical dialogical interaction with an "internal" other as inner life imitates "outer" life.

The dialogical self as complex metaphor

However, the importance Voloshinov and Bakhtin attribute to words in inner life may overestimate the importance of conscious reflective thought in consciousness as a whole. Weigand (2002a, 2002b) and Lakoff and Johnson (1999) have described some of the numerous processes that operate outside conscious awareness in even the simplest dialogic interaction. From a psychotherapy perspective, the highly significant role that Lakoff and Johnson ascribe to metaphor in the "cognitive unconscious" is interesting both because these metaphors influence and structure how we see and experience the world and because they illustrate how thought and language are simultaneously structured and constrained by embodiment. Primary metaphors function automatically and outside conscious awareness in everyday experience. They are embodied as they conflate sensorimotor experience with subjective, non-sensorimotor experience from early childhood and the neural connections laid down at this stage persist throughout life, even when these different domains of experience can be differentiated.[7] They are not social in a Bakhtinian sense or primarily semiotic in origin, although they may be expressed in language:

> Contrary to long-standing opinion about metaphor, primary metaphor is not the result of a conscious multi-stage process of interpretation. Rather it is part of immediate conceptual mapping via neural connections. [Lakoff & Johnson, 1999, p. 57]

More complex metaphors develop from primary metaphors, which are more culturally specific. Again these structure experience and are the basis of taken-for-granted assumptions about everyday life that operate largely outside conscious awareness. An example of a complex metaphor common in Anglo-American culture is life as a journey, with goals as destinations, and a person living a purposeful life as a traveller. People seen as lacking in purpose are commonly said to "have lost their way" and those seen as acting too slowly are said to have "missed the boat". An example of a more complex metaphor is of a relationship as a vehicle going on a journey as evidenced by such comments as "we hit a rocky patch", "we've come a long way" or "we're breaking up". The "narrative self" is another complex metaphor in which a life is seen as having a teleological structure directed by the meaning attached to life experiences. Complex metaphors are built from primary metaphors that are grounded in early subjective and sensorimotor experiences, although they are expressed in language. Lakoff & Johnson argue therefore that speech, whether internal or external, is only the tip of the iceberg, being only a small part of psychic experience, most of which operates unconsciously as embodied conceptual reason. Dialogical consciousness, understood in linguistic terms, may therefore be only a small part of psychic life.

All theories of self, as they are reflected in everyday language and psychotherapy, are based on complex metaphors. This echoes Rorty's (1980, cited in Shotter, 1993) observation that it is pictures and metaphors, rather than statements or propositions, that mostly determine philosophical convictions and seems to account for what Shotter (1993) refers to as the unexplained but nevertheless specific ways of talking that shape our perceptions of the world as well as our thinking, evaluations, and activities so that common or shared understandings seem to be rooted or situated in a particular context. In psychotherapy, entities such as the ego, inner self, inner voice, true and false self, self-state, self-object, and so forth are not tangible and have no existence outside language. As Lakoff & Johnson (1999) observe, it is almost impossible to talk about the mind or the self in any meaningful way without metaphorical concepts. In psychotherapy, as in everyday speech, there are several different metaphorical systems in operation that are often inconsistent with each other. The dialogical self is primarily a combination of the "thought as language metaphor" as it applies to the concept of mind and the "social self metaphor" and the "multiple selves metaphor" as applied to the self. The thought as language metaphor is one of a subset of metaphors about the mind that is fundamental to Anglo-American analytic philosophy. It involves thinking as a form of linguistic activity, in which thought is conceptualised in terms of a linear sequence of symbols and is therefore external and public.[8] In positing the idea of thought as inner speech, Voloshinov and Bakhtin, unlike Weigand, whose analysis is based only on observable external speech, are treating thought as inner speech as an entity that has an independent objective existence. As Lakoff & Johnson (1999) illustrate, this is merely an intuition based on embodied conceptual systems. The thought as language metaphor has gained prominence following the linguistic turn in analytic philosophy but other mutually inconsistent metaphors of mind are also prevalent: thought as mathematical calculation, thought as movement, thinking as perceiving, thinking as object manipulation, ideas as food, and mind as a machine. Nevertheless such metaphors are central to the conception of mind, thought and reason:

> Would ideas be ideas if we could not grasp them, look at them carefully, and take them apart? What would reason be if we could not reach conclusions, or go step by step, or come directly to the point? Would ideas be the same if you couldn't let them simmer for a while . . . or digest them. Would thinking be the same if you could not make mental notes, translate your vague ideas into plans, sum up an argument, or crank out ideas? [Lakoff & Johnson, 1999, p. 248]

The social self metaphor as described by Lakoff & Johnson is similar to the psychoanalytic concept of Object Relations in which a subject or "I" has an evaluative relationship with a "me" or self and is derived from early interpersonal relationships. This leads to a correlation throughout life between the experience of evaluative social relationships between self and others and a similar relationship between subject and self. In this metaphor the subject is conceived as a person and the self as another person. Closely related to this is the multiple self metaphor, in which different selves are associated with the social roles attached to different values, which are conceptualised as being in different places.

An examination of any model of psychotherapy or self will invariably reveal numerous, less dominant metaphors. Experiences, particularly formative relational experiences, are "internalised": here the metaphor is of the self as a container with an outside and an inside. It is also common in psychotherapy to speak of "containment", the metaphor here being the self as a body at risk of fragmenting or exceeding its boundaries and needing to be held together. Terms such as integration and self-coherence are based on the same metaphor. Positioning is another significant metaphorical concept in the dialogical self, in that different "voices" address each other from different locations in space. In dialogical therapy, the self can be conceived of as a "process" that evolves over time and as a structure that requires adjustment.

The concept of the dialogical self is both metaphorically rich and inconsistent, as this sentence taken from Bromberg (2004) illustrates (bracketed sections are the present author's comments):

> From my perspective (self as a location) the capacity (self as a container) for self-reflection (self as two persons) is a matter

of the degree (self as something that can be measured) to which self-states (self as multiple) are disassociated (self as a structure) from one another. [Bromberg, 2004, p. 145]

However, inconsistency should not be seen as a problem, as such inconsistencies are pervasive, being intrinsic to the process in which primary metaphors are acquired in early subjective and sensorimotor experience. The dialogical self is an extended and extremely complex metaphor for the self that is particularly useful in contemporary psychotherapy because of the importance it accords to language in the experience of self and to relationships with other people. However, like all metaphors, as a product of embodied conceptual systems it has no objective, independent truth. Like the psychoanalytic self, another rich but inconsistent complex metaphor, it is a product of a particular cultural context, which could be said to be characterised by social and geographic mobility that leads to: numerous transitory and fragmented interpersonal relationships; varying degrees of social instability and conflict; and varying degrees of economic uncertainty and insecurity. Conceiving of the self as different "voices" positioned in different locations in time and space may be a profoundly helpful way of making sense of complex contemporary experience.

Conclusion

In this chapter I have attempted to demonstrate that Girardian mimetic theory and the Bakhtinian concept of the dialogical self are more than just complementary ways of approaching the problem of consciousness and the self. They could also be interdependent on each other insofar as the embodied capacity to imitate is an essential precondition for dialogical understanding and interaction and dialogical discourse is the primary means whereby mimetic desires are expressed. Recent findings in infant and child observation, linguistics and cognitive science both lend support to and deepen the concept of mimetic theory as derived from literature, social anthropology, and theology, and the concept of the dialogical self, which is largely derived from literature and philosophy. These developments appear to demonstrate the interdependence of the two concepts in neurobiological terms as well as in emotional and social life.

The abilities needed to interact dialogically in different ways are embodied and are both present at birth and learnt or acquired through imitation. Responsive understanding, which Bakhtin views as an essential component of meaning, depends on the ability to empathise, an ability that depends on our recognition that the other is the same as us but also different and separate from us, a form of knowledge that is acquired, as Meltzoff (2002) demonstrates, through imitation. Even the simplest dialogical interaction requires a complex integration of different biological and cognitive abilities and processes, most of which take place outside the conscious awareness of the interlocutors and are not immediately apparent to an external observer.

Weigand brings an evolutionary and biological perspective to Voloshinov's (1986) and Bakhtin's (1984) description of dialogical discourse, focusing on the individual using language purposefully to communicate their desires and further their interests and claims to truth. She shows us how language is not an isolated and separate human ability but part of a continuum of dialogically interactive abilities. She also demonstrates that words as signs are only a part of a complex phenomenon and that meaning is both unstable and indeterminable, and therefore that misunderstanding is an inevitable and constituent aspect of dialogical interaction. Of particular significance is Weigand's claim that treating language as a natural phenomenon from a scientific perspective[9] necessarily involves embracing its complexity, including its irrational and emotional aspects as well as its uncertainty and unpredictability.

Whereas Weigand analyses the complexity of dialogue at the minimal level of two individuals interacting, Bakhtin and Voloshinov use a sociological perspective to draw attention to the importance of the cultural and historical context of dialogue. In doing so they deepen and broaden Weigand's account at the contextual level by stressing the influence of the sociol/historical and political forces on the psychic life of the individual: that when expressed in language, or even when experienced subjectively, human needs and desires are always refracted through ideology. At the linguistic level, Bakhtin deepens Weigand's account as he shows us how words and utterances are infused with the meanings and intentions of previous users and earlier contexts, an aspect which is consistent with Weigand's instability of meaning. Individual intentions and desires not only interact or conflict with the intentions, desires, different abilities and different life experiences of the interlocutor but also with the intentions, desires, differences, and abilities present in countless previous dialogical interactions.

In positing an inner life of thought that is inherently dialogical, the existence of conscious yet unspoken dialogue that is not observable to either the interlocutor or an outside observer, Bakhtin and Voloshinov, in contrast to Weigand, depart from what is empirically observable but enrich her account at the metaphorical level. Thought as language or internal conversation, or the concept of mental life being dialogical, are both complex metaphors derived from embodied conceptual systems. The metaphorical richness of the dialogical self in psychotherapy is enhanced by its ability to encompass different models that contain different metaphors. Lakoff and Johnson and Weigand, in drawing attention to largely unconscious cognitive processes and the complex integration of abilities involved in language use, highlight the embodied nature of mind, self, and dialogical interaction. The dialogical self, understood only in semiotic terms, is a partial self, as it appears to take insufficient account of the embodied nature of the abilities needed for dialogical interaction and the non-semiotic aspects of consciousness. Imitation and desire are also important and related ways in which human beings are interconnected at the level of observable behaviour and at the symbolic level.

This chapter has attempted to illustrate the convergence of discourses from different disciplines on the themes of intersubjectivity, embodiment, individual difference, and dialogical consciousness. It has also attempted to show how discourses from other disciplines have the potential to contribute to conceptualisations of such phenomena in psychotherapy. Mimetic or interdividual psychology, itself an outcome of knowledge from different disciplinary backgrounds, is both strengthened and modified by research in developmental psychology that demonstrates the innate capacity for imitation and its crucial role in social and emotional learning. By suggesting how the human capacity to imitate is fundamental to a theory of mind and therefore the ability to empathise with and understand the feelings of others, imitation research "legitimises" the desire to imitate others and modifies Girard's apparent emphasis on the destructive aspects of imitation and our consequent attempts to disguise it, as well as our displeasure when others seem to imitate us. Without an "imitative" mind it is impossible to imagine how another might feel. The phenomena of projection and projective identification could be reinterpreted as an ability to perceive and interpret subliminal non-verbal clues as to the feelings of another such as intonation, facial expression, and gestures, which rely on our own experiences of similar feelings and the proprioceptive feedback from the sensorimotor manifestations of these feelings. These in turn are fundamental to the ability to recognise and work with transference and countertransference.

Research into the Mirror Neurons System, as yet in its early stages, lends tentative support to both mimetic psychology and the observations of researchers in developmental psychology about childhood imitation from a neurological/biological perspective. It suggests that imitation is a biological as well as a social phenomenon and that there is a neurological basis for human social and dialogical consciousness. If, as some researchers argue, the MNS is instrumental in the human language ability, it deepens our understanding of the complex human abilities needed to communicate with each other and modifies the linguistic account of dialogical interaction proposed by Voloshinov. In taking into account the numerous individual human as well as the immediate contextual factors involved in dialogical interaction, Weigand demonstrates the significance of the biological abilities and emotional influences in human communication.

Dialogical conceptions of subjectivity informed by Bakhtin have so far emphasised the linguistic and the semiotic in consciousness, with a consequent neglect of corporeal experience and desire. Human beings are interconnected in different ways and language, although a major factor, is not the only dimension of human social life. In the next chapter I will discuss the importance of the body in Bakhtin's thought and its centrality to his ethics of intersubjective relations.

Notes

1 The distinction between innate and learnt abilities is disputed by some neuroscientists who have found that some neural pathways are present at birth but disappear in infancy, while new pathways

are laid down at later stages in development (Lakoff & Johnson, 1999). It may be more accurate to describe this early ability to imitate as being present at birth. This may explain why the tendency of infants to imitate in the way described by Meltzoff and his colleagues disappears after the first few months and then re-emerges as goal directed imitation.

2 As the human individual grows older imitation is progressively controlled and restrained as the prefrontal lobes develop to maturity. People with damage to this part of the brain can exhibit unrestrained and often meaningless imitative behaviour. People under stress are also prone to involuntary imitation for example a passenger in a car going too fast puts their foot on an imaginary brake (Kinsbourne, 2002). Rizzolatti et al (2002) gives the example of people caught up in the excitement of a boxing match making involuntary boxing movements with their arms.

3 The human infants response to rhythmic behaviour and reciprocal imitation is not found in other species (Prinz, 1993 cited in Kinsbourne, 2002) and rhythmic activity between infant and carer has also been interpreted as an early form of dialogical relatedness (Bertau, 2004). Dancing is a form of rhythmic movement that invites reciprocal imitation, as does chanting and other forms of musical activity that seem to engender a primitive sense of belonging. Affiliation to groups and individuals may therefore have a neuro-biological basis mediated by imitation (Kinsbourne, 2002).

4 Taken from Vossler (1910) Grammatika istoriija jaka, Logos, 1, 170.

5 This has implications for the understanding of a "semiotic position" (Leiman 2004) which will be discussed in the concluding chapter.

6 Earlier cognitive science regarded the brain as analogous to a computer and took for granted the a priori Cartesian philosophical assumptions of Anglo-American analytical philosophy. Second generation cognitive science (discussed further below) abandoned these "cognitivist" assumptions in the light of research that revealed the dependence of concepts and reason on the body and the central role of imaginary processes such as metaphor in conceptualization and reason (Lakoff & Johnson, 1999).

7 Lakoff & Johnson give many examples, too many to reproduce here. Three examples are:

Knowing is seeing. Subjective judgement: Knowledge. Sensorimotor Domain: Vision. Example "I see what you mean". Primary Experience: Getting information through vision.

Understanding is grasping. Subjective judgement: Comprehension. Sensorimotor Domain: Object Manipulation. Example: "I've never been able to grasp transfinite numbers". Primary Experience: Getting information about an object by grasping and manipulating it. (pp. 53–54).

Affection is warmth. Subjective Judgement: Affection. Sensorimotor Domain: Temperature:

Example: "They greeted me *warmly.*" Primary Experience: Feeling warm while being held affectionately (p. 50).

8 The idea that thought is always dialogic or conversational from another perspective is slightly bizarre. It is a particular type of thought concerned with weighing things up, reaching a decision or reconciling conflicting views. Even conscious thought is far more chaotic in Strawson's (2002) words:

For most people, inner thought is broken and hiccupy. There are gaps and fadings and fugues. It seizes up, it flies off, it suddenly flashes with extraneous matter. It fits Daniel Dennett's pandemonium model of the mind-brain, which depicts not yet conscious words, ideas, mood-tones, thoughts, impulses of all sorts jostling competitively for emergence into consciousness (Strawson, 2002, p. 10).

9 The idea that linguistics can be treated as a natural science is contentious and one that Voloshinov with which would strongly disagreed. Ian Hacking (1999) argues that as human beings are interactive, that is they respond to how they are categorized or defined and may in doing so change the behaviour being studied, the methodology of the natural sciences is not appropriate for studying them. However, given that communication involves more than just words and requires the integration of different biological, perceptual and cognitive abilities, many of which operate outside of conscious awareness, as well as being the product of communication between socially organized persons, there seems to be a strong case for the knowledge gained through the natural sciences to be integrated with sociological, literary and philosophical perspectives.

CHAPTER SEVEN

Bakhtin's Ethics and Psychotherapy

The previous chapter discussed how human interaction and communication is a complex but integrated phenomenon of which language itself is only a part. In focusing only on the dialogical in Bakhtin, psychotherapy misses the full significance of the contextual matrix in which dialogical consciousness is embedded in Bakhtin's thought as a whole, leading to an overly linguistic view of consciousness. The human body was a central and recurring theme in Bakhtin's thought, although he approached it from an ethical and philosophical perspective that is very different to the perspectives discussed in the last chapter. This chapter will discuss a theme that is widely seen as being common to all Bakhtin's writing, which is an ethics of interpersonal relatedness that is grounded in the principle of incarnation, i.e. the Word made flesh. In Bakhtin's thought dialogism is superior to monologism (PDP, pp. 81–82), closed systems of thinking such as abstract theory are inferior to those that are open as a result of human activity (Bakhtin, 1990, 194), the official is inferior to the unofficial, and dogma or fixed codes of any kind, from an ethical perspective, are inferior to the unique and unrepeatable concrete event (Bakhtin, 1993, pp. 23–24). Bakhtin (1990, 1993) is concerned with the particular rather than the general, lived experience rather than abstract ideals. Love and forgiveness in the context of the intimate I and Thou relationship, with what Holquist (1993) identifies as their associated themes of "authoring," "responsibility," "outsideness" and "participatory thinking," are for Bakhtin far more important than the impersonal values of justice or fairness. Bakhtin would have abhorred the blanket generalisations about human subjectivity that passes for "scientific" research in clinical psychology and psychiatry.

From a psychotherapy perspective, to focus only on the dialogical in linguistic terms does not do justice to Bakhtin's thinking about the ethics of interpersonal relatedness, about our responsibility for our own actions and towards others. His thinking in this respect is of particular relevance to psychotherapy because of its exclusive focus on intersubjectivity. However, as Emerson (2001) points out, Bakhtin's ethics do not extend beyond the confines of the interpersonal relationship and his views on other moral issues are not known (although, if Bakhtin is understood as a sympathiser with Marxism in its broadest sense, they might be inferred). In contemporary Western societies his ethical stance might be considered unfashionable with its emphasis on humility, self-forgetfulness, responsibility, love, insistence on the singularity of each person, and on obligations rather than on rights and individual fulfilment. As noted earlier, Bakhtin neither thought nor wrote in isolation and his work on ethics was influenced by a complex mix of sources: while it seems unlikely that the Christian Bakhtin was an orthodox, Soviet-style Marxist, he was probably a fellow traveller with Marxism, perhaps more concerned with the cultural and philosophical aspects than the economic. The neo-Kantian philosophers he admired were also religious thinkers of left-leaning persuasions and, as previously noted, Bakhtin was influenced by Voloshinov, who incorporated developments in neo-Kantian philosophy into his more overtly Marxist approach to language. However the strand of influence on Bakhtin's thought I would like to pursue here is the influence of Orthodoxy, as I imagine it will be less familiar to many readers and because of its distinctness from the Roman Catholicism of Girard and from European Protestantism.

The Influence of the Orthodox Church

Scholars who prefer to view Bakhtin solely through the prism of Marxism are often dismayed by Christian interpretations, as if the latter cancelled out the former, but the ethics of Orthodoxy do not seem to be inimical to a Marxist conception of social justice. Most Russian Bakhtin scholars and many non-Russians now consider that not only was Bakhtin a religious man but that his Eastern Orthodox Christian beliefs were one of the most important influences in his thinking. Ruth Coates and Graham Pechey are two non-Russian scholars who have identified Christian themes and influence throughout Bakhtin's work. Coates (1998) finds the Christian motifs of the Creation, the Fall and the Incarnation throughout the whole of Bakhtin's writing.[1] The Incarnation in Orthodox theology is the central paradigm for the dialogical in that Christ embodied a *hypostasis of* both human and divine natures without division or separation; so the word is a *hypostasis* of at least two voices (Lock, 2001). Similarly, the doctrine of the Trinity[2] is the paradigm for the pluralistic world view of many unmerged souls that Bakhtin found in Dostoevsky (Poole, 2001b). The Orthodox concept of the Trinity, in which the Father is the origin of both the Son and the Spirit,[3] is also the paradigm for Bakhtin's concept of the "superaddressee", the third absent other who is addressed in dialogical discourse and whose responsive understanding we assume or hope for. This third other can be God but not necessarily (Bakhtin, 1986, p. 126). Pechey (2007) argues that the Trinity is the inspiration for Bakhtin's early phenomenology, with its interrelationship between the cognitive, ethical, and aesthetic in human activity. This apparent Christian bias may pose difficulties for some psychotherapists but Bakthtin's ethics does not have to entail a belief in a deity, even less a specifically Christian one. Bakhtin's Christian beliefs are understated, implied rather than explicit and they appear to influence rather than determine the shape of his ideas. Morson and Emerson (1989) argue that in divorcing ethics from rules, Bakhtin makes a principled refusal to make ethics a part of religion. Bakhtin is at the other end of the spectrum from prescriptive right wing evangelical Christianity and, like all the best representatives of religious faiths, inspired others by the life he led, his being in the world, rather than by preaching or moralising, but that does not mean that his beliefs are irrelevant to an enhanced understanding of his work in total. Orthodoxy may not be at the centre of Bakhtin but it is found throughout his work on the periphery (Lock, 1991).

In Orthodox thinking everything is material and all matter is sacred. There is no conflict between faith and reason, between the senses and the intellect or between body and spirit (Emerson, 2001). There is diversity within unity rather than the conflict and turmoil that result from the divisions associated with Western theology. As Timothy Ware describes it:

> The human being is a single united whole; not only the human mind but the whole person was created in the image of God. Our body is not an enemy, but partner and collaborator with our soul. Christ, by taking a human body at the Incarnation, has "made the flesh an inexhaustible source of sanctification." [Ware, 1997, p. 67]

Bakhtin's view of the person, as well as his disapprobation of theory, appears to be strongly related to the Orthodox view of God, which is characterised by apophatic or negative theology; as God is fundamentally unknowable, beyond human conception, theology can only talk about what God is not. There is no clear boundary between mysticism and theology and between theology and everyday experience (Vossky, 1957, cited in Pechey, 1998), which suggests that priests and theologians have no privileged access to God. As Randall Poole (2001) points out, there is no room here for abstract or purely intellectual theology, and as human beings are made in the image of God, the human being is also ultimately unknowable. For Bakhtin, there is something irreducible about the person that is not amenable to systemisation or theory (Coates, 1998) and it is the human body that ensures the uniqueness of each individual and the otherness of each individual to every other individual, not only in its own particularity but in its own specific location in time and space. There are ethical implications consequent upon the uniqueness of each individual in terms of how we should act towards our fellow human beings, respecting the other's unique point of view and unique experiences. Each act, like each individual and each word, is unique and unrepeatable and cannot therefore be subject to rules, norms or theories. To seek the answers to questions of meaning and responsibility from theory or religion is itself an abdication of responsibility. Bakhtin has no difficulty in reconciling the concept of consciousness as social or being "on the border" between self and other with the unique position and experience of each individual that is guaranteed by embodiment. In focusing on the body, Bakhtin describes how the world is experienced concretely through the senses.

It is a world that is seen, heard, touched, and thought, a world permeated in its entirety with the emotional-volitional tones of the affirmed validity of values. [Bakhtin, 1993, p. 56]

From this it can be seen that Bakhtin resists any form of category distinctions or attempts to isolate phenomena or place them in a hierarchy; sense experiences, thoughts and values exist on the same plane and his extensive use of what Lakoff and Johnson (1999) have identified as "primary metaphor" lends particular credence to the centrality of the body in personhood:

> Planes that are different from the abstract point of view (spatial-temporal determinateness, emotional-volitional tones, meanings) are contracted and concentrated here to form a concrete and unique unity. "High", "above", "below", "finally", "as yet", "already", "its necessary", "ought to", "farther", "nearer", etc—all these expressions acquire not just a content/sense . . . but acquire an actual, lived-experienced, heavy and compelling concretely determinate validity or operativeness from the unique place of my participating in Being-as-event. [Bakhtin, 1993, p. 57]

Bakhtin's ethics are a materialist ethics characterised by a refusal of systematisation and a unity of experience alongside an overriding insistence on individual difference and the ultimate unknowability or mystery of each human being. It is this singularity of each individual that means that we cannot justify our behaviour in terms of roles or rules, theories or knowledge.[4] These are all "alibis for being", a pretence at an authentic engagement with the world. To be answerable for one's own action requires that thinking about it is not divorced from its content. This is participatory thinking as opposed to abstract theoretical thinking. Understanding of theoretical thinking can only be reached in the context of specific actions (Bender, 1998):

> An answerable act or deed is precisely that act which is performed on the basis of an acknowledgement of my obligative (ought-to-be) uniqueness. It is this affirmation of my non-alibi in Being that constitutes the basis of my life being

actually and compellently given as well as being as its being actually and compellently projected as something yet-to-be achieved. It is only my non-alibi in Being that transforms an empty possibility into an actual answerable act or deed. [Bakhtin, 1993, p. 42]

This uniqueness or specificity can be understood not only in terms of the particularity of each human body, but also in terms of each person's position in time and space, according to Bakhtin's original concept of the chronotope.

The chronotope

The chronotope,[5] which has received less critical attention than some of Bakhtin's better known concepts such as dialogism, polyphony, and carnival could, by situating human life in a physical geographical space and a historical time (Morris, 1994), be used to overcome some of the limitations of an overly dialogic/linguistic account of consciousness. Bakhtin appropriated the German word "chronotope" to refer to the temporal and spatial dimensions of narrative and plot in fiction. Another way of understanding it is as the organising structure of the narrative element in the novel or a life, which is the context for the dialogical element or the presence of different "voices". Dialogism and the chronotope are inseparable. Even in the most "stream of consciousness" novel or the most uneventful life, things happen at particular intersections of space and time. In his essay *Forms of Time and of the Chronotope,* Bakhtin describes it thus:

> We will give the name chronotope (literally "time space") to the intrinsic connectedness of temporal and spatial relationships that are artistically expressed in literature. This term (space-time) is employed in mathematics, and was introduced as part of Einstein's Theory of Relativity ... In the literary and artistic chronotope, spatial and temporal indicators are fused into one carefully thought-out, concrete whole. Time as it were thickens, takes on flesh, becomes artistically visible: likewise, space becomes charged and responsive to the movement of time, plot and history. [Bakhtin, 1981, p. 84]

Space and time are simultaneous in relativity theory and dialogism but there is no Newtonian absolute, no one truth, no certainties, and no single vantage point for observation. Choices have to be made and choice implies value (Holquist, 1990). Holquist draws attention to the importance of simultaneity and relationship in relativity theory and dialogism. Einstein is not concerned with things but the relationships between things. People and things are not static or isolated but active simultaneous *events*. For Bakhtin, human *being* is an event or an activity. To be is to actively perceive and in that process be judging, creating meaning and assigning value. There is no such thing as passivity; for Bakhtin to be conscious is to be active.

The concept of the chronotope, whether employed to understand the artistic structure of a novel or to illuminate an individual life, allows us to appreciate the unique qualities of our selves—only I can stand in this place at this particular juncture of space-time—and also how this unique position is defined by my relationships to other people, as well as to objects and the natural environment. Time and space are relational concepts. Our sense of time is governed by before and after and our sense of space is governed by the location of other people and objects in relation to ourselves. As Holquist points out, the chronotope, like the utterance, is a particular rather than a general concept:

> It must be a chronotope of someone for someone about someone. It is ineluctably tied to someone who is in a situation. [Holquist, 1990, p. 151]

The term situation, itself, can only be understood in reference to other things or events and always refers to a particular combination of circumstances:

> Chronotope, like situation, always combines spatial and temporal factors with an evaluation of their significance as judged from a particular point of view. [Holquist, 1990, p. 152]

The values attached to the dimensions of space and time as experienced by human subjects is an essential aspect of the chronotope. There is no such thing as perception uncoloured by a judgement. However, this individualised chronotope is a relatively recent one, which marks out the private sphere from the public sphere and people from their natural environment. It is associated with the rise of capitalism, the separation of the means of production from other aspects of daily life, and the displacement of popular culture with various forms of the commodity, leading to an increasingly fragmented social world (Aronowitz, 1995). Time itself takes on many different forms. For example, in pre-industrial societies time is collective in that it is differentiated only by the events of collective life:

> The progression of events in an individual life have not been isolated (the interior time of an individual life does not yet exist, the individuum lives completely on the surface, within a collective whole). [Bakhtin, 1981, pp. 206–7]

The replacement of the social or collective chronotope with the individual chronotope is reflected both in the artistic form of the modern novel and in the social practice of psychotherapy in its various forms. Time and space are not immutable but take on different forms as part of the created order. The human individual's experience is therefore delimited by its temporal and spatial aspects rather than being "transcendent" over them, and knowledge is knowledge of difference based on spatial differentiation and temporal deferral (Lock, 2001). Ideas, knowledge, and truth are not abstract concepts but are embodied in the individual according to their temporal and spatial location in the world. There can therefore be no such thing as absolute disembodied truth or pure reason. Bakhtin's view here seems to coincide with Lakoff and Johnson's (1999) arguments discussed in the previous chapter; that all perception and cognition is constrained and shaped by the body. Bakhtin therefore advocates a descriptive rather than a prescriptive view of the world that allows for *emotional-volitional* judgements as well as rational assessment (Coates, 1998).

Interdependency and outsideness

As well as being unique, individuals are also incomplete and therefore interdependent on one another. As Hirschkop (1999) observes, intersubjectivity on its own does not imply any moral obligations;

rather it is interdependency, human inadequacy, and the consequent need for other people that carries with it awareness both of our own dependency on the other and our consequent obligations towards them. As Bakhtin conceives of consciousness as being "between" people rather than "inside" them, it follows that the isolated individual cannot be fully conscious to themselves. Our experience of ourselves is formless and we need the benevolent form-shaping activity of dialogue with another person in order to come to know ourselves. A pre-condition of this activity through which we come to know ourselves through another is "outsideness", a term that refers to the externality of our bodily location in relation to other people and the perspective or "excess of seeing" this position grants us. In *Author and Hero,* Bakhtin describes it as follows:

> When I contemplate a whole human being who is situated outside and over and against me, our concrete, actually experienced horizons do not coincide. For at each moment, regardless of the position and the proximity to me of this other human being who I am contemplating, I shall always see and know something that he, from his place outside me ... cannot see for himself. [1990, pp. 22–23]

He conceives of the interdependent nature of individuals as a three-way dynamic:

> These basic moments, are I-for-myself, the other for me, and I-for-the-other. All the values of actual life and culture are arranged around the basic architectonic points of the actual world of the performed act or deed. [Bakhtin, 1993, p. 54]

I-for-myself alone is fragmentary and fluid; security and stability can only be bestowed by others who are outside me (Emerson, 1997). The spatial and temporal uniqueness of each person means that we all occupy a position of outsideness in relation to other people and consequently have a "surplus" of vision that enables us to see what the other cannot see for his or herself. Ann Jefferson (1989) stresses the importance of subjective bodily experience in outsideness; our experience of ourselves is limited to inner sensation and fragments of what the other can see. Only the other can see our body as a whole object in the world.⁶ Outsideness means that our relationship with others is always asymmetrical—we know ourselves from the inside but others can only know us from the outside. Bakhtin was opposed to the idea of interiority as the highest form of self-knowledge; knowledge of ourselves comes from outside; our selves and our subjectivity is given to us by other people. Outsideness rather than transcendence is the only true source of knowledge. There is no inner reality separate from outward appearance. Outsideness is the trope of the Incarnation and iconography (Lock, 2001).⁷

Unfortunately outsideness also has connotations of separateness, aloofness and isolation. Emerson (1997) cites the work of Russian scholar Elena Volkova, who attempts to refine Bakhtin's concept and rescue it from possible misunderstanding. She regards the healthy self as both able to be vulnerable and involved with others without presuming to enter or identify entirely with another's experience. We must maintain or return to our own position in order to see what the other cannot see, and in order to learn about ourselves we need to expose ourselves to the gaze of as many and as varied people as possible. In *Author and Hero* Bakhtin saw the author as having a benevolent "surplus" of vision that "finalised" or completed his heroes (Bakhtin, 1990, p. 12). The creative activity of authoring is a paradigm for the relationship between God and man as well as the relationship between people (1990, p. 56). As I-for-myself is inchoate and formless, I rely on the other to give form to me or "author" me. As Emerson (1997) points out, Bakhtin assumes that the outsideness of others and their consequent surplus of vision will be useful to us, even if not always benevolent. He appears to take no account of the human capacity for self-deception and the less honourable feelings and unconscious motivations that can influence the way we conduct our relationships. While the intentional act towards the other is at the heart of Bakhtin's ethics (Brandist, 2002), the early Bakhtin does not seem to question how well we know what our intentions are.

However, the nature of this creative authoring changed in the *Dostoevsky* book where use of the "surplus" was no longer necessarily seen as benevolent and where "finalising" another is seen as preventing them finding their own truth for themselves (1984, p. 58). The polyphonic author is merely a conduit for his heroes' discourses; he orchestrates rather than composes. The polyphonic author "allows" his characters freedom, even if this is at the expense of happiness. Bakhtin sees Dostoevsky's struggle as being against the reification of human beings, their values and relationships and his authorial position is a

> ... fully realised and thoroughly consistent dialogic position, one that confirms the independence, internal freedom, unfinalisability, and indeterminacy of the hero ... (1984, p. 63)

Here, Bakhtin's ethics imply that a responsible acceptance of mutual dependency must eschew attempts to influence or control the moral choices of others, how ever well motivated. In his 1961 notes that accompanied the revised edition of the *Dostoevsky* book, Bakhtin seeks to clarify the relationship of outsideness with the responsible use of the surplus:

> Not merging with another, but preserving one's own position of extralocality and the surplus of vision and understanding connected with it. But the real question is Dostoevsky's use of this surplus. Not for materialisation and finalisation. The most important aspect of this surplus is love ... and then confession, forgiveness ... finally, simply an active (not a duplicating) understanding, a willingness to listen. This surplus is never used as an ambush, as a chance to sneak up and attack from behind. This is an open and honest surplus, dialogically revealed to the other person, a surplus expressed by the addressed and not by the secondhand word. [1984, p. 299]

Despite this description, Bakhtin does not explain how we can reach an understanding of someone without duplicating or empathising with their experience. Without empathy our understanding can only be a detached and unemotional one.[8] Alan Jacobs (2001) draws attention to the absence of a universal humanity throughout Bakhtin's writing and in doing so denies the possibility that we can love someone and understand them, at least partly, because of what we have in common or the ways in which they are similar to us. Tellingly he draws attention to a scene in the *Brothers Karamazov* where Lise reproaches Alyosha for presuming to predict that Captain Snegirev will accept money from him, which he has just refused, when it is offered to him again the next day. Bakhtin agrees with Lise that it is degrading and wrong to "finalise" someone in this way but fails to mention Alyosha's reply to Lise:

> No Lise, there is no contempt in it. . . . Consider what contempt can there be if we ourselves are just the same as he is? Because we are just the same not better. And even if were better, we would still be the same in his place . . .

Jacobs speculates that Bakhtin's apparent antipathy to the idea of humanity in general is because, in his view, moral decisions cannot be reached on the basis of an abstraction but only on the particularity of each situation and each person. Over-identification with another is an abdication of our unique responsibility to bring our own evaluation and perspective to each situation, an "alibi for being" (Bakhtin, 1993, p. 15; pp. 40–42). Each encounter with another requires a *kenotic* humility and self-discipline, a letting go of any claims to authoritative truth, together with an active rather than a passive understanding of the other. For Bakhtin (1990, pp. 50–51), failing to attend actively to another is a failure of love.

The uniqueness of each individual conferred by embodiment does not erase the shared human characteristic of interdependency, and acknowledgement of interdependency means letting go of illusions of autonomy. The quest for self-sufficiency that Girard regards as a form of pathology is also regarded by Bakhtin as destructive of the self and society; the pride of autonomy must give way to the humility of personal responsibility and participation, a *kenotic*[9] emptying of self (Coates, 1998, 2001). The influence of Orthodoxy is apparent in the emphasis on the collectivity held together by mutual interdependence that would regard any claims to self-sufficiency as sinful (Good, 2001). There are no absolute ethical values outside of lived experience, and lived experience is collective social experience. A genuine moral engagement with the world involves self-forgetting and orientation towards the other:

> Ethics, when it is reduced to itself, left to itself, becomes a desolated ethics, for the ethical principle is a mode of relating to values, and not a source of values. [Bakhtin, 1993, p. 84]

The deceitful word

The early Bakhtin appears to have a near absolute faith in the human potential for goodness and the healing power of dialogue. It is possible that his subsequent experiences of arrest and exile under Stalin as well as the execution and disappearance of many of his contemporaries, coupled with the guilt he might have felt about his own survival, caused him to question these beliefs. Coates (1998, 2001) argues that the Fall motif in Bakhtin's work is in evidence not only by the Fall from Grace that results from the arrogance of self-sufficiency when the shame associated with the actual condition of human incompleteness and dependency is revealed, but also because the author himself "falls silent" as his faith in discourse is shaken. He can no longer trust his own creative activity and instead allows the discourses of others to speak through him. The word becomes alien contaminated with the values and intentions of previous use. The author's intent is subverted by the condition of heteroglossia. His position of "outsideness" is no longer tenable:

> For the novelist working in prose, the object is always entangled in someone else's discourse about it, it is already present with qualifications, an object of dispute that is conceptualised and evaluated variously, inseparable from the heteroglot social apperception of it. [Bakhtin, 1981, p. 330]

The author can be no more successful than his heroes in the fruitless struggle for semantic autonomy and his outsideness no longer guarantees his benevolence; that his own selfish interests will not subvert his attempt to give form to the other. Even if his intentions are totally selfless, the words available to him are not value free and their meaning is already partly determined. Bakhtin (1981) writes that the prose writer describes and measures his own experience in an alien language. Each word *tastes* of the contexts of its previous usage in socially charged situations, is *overpopulated* with the intentions of others. This complicates the relationship between the author and language, he has to distance himself from it to *play* with it; he cannot give himself up to it but at the same time has to try to mould it to his own intentions. As the author must resort to the use of parody and irony, direct authorial discourse as a vehicle for truth is no longer to be trusted. The author (Rabelais)

> ... taunts the deceptive human word by a parodic destruction of syntactic structures ... Turning away from language (by means of language of course), discrediting any direct or unmediated intentionality or expressive excess (any weighty seriousness) that might adhere in ideological discourse, presuming that all language is conventional and false, maliciously inadequate to reality. [Bakhtin, 1981, p. 309]

Bakhtin appears to turn his attention away from the possibility of a straightforward, honest discourse and is concerned instead with the potential of discourse to deceive and manipulate:

> The word frightens, promises, raises hopes, praises or blames (the fusion of praise or blame neutralises the lie)

and

> The genuinely good, impartial and loving person has not yet spoken, he has realised himself in the spheres of everyday life, he has not touched the official word, infected with violence and falsehood, he does not become a writer. [cited in Coates 1998, p. 118][10]

Modern man can only speak with reservations (Bakhtin, 1986). Honest and straightforward expression of our own intentions is no longer possible and it is impossible to speak about others without objectifying them or undermining their own experience of themselves. Here Bakhtin seems close to a Girardian position in which language can be used or misused to pursue and disguise the pursuit of mimetic desire in its various forms in the interests of deceiving both others and our selves. Discourse, however subtly employed, becomes a means of violent self-assertion. This could be equivalent to what Coates (1998) argues is "fallenness", reinscribed into a theory of discourse, in which monoglossia, the striving for hegemony and ideological closure is a threat to the multiplicity of discourses and ideologies in heteroglossia.

Despite this bleak vision of the reduced possibilities of language, the potential for straightforward, honest communication is redeemed in two ways. The first is when the human desire to establish oneself in discourse gives way to a superior discourse wholly directed towards the interests of the other. This is only a partial redemption, as the qualities needed are exceptional rather than ordinary. There needs to be an attitude characterised by humility and the willingness to acknowledge human weakness. For Bakhtin these are the qualities of Dostoevsky's more spiritual heroes, who have surrendered their own authority to God and can therefore be the bearers of "penetrative" or "inwardly persuasive" discourse which is both selfless and entirely oriented towards helping the other find their own truth. Inwardly persuasive discourse here is the ability to speak to the other in a way that the words are assimilated and become their own despite previous contradictory or conflicting positions they might have had (Bakhtin 1984, p. 242). Despite his later opposition to "finalising" the other, Bakhtin finds a "loophole" in the surrender to the authority of a higher authority or God, who can also speak through a human other (Coates, 1998).

Carnival, laughter and the grotesque body

The second redemption is through laughter. In Bakhtin's study of Rabelais,[11] the human body is defined not by its separateness from others but by what Tihanov (2001) refers to as its *transgressive togetherness* (p. 114). It is a body that is still, in a collective sense, spiritual that through its laughter overcomes the division between nature and culture. Its relevance to and continuity with Bakhtin's previous ethical concerns is not obvious. As Emerson (1997) suggests, there are apparent contradictions between dialogue, which individuates, and carnival, which effaces difference, and between the mortal speaking body and the immortal *grotesque* body; nevertheless the implications of carnival for psychotherapy practice are deserving of serious consideration to bring balance and an overall coherence to the linguistically oriented dialogic approach to communication and meaning. Lock (2001b) suggests that the development of Bakhtin's ideas after the *Dostoevsky* book were an excavation for the origins of the dialogical which is merely a *discursive displacement* (p. 87) of the carnivalesque. While any word is a *hypostasis* of at least two voices (Lock, 2001a), human nature is a *hypostasis* of the official and the unofficial or of laughter and seriousness. Bakhtin (1984b), with reference to Aristotle, writes that not only is foolishness inherent in people but that it is laughter itself that makes us human and distinguishes us from other animals. Formal systems of ethics, the law and religious prohibitions are all associated with high seriousness. As previously discussed, they deal only with the abstract and cannot address the particularity of lived experience and can therefore only give us partial access to reality. Bakhtin cites Engel's critical comment about the Enlightenment in which

> Cogitative reason became the yardstick of all that existed[12]

From Aristotle's Poetics onwards seriousness in literature has always been privileged in relation to comedy, which as Lodge (2006) highlights may well be due to the loss of the part of the Poetics concerned with comedy. In tracing the pre-history of the novel in classical comedy and the medieval carnival tradition of parody and irreverence, Bakhtin reinstates the importance of comedy as a counterbalance to serious authoritative totalising discourses. The comic is far more than light relief from the main business in life of being serious, it is an essential and complex response to seriousness that is of equal value in matters of understanding and truth, particularly progressive and liberating truths.

With its inversion of social hierarchies, its opposition to official culture and the apparent celebration of bodily indulgence, carnival has also been seen as potentially the most subversive of Bakhtin's ideas, due to its opposition to both organised religion and Stalinist bureaucracy. However, the anti-clericalism in *Rabelais and his World* is directed at the Roman Catholic Church with its Neo-Platonist insistence on the divisions between mind and body, spirit and matter, reason and sense, the former always being elevated above the latter, rather than Eastern Orthodoxy, in which the Incarnation, the Word becoming flesh, invalidates these dichotomies (Lock, 1991).

This joyful anarchy of the body was suppressed by the rise of rationalism and Cartesian dualism from the 17th century onwards (Bakhtin, 1984b, p. 115). Carnival means far more than just feasts and celebrations and refers to the whole of popular festive culture as reflected in the everyday language and behaviour of ordinary people, that is people who are not part of a political, religious or social elite. In this context, popular humour and irreverence are the mirror image of official seriousness in which the certainties of authority are inverted or parodied. Humour and laughter are also the counterpoints to the cosmic fear that stalked the imagination of the medieval world. This laughter is not cruel or rebellious but represents liberation from socially or religiously imposed roles and inhibitions. The medieval church forbade laughter, which for Bakhtin is part of human nature and legitimising laughter is therefore merely freeing people to be themselves. The liberating effect of laughter is discussed by Serge Averintsev (2001) in relation to the Christian tradition that Christ never laughed. He reminds us that real laughter is a spontaneous, dynamic event that affects the whole body and, as it is provoked or manipulated by something or someone outside of ourselves, it is a passive phenomenon that involves a suspension of personal will. It is also a transitional phenomenon, as Averintsev argues, from a state of fear or anxiety into a state which is less fearful though not free of fear. To be entirely free from fear is the ultimate freedom and wisdom that only Christ embodied. Laughing at ourselves, self-ridicule, is a way of getting our self-importance into perspective, while also revealing the self as divided; one of the ways in which the culture of laughter was crucial to the development of double and multi-voiced discourse in literature (Brouwer, 1999).[13] Laughter is also fluid, infectious and indeterminate; once we began to laugh the object of our laughter can change course in unpredictable ways. Rabelais' laughter is universal, it is a philosophy of laughter that belongs to everyone and no one. Laughter is related to truth because it reveals aspects of life and the world which would otherwise be hidden. In its critical resistance to dogma and the official world, laughter is a test of truth (Poole, 1998). According to Bakhtin, true seriousness, free of narrow dogmatism, is capable of being tested in the *crucible* of laughter:

> True ambivalent and universal laughter does not deny seriousness but purifies and completes it. Laughter purifies from dogmatism, from the intolerant and the petrified; it liberates from fanaticism and pedantry, from fear and intimidation, from didacticism, naïveté and illusion.... It restores the ambivalent wholeness. [Bakhtin, 1984b, p. 123]

By liberating people from not only external authority but internal censorship, from the fears of breaking sacred and official prohibitions, laughter reveals interior truths that higher authorities may prefer us not to know. Hub Zwart (1999) refers to official or scholarly discourses as "truth games" in which the discourse that is permitted is restricted, so limiting what is accepted as being true. He describes how the young ascetic Martin Luther became depressed, due to the guilt he felt because of the punitive official discourse of Roman Catholicism, and was liberated when he understood the justice of God as being a source of salvation rather than punishment, an apparently sudden insight that came to him while struggling with constipation on the monk's privy. In this unlikely setting, official Catholic theology of hell and damnation was turned upside down and the gloomy monk was transformed into the jolly, uninhibited Protestant whose voluminous writings were full of scatological metaphors and abuses. Luther's humourous abuse of the Roman Catholic hierarchy was not malicious but designed to reduce the vertical distance between them and ordinary people by demonstrating that their bodily functions were the same as everyone else's. By translating ascetic or classical theological discourse into the everyday language of ordinary life, Luther[14] revolutionised the theology of his time. This theology had become an inflexible intellectual game entirely removed from corporeal life[15] and he revitalised it by reinterpreting it in the vernacular, the language of the original gospels.[16]

Laughter and carnivalised language can reveal a different truth from below. In this sense laughter gives a voice to people who might otherwise struggle to find one, whose languages are suppressed by the centripetal monologising forces of officialdom and as such could be considered an essential element of heteroglossia. Laughter importantly restores philosophy to ordinary situations in everyday life, even those that might be considered, from the perspective of high seriousness, to be bestial, immoral, frivolous or irrelevant, and partially redresses the grievances of relative powerlessness.

Menippean[17] satire is fundamental to a carnivalised view of the world. In the menippea apparently heterogeneous and incompatible elements are combined into an organic whole; philosophical dialogue, symbolic systems, *slum naturalism* and improbable adventures are all seamlessly present in the same narrative in what amounts to a philosophical universalism:

The adventures of truth on earth take place on the high road, in brothels, in the dens of thieves, in taverns, marketplaces, prisons, in the erotic orgies of secret cults and so forth. The idea here fears no slum, is not afraid of life's filth. The man of the idea—the wise man—collides with worldly evil, depravity, baseness and vulgarity in their most extreme expression. [Bakhtin, 1984, p. 115]

From a historical perspective the menippea was the first genre to attempt to represent the moral and psychological complexity of the human individual, a complexity that destroys the illusion of epic or tragic heroism. For the first time there was an attempt to portray human psychological frailty with its predilection for unrestrained daydreaming, out-of-control passions, suicidal despair, and what in contemporary psychological discourse is sometimes referred to as "personality disorder". The significance of this for Bakhtin (1984) is that the person no longer coincides with her/his self, is revealed as unfinalised and therefore needs and is open to the possibility of another in her/him self. In other words s/he is in possession of a dialogical consciousness. The important aspect of this is not to illustrate individual pathology but universal aspects of the human condition.

Like the menippea, carnival is fluid, ambivalent and ambiguous. Degradation of the body is also the source of renewal; death cannot be separated from birth or life from death. Ambivalence is also characteristic of the ironic and playful banter of the "market place" the everyday context for carnivalised language where praise can be simultaneously abuse and vice versa. The *grotesque* body of carnival is not static but a body that is always becoming something else in the processes of copulation, birth and death, eating, drinking, and defecation. The focus is on the orifices of the body, the mouth, nose, anus, and genitalia, that are most often subject to grotesque, carnivalised, exaggeration. This is where the boundaries between the body and the rest of the world break down as the world is both ingested and expelled. It is also these organs that are most frequently referred to and have the most varied terminology in everyday speech. Bakhtin's apparent opposition to the idea of a common humanity breaks down when it comes to the body, which is universal to everyone:

It is presented not in a private, egoistic form, severed from the other spheres of life, but as something universal representing all people. [Bakhtin, 1984, p. 19]

However, universality does not deny the singularity or irreplaceability of each person, which he sees as imposing a moral obligation, but it does deny the body as private property, isolated from the rest of the world and other people. The *grotesque* body is a point of transition in the eternal renewal of life in the cycle of birth and death and is also inseparable from the rest of the world:

... it is cosmic and universal. It stresses elements common to the entire cosmos: earth water, fire air; it is directly related to the sun, to the stars. It contains the signs of the zodiac. It reflects cosmic hierarchy. This body can merge with various natural phenomena, with mountains, rivers, seas, islands and continents. It can fill the entire universe. [Bakhtin,1984b, p. 317]

Bakhtin contrasts this universal body that is at one with the natural environment with the modern classical body of smooth surfaces and closed orifices that is self-contained, separate from the rest of the world and other bodies. The events and actions of this classical body have a single meaning confined to the life of one individual. Death is final and does not coincide with birth. The activities of bodily orifices are transferred to the private and psychological sphere, where they are shorn of their wider philosophical implications and their relationship to communal life and the cosmos. The emphasis is on the individualising aspects of the body, particularly the face, and to the place of the body in the external world. Despite Luther's radical insistence on the inseparability of corporeal and spiritual life, as Hirschkop (1999) points out, this private body was later typified by the Puritan capitalists, in their refusal to integrate with the life of humanity as a whole. The neo-classical body seeks both to differentiate itself from and place itself above other people, analogous to the quest of Girardian mimetic desire for absolute difference. The body becomes private property in which thought, ideas, spirit and reason are disembodied. By contrast, the *grotesque* body is imperfect and needy and therefore cannot exist in isolation. Satisfaction of bodily needs is a cause for celebration, rather than a shameful reminder of the body's lack of self-sufficiency. Lock (1991) writes that for Bakhtin, who as Emerson (1997) reminds us was no stranger to hunger, food was always an occasion for celebration:

> Man's encounter with the world in the act of eating is joyful, triumphant, he triumphs over the world, devours it without being devoured himself. [Bakhtin, 1984b, p. 281]
>
> No meal can ever be sad. Sadness and food are incompatible (while death and food are perfectly compatible). [Bakhtin, 1984b, p. 283]

The alienation that women in Western societies in particular experience in relation to their own bodies and their ambivalent relationship to food form no part of this vision of a healthy, joyful relationship to eating. Bakhtin does not address the significance of the body that is fed back to us through the perceptions of others, the varying amounts of "symbolic capital" (Crossley, 2001) that are granted to us by different bodily attributes. Lack of symbolic capital can lead to the body being a source of shame, disgust, and the object of self-destructive behaviour. Merely having or being a body is not seen as sufficient to deserve respect and recognition as an other. The body is both privatised, insofar as we are expected to act on it and control it so as to conform to societal demands and expectations, and public, insofar as it is available for general inspection, granting either approval or condemnation. The downside of the recent assault on Cartesian dualism in academia is that we can no longer claim to live in a rarefied world of consciousness separate from our bodies; we are our bodies and nothing else. But the contemporary Western body is not granted sacramental status as it is in Orthodox theology, in which all matter is sacred and there can be therefore no hierarchy of matter (Lock, 1991) or differences of value between different bodies.

Without this spiritual recognition, the body is reduced to private property for which the individual is uniquely responsible, a source of pride or shame that in turn makes it acutely vulnerable to exploitation, economic and sexual. In this respect contemporary Western culture has not yet thrown away the solipsistic illusion of the privatised and individualised body, a legacy of rationalism and the Enlightenment. It accords with the ideals of individual as opposed to communal freedom and individual rather than communal responsibility, as well as the marginilisation and exclusion of the imperfect and non-conforming body. It leads to an instrumentalist relationship to the world which has to be dominated and controlled (Gardiner, 1998). It both helps to create the conditions for and contributes to the pathologisation of mental distress as individual psychological disorder. Some parallells can be drawn here with the opposition of dialogism and monologism: the classical body could be seen as exhibiting some of the static, univocal aspects of monologism and the *grotesque* body could be seen as being in a dialogical relationship with other bodies and the cosmos. Carnival, with its valorisation of bodies that are simultaneously universal and diverse, is a centrifugal force in contrast to the centripetal ideology of the state or established church. As Birkett (1998) suggests, carnival, in its subversion of authority, reveals the heteroglossia that is central to language and socio-historical relations and that official power tries to suppress.

Without getting over-involved in the many disputes between Bakhtin scholars over the interpretation of carnival, it is important to draw attention to the limits of his analysis. Much, though not all, of what Bakhtin writes about human nature seems curiously innocent of its more extreme, disturbing, and malign aspects. Nowhere is this truer than in his treatment of the phenomenon of laughter. For Bakhtin (1984b) there is no violence, hypocrisy or cruelty in laughter; even mocking, ironic and parodic laughter is ultimately harmless and liberating. He does not address how laughter can become an instrument of oppression and torture, entirely destructive of human dignity and bodily integrity. Averintsev (2001) draws attention to how carnival forms were used by Ivan the Terrible, Stalin and Mussolini as examples of the direct connection between laughter, violence, carnival, and authoritarianism. Natalia Reed said in relation to Bakhtin's assertion that the Gospels were carnival that:

> Indeed they are. Up to and including the mob-lynching of Christ. [cited in Emerson, 1997, p. 175]

A horrific recent example is the mockery used in the torture of Iraqi Muslim prisoners by American and British soldiers. At a less extreme level, but nevertheless on the same continuum, is the use of carnival laughter to reduce the fears of psychiatric practitioners by mocking their patients, a process vividly described by Good (2001). By laughing at their patients' "madness" these practitioners "liberated" themselves from their own fears of insanity but in doing so reduced their capacity for empathic or imaginative understanding, thereby objectifying their patients and boosting their own standing. What we laugh at in others is what we most fear in ourselves. Fear and anxiety can be an appropriate dialogical response to another who is in distress.

Another valid criticism is how carnivalised forms can easily become mainstream and lose their subversive and democratising effects, or tolerated and even sanctioned by officialdom and therefore function merely as a safety valve in which legitimate critical viewpoints are siphoned off and rendered "harmless" and ineffectual. Carnival effigies and coarse language have long been a standard feature of radical political protests and demonstrations that have seeped into mainstream political campaigning, where their effect is to provoke derision and contempt rather than liberation from the stranglehold of official discourse.

Nevertheless, Bakhtin's carnival, with its valorisation of the unofficial and subversive aspects of culture could be seen as a critical challenge to the serious discourses and monological tendencies of therapeutic movements. Therapeutic concepts and theories are frequently couched in language that is inaccessible to the non-specialist. Translating these into ordinary language that anyone can understand can be both comical and demystifying, thereby reducing the distance between "expert" practitioners and patients. As Zwart (1999) points out, terminology can become fixed and mechanical; making fun of it in the way that Luther and Rabelais did of Catholicism with their grotesque and scatological parodies flattens the hierarchical or vertical dimension in discourse and stretches it out on a horizontal plane. Established ideas become open to dispute from different perspectives and the gap between the Word and the body is reduced. Dialogism in its broadest sense implies full acceptance or even celebration of uncertainty, unknowability, messiness, and unpredictability as the preconditions for freedom and of the speciousness of all claims, particularly those relating to the human psyche, to absolute knowledge.

Commonality versus difference

There is a contradiction in attempting to bring theory of any kind into an interrelationship with Bakhtin's ethics. For Bakhtin, the act, like the word, is unique and unrepeatable and cannot therefore be adequately described by or accounted for by theory. Theoretical boundaries are arbitrary and, wherever they are drawn, limit what can be spoken about. Ethics can never be transcendental and our response can only be determined by the particularities of any given event or situation. There is much value in this kind of thinking for psychotherapy, as attempts to diagnose and fit people into theoretical models are inevitably demeaning and reductive, however helpful it might be for clinicians to attempt make sense of their patients in this way. Theory, however broad and integrated and however flexibly applied, will draw a boundary at some point and will therefore fail to take account of the whole unique person.

Like theory, ethical codes of practice cannot account for the irreducibility of each person and the nuances of interdependency in each situation.

However, Bakhtin's ethics, in which uniqueness and difference are privileged over similarity and the idea of "common humanity", risks becoming yet another abstraction, in which the I and Thou encounter is isolated from its social context. There seems to be an idealistic optimism about individual altruism, sensitivity, and goodness, a failure to fully acknowledge the murkiness as well as the complexity of human motivation; that acting towards someone with the best of intentions can have harmful consequences. Irreducibility is not an absolute quality of human beings. If it were, there could be no intersubjectivity and no basis for empathy or understanding. Irreducibility has to be counterbalanced by recognition of basic human similarity. Intersubjective ethics cannot be entirely based on the particularity of each encounter with another human being. A common basic consensus about morality is needed around which the differences inherent in each person and each situation can be understood and considered. Particularity needs to be modified by sameness and the potential for goodness, and altruism needs to be modified by a realistic acknowledgement of human failings. Another weakness in Bakhtin's account of intersubjectivity is, as Hirschkop (1999) points out, his overestimation of the importance of Christian forgiveness in relation to the numerous other responses —practical, political, scientific etc—that are equally significant in complex societies.

Bakhtin's existential phenomenology could be both strengthened and modified when reconsidered in the light of imitation research and the discovery of the Mirror Neurons System. The previous chapter discussed how our learning about our selves, others, and the world is not only facilitated but could not happen at all without the capacity to imitate. As this develops from a simple capacity to copy the motor actions of others into a more complex ability to infer the goals of these actions, we begin to learn about the desires of others and to model ourselves on what others around us consider desirable. As Girard has shown, the objects or goals of desire can be infinitely variable, but the phenomenon of desire itself is not and it can therefore be part of the basis of mutual understanding. However, in order to reach such an understanding of another, we need to be aware of the workings of our own desire, which could otherwise interfere with an ethical response in the intersubjective encounter. Rules are necessary as a safeguard against, even if they cannot prevent, mimetic desire interfering with the need to give absolute priority to the needs of the other. Bakhtin's carnival, in which the universal aspects of the body are stressed, is needed to modify the concept of absolute outsideness and to overcome what Holquist (1993) identifies as the conflict between outsideness and empathy.

Imitation research suggests that it is proprioceptive feedback from our own bodies that enables us to read or infer the feelings or emotions of another, something we would be unable to do without a basic similarity to others. This is not to say that misunderstandings do not occur—as Weigand (1999) has shown, they are an inevitable feature of dialogical interaction. Nevertheless communication and understanding are not possible without similarity. The way in which the mirror neurons function also adds weight to the concept of the universal body, suggesting that physiological processes in our brains are interconnected in an immediate rather than a mediated way, which could itself constitute a further modification to outsideness.

If people as a whole were not characterised by similar bodies and emotions, it would not be possible to talk about human beings as a category at all. None of the human and biological sciences and the practices that have developed from them would exist and, whatever the artificial nature of the boundaries that have been drawn to demarcate different disciplines and at whatever level of abstraction their theories have been pitched, they have also created a vast body of knowledge, that includes our knowledge of the conceptual tools with which to criticiwe them. At a very basic level we need a theory of mind to operate at all in the social environment, a theory that allows us to predict how others might respond to us and to guide our own behaviour, according to our goals or aims. The usefulness of such a modified concept of outsideness is an injunction to think beyond and outside theories, rules and categories as well as with them, and to consider the particular qualities and aspects of each person, as well as and alongside the ways in which we are the same as them.

The importance Bakhtin accords to the body, its centrality in shaping our experience and our perceptions of others and ourselves, is lent considerable support by the cognitive scientific research described by Lakoff and Johnson (1999), which suggests that human language, cognition, and the conceptual categories we think with are governed by embodiment. The embodied mind is not merely an organ within the body; our bodily experience and interactions are a scaffold for the metaphors that populate all systems of thought, including ethical and moral ones. Outsideness is itself a primary metaphor, derived from the experience of our bodies being distinct and separate from the bodies of other people.

The account of Bakhtin's intersubjective ethics I have outlined here is premised on my view that there is an overall ethical coherence to his writing at different stages, despite the apparent transition from ethics and aesthetics in his early work to his later concerns with language and sociology. Although I have focused more on the influence of Russian Orthodoxy, it is important to remember, as discussed in Chapter Two, that Bakhtin's philosophical position with regard to self and other arose in the context of an intellectual climate that owed as much to Kant and Marx as it did to Orthodoxy (Hirschkop, 1999). From a psychotherapy perspective, the significance of Bakhtin's thinking about embodiment is that it potentially extends and modifies the dialogical and social model of consciousness by its insistence on the inseparability of corporeal and chronotopic aspects of experience from its cognitive and emotional aspects. Lakoff and

Johnson's (1999) work on embodied cognition lends retrospective confirmation to Bakhtin's ideas, which were derived from philosophy and literature from their cognitive science perspective: and Bakhtin's extensive use of primary and complex metaphor derived from the conflation of early emotional and sensorimotor experience is a vivid illustration of embodied cognition.

Ethics divorced from embodied existence are meaningless and Bakhtin's meditations on the implications of corporeal experience in terms of difference and sameness seem in many ways to be stating what is obvious. However, it does seem that the prevalence of dualistic thinking in Western thought, in which ethics and reason are traditionally categorised separately from corporeal existence and emotions, has made such thinking habitual and Bakhtin's restatement of the obvious seem startlingly original. His work on Rabelais adds a moral dimension to the primary metaphorical categories of "high" and "low" as applied to culture and social life in that the life of the body, particularly to what Bakhtin refers to as the "lower bodily strata," is split off from anything considered to be "high" and serious. In emphasising the universal nature of corporeal life, Bakhtin reduces the vertical hierarchy of authority and officialdom whether in the state, the church or other social institutions. From a religious or spiritual perspective he brings an Orthodox, horizontalising modification to Girard's vertical Roman Catholicism. The centrality of embodiment, rather than abstract beliefs, to Bakhtin's ethics makes his ideas both potentially appealing to and applicable to all human encounters, regardless of religious affiliation, whereas Girard's overtly religious standpoint may limit the extent to which non-Roman Catholics and, even more so, non-Christians have been able to engage with his ideas.

The next and final chapter will consider the implications of the convergent discourses discussed in this chapter and the previous chapters for the theory and practice of psychotherapy.

Notes

1 Coates approaches Bakhtin from a Western protestant perspective and looks for evidence in Bakhtin's writing that his thinking was influenced by his Christian, as opposed to specifically Orthodox,

beliefs. She acknowledges that her own ignorance of Orthodoxy may have lead her to overlook its influence.
2. The doctrine of the Trinity holds that God is union or unity of three persons: Father, Son and Holy Spirit and so encompasses diversity within unity.
3. The Orthodox doctrine differs from the Latin and Protestant churches in that the Spirit *proceeds* only from the father and not from the Father and the Son. This preserves the Father as "the unique origin and source of the Godhead" (Ware, 1997, p. 213) and thus keeps the principle of unity in the person of the Father (Ware, 1997). Differing doctrines of the Trinity were highly significant in the schism between the Papacy and the Eastern Church in the 11th century.
4. This does not mean that knowledge is not relevant, it means that it must be *acknowledged* and evaluated according to the particular situation. Theoretical validity on its own is like a document without a signature according to Bakhtin (1993). Bakhtin's critique of *theoretism* is not primarily directed towards scientific instrumentality but Kantian formalism in ethics, his point being that laws alone are not enough as they can only deal in generalities and therefore do not generate the moral obligation that arises in a particular situation (Hirsckhop, 1999).
5. The concept of the chronotope was developed much later than his earlier ideas about ethics and responsibility. It is being discussed at this stage because it lends retrospective clarification to his ideas on the uniqueness of the person and the act. It could also, as Morson & Emerson (1989) imply, replace his earlier less precise concept of "architectonics" (Bakhtin, 1990), an attempt to endow the particular situation with a structure and avoid generalizing by reference to systems.
6. The camera and particularly the video camera have meant that people have more access than in previous eras to how other people see them and their popularity may be partly due to the extent to which such devices give us an illusion of control in this respect.
7. Lock relates Bakhtin's concept of outsideness to the Orthodox concept of *diastema* or that which is created and can be known and is changeable over time and space. The Creator is outside *diastema* and cannot be known. Human consciousness is created and subject to mutability and therefore intelligence and reason can have no privileged or transcendent position. Insofar as language is constitutive of consciousness, consciousness itself will change as language

evolves and mutates. This amounts to "... an externalization and a historicization of consciousness, that inscription of consciousness in time and space that has been most vigorously resisted by the entire tradition of Western philosophy that would secure consciousness in the realm of ideas and treat even time and space as merely contingent to the intelligence" (Lock, 2001, p. 103). Bakhtin said that the novel was the first new form of writing since writing began and Lock (2001b) implies that the novel, itself, has created a world of silent discourse that requires private space and separation from others in a way that has profoundly shaped modern consciousness.

8 Holquist (1993) suggests that Bakhtin was unable to resolve the contradiction between complete empathy with another, coinciding with another, and maintaining one's unique position. The possibility of empathy is in some ways denied by Bakhtin's concept of outsideness in that we have no direct access to the inner life of another.

9 Coates (1998) and Jacobs (2001) use the term *kenosis* in slightly different ways. Jacobs argues that Bakhtin's use of the term does not imply forgetfulness of self in the sense of giving oneself over entirely to other's position but rather to cultivate a disinterested active attentiveness to the other, while maintaining one's own position.

10 From Draft Exercise books 1992 untranslated. Emerson (1997) offers a longer version with a slightly different translation into English:

The lie is today's most ever present form of evil, The word does not know whom it serves. It emerges from the dark and does not know its own roots. Its serious link with terror and violence. The authentically kind, unselfish and loving person has not yet spoken, he has realized himself in the spheres of everyday life, he has not attached himself to the official word, infected with violence and the lie; he is not becoming a writer (Emerson, 1997, p. 170).

11 Bakhtin's work on Rabelais and the concept of carnival in general has been the subject of considerable scholarly debate and disagreement. Emerson (1997) offers a useful summary of these discussions which will be largely avoided here as the purpose of the present discussion is to highlight ethical implications of relevance to psychotherapy. The concept of carnival has been widely appropriated by the left and particularly by feminists and post-colonial theorists, although it is fiercely debated as to whether the inversions of carnival

are actually subversive or merely a safety valve that serves to contain frustration and resistance.

12 Marx and Engels, Works: Vol. 5, 16.
13 Brouwer draws attention to the different cultures of laughter in Europe and Russia, where there was no equivalent of the Renaissance. The opposition between laughter and official culture did not exist in the same way in medieval Russia and therefore had a different influence in Russian literature that was not influenced by Western European culture.
14 The Reformation inspired by Luther became a widely popular movement, probably due to its carnivalised view of the world in contrast to the Renaissance which did not extend beyond the aristocracy (see Brandist, 2002, 31).
15 Catholic doctrine had nothing to say about the natural functions of the body, and enjoyment of these was entirely shunned in ascetic idealism and sexuality was denigrated. Such repression inevitably lead to its opposite of crude debauchery (Bakhtin, 1981).
16 Luther's frankness about his own and other peoples' bodily processes, the coarse "carnivalised" language in which he wrote his account of the birth of Protestanism became an embarrassment to his later "Puritan" followers who expunged it from his writing (Zwart, 1999).
17 The genre takes its name from the Greek philosopher Menippus who lived in the 3rd century BC. It developed out of Socratic dialogue with its serio-comical inversions and features legendary figures who have fantastical adventures in order to illustrate or provoke discussion about a philosophical truth or idea. The most well known example is Lucian's story of the Golden ass.

CHAPTER EIGHT

Towards a Bakhtinian Practice of Psychotherapy

> ... the embodiment of meaning in mortal flesh—is born and dies in the world and for the world; it is totally given in the world and can be consummated in the world ... As such ... it can be a hero. [Bakhtin, 1990, p. 111]

In this concluding chapter I will discuss how a more inclusive reading of Bakhtin, together with a qualified reading of Girard, could contribute towards finding a direction for a practice of psychotherapy inspired by Bakhtinian ethics. The dialogical aspects of Bakhtin have already been widely used to inform theory and practice in psychotherapy as discussed in Chapter Three. In this chapter I will focus on the other aspects of Bakhtin's thinking that I think are the contextual background in which the dialogical should be understood.

As previously discussed, there are many conflicting interpretations of Bakhtin and therefore when using his concepts in psychotherapy there is a need to be explicit about our own chosen interpretation. It is first necessary to return to the difficulties posed about the use of Bakhtin in psychotherapy theory and practice discussed in Chapter One. Two main questions emerged: given the uncertainty about the meaning of Bakhtin's most important concepts, how can psychotherapists justify the use of one meaning over any other? If there is an overall coherence to Bakhtin's works, can psychotherapists selectively appropriate particular concepts without distortion by removal from their wider context?

I have attempted to give the reader an overview of the differing interpretations of Bakhtin and the way some of his ideas have been appropriated in the fields of psychology and psychotherapy. My own understanding of Bakhtin is that he lies beyond glib classifications but his ideas are congruent with non-doctrinaire Marxism, a liberal acceptance and celebration of human cultural and religious diversity, as well as radical and progressive currents within Christianity. Christian beliefs and values are apparently implicit and sometimes explicit in Bakhtin's writing and to represent him otherwise would be to do him a disservice. Christian values and beliefs are more overt and explicit in Girard's writing. However, as these values are not exclusively Christian and are used primarily by both thinkers to think through intersubjectivity and the nature of selfhood, a belief in a deity or other supernatural phenomena is neither a necessary precondition for nor an obstacle to their use in psychotherapy. A holistic approach cannot divorce religious beliefs and spiritual concerns from other aspects of well-being. With his emphasis on plurality and the conflicting discourses of heteroglossia and, by implication, the diverse interests of oppressed and marginalised groups in society with their different political and religious beliefs, Bakhtin inspires revolt rather than revolution (Pechey, 2007); a revolt against any attempt to impose uniformity or conformity. This is not, however, an absolution from responsibility, but could be understood as what Barsky (1998) argues is Bakhtin's implicit support for an anti-authoritarian as opposed to an irresponsible anarchism.

Despite the controversy and conflict that surrounds interpretations of Bakhtin, he can be made to elide smoothly with current concerns with narrative, discourse and identity, as well as with more pessimistic "postmodern" concerns with social and individual disintegration, fragmentation, and meaninglessness. Dialogical discourse allows, in theory at least, for the possibility of infinite meanings but also, if abstracted from the rest of life, infinite misunderstanding.

The dialogical has to be seen in the context of Bakhtin's thought as a whole. Otherwise, as Hirschkop (1999) suggests, there is a risk of idealising dialogue and expecting too much from a detailed analysis of it, while overlooking the historical background that shaped it.

In the recognition and importance Bakhtin accords to the body, he implies a constraint on the range of meanings that are possible and counterbalanced human difference with human similarity. However, Bakhtin did not follow all these implications through. Taking Bakhtin's insistence on the irreducibility of each person through to its logical conclusion would lead to a fantasy world of "absolute difference" in which relationships of any kind would be impossible. Human interrelationships are partially based on what people feel or perceive they have in common with each other, if only the minimal fact of being fellow human beings. Differences are not absolute but arise out of a field of sameness (Alison, 1997). Empathy, a sense of community, and the concept of "kindness" are all based on a shared understanding of, if not always fully conscious and articulated, similarity. Alongside a growing awareness of the varieties and complexity of human differences, globalisation has brought about a growing realisation that human beings are interdependent with one another and the environments that they share. Recognition of the sameness and equality of human biological, social, and psychological needs is as important as respect for the right of people to express and attempt to pursue these in different ways. On this basis it is argued that the original Bakhtinian self, with its emphasis on what is unique about the person, needs to be supplemented with a Girardian understanding of the ways in which people are the same. While it could be objected that such a modified version could no longer claim to be Bakhtinian, if Bakhtin is understood as having bequeathed a methodology of enquiry in the form of internally persuasive discourse as well as a descriptive account of consciousness, then the approach to the self described below could claim to be inspired by Bakhtin, while eschewing any claims to be anywhere near complete or finalised. However we choose to interpret Bakhtin, it is important to engage with him critically, otherwise he risks being misrepresented as another authoritative monological discourse, left to stand alone on a pedestal unchallenged and static (Pollard et al, 2006).

Towards a Bakhtinian conception of self

> ... the author's creative consciousness is not a language-consciousness; ... language consciousness is merely a passive constituent in creative activity—an immanently surmounted material. [Bakhtin, 1990, p. 194]

That human beings, not just language, are fundamentally dialogical in their orientation towards each other is supported by the research discussed in Chapter Six. Imitation is also dialogical in that it involves the recognition of and a response to the actions of another. And, as desire, according to Girard, is mimetic, it is also dialogical in that it is always a response to the perceived or imagined desire of another.

A Bakhtinian self can only be conceived of in relation to other selves and possesses a consciousness that lies on the "borderline" between self and other. The idea that consciousness is a "borderline" phenomenon is a metaphor that conveys the thoroughly social nature of consciousness; without other people, our awareness of ourselves as conscious beings would not be possible and the production of meaning is always a shared activity. Consciousness is an inter-subjective phenomenon and selfhood is interdependent on other selves, which means that the Bakhtinian self is also a moral agent with unique responsibilities for its own actions and towards the other. As co-creators of meaning, the participants in an intersubjective relationship are also the "authors" of each other's identity and subjectivity. Both have a "surplus" or excess of seeing in relation to the other and possess knowledge of the other that the other cannot know for themselves. This "surplus" is a consequence of the unique vantage point in the world, possessed by each person, that is guaranteed by embodiment. The body is central to a Bakhtinian understanding of selfhood. While consciousness is fluid, mobile, and shared between selves, the body is the more stable referent for the individual self. However, this stability is only relative. The body itself is not only mobile, voluntarily or involuntarily, a fact that emphasises the importance of the chronotopicity of experience, but is perpetually in a state of transition between birth and death, growth and decline, health and illness, sleeping and waking. It is also permeable and in constant interaction with the environment and hence with other bodies.

Bakhtin stressed not only the vital role of the other for the self but the radical otherness of the other. As Cheyne and Tarulli (1999) note, Bakhtin entirely rejects the notion of shared perceptions or shared goals and maintains that the value of the other for the self is based solely on what the other can see and know that the self cannot. Once we see people as a category rather than as a unique individual, we see them and treat them as less than fully human. However, in his apparent rejection of the idea of a common humanity, Bakhtin fails to fully acknowledge how our ability to understand and empathise with others is based on similarity and shared experiences, and without a shared basic common humanity communication and understanding would not be possible at all. A theory of mind, our capacity to learn by imitation and to infer the desires, goals and feelings of others and to respond to them; our reliance on primary metaphors to express our feelings and thoughts to one another: all these are based on a commonality of embodied experiences.

Despite the recognition Bakhtin gave to the body, his account of consciousness, as discussed in Chapter Four, is devoid of actual content and fails to account for either violence or desire. Although Reed (1999) frames this observation as a criticism of Bakhtin, it can also be used creatively to bring him into dialogue with Girard. Bakhtin and Girard could be described as having a relationship of radical outsideness in relation to each other: Girard would see mimetic desire expressed or denied in dialogical discourse and Bakhtin would see dialogicality in the convoluted discourse of mimetic desire. Dialogism describes the dynamic and structural aspects of consciousness, but not its contents, the desires and emotions that are directly or indirectly, consciously or unconsciously, expressed. To ignore content is to embrace the abstract theory that Bakhtin abhorred. Stallybrass and White (1986) make an implicit link between the neo-classical body with its smooth surfaces and closed orifices and "rigorous" academic theory that is contemptuous of content, which it regards as obvious and vulgar. Such abstract theory is a discursive mirroring of the myth of the bourgeois subject, whose rational disinterest and clear-sighted objectivity is both superior to and a negation of the emotional and subjective discourses of women and other minoritised groups, and a rationale for their subjugation.

A Bakhtinian understanding of self needs to be supplemented with a balancing of difference with similarity, the acknowledgement of specific "contents", particularly desire, sexuality, and the human propensity for violence.

A Girardian addendum to the Bakhtinian self

Whereas Bakhtin stresses the radical otherness of the other for the self, Girard emphasises the essential sameness of human beings, despite or even because of their strivings to assert their differences. The two highly significant aspects of subjectivity to which Girard draws our attention are desire and mimesis, and also the ways in which they are related. Desire and thwarted desire are fundamental to human emotional and social experience but they have fallen off the maps of most contemporary models of psychotherapy. Just as Bakhtin exposes the myth of human passivity, that it is impossible not to act, Girard exposes the myth of consciousness without contents, e.g. that it is possible to be free of desire. Even wishing to be free of desire and be self-sufficient is itself a form of desire. Desire, in Girardian terms, is distinct from need and only indirectly related to pleasure, sexual or otherwise, and is a purely mimetic, symbolic, and social phenomenon.

From a psychotherapy perspective, it is important to distinguish between the two types of mimetic desire that Girard proposes: externally mediated desire, where the model is not in competition with the subject for the same "object" and the relationship is therefore non-conflictual; and internally mediated desire, where the pursuit of the desired object is a threat to the model and subject and model become rivals whose identical desires erode the differences between them, making them "doubles" of each other. Neurosis can result when the subject, who experiences mimetic desire that is externally mediated and does not perceive her or himself as a rival to the model, finds that their imitation born out of admiration or respect is perceived as a threat and subject to criticism or prohibition, the so-called double bind. The model that both designates what is desirable and obstructs us from obtaining it, serves only to intensify our desires as well as our sense of personal inadequacy if we fail to satisfy them. The most extreme form of mimetic desire is "metaphysical desire" that is born out of a deep sense of what is lacking in ourselves that we imagine the other possesses. Narcissism, according to Girard, is both a strategy for concealment of this felt inadequacy while feigning self-love in order to attract the desire of the other. "Metaphysical desire", because it can never be realised, leads to enslavement, failure, and shame. As such, its unrelenting pursuit is a form of masochism in which the very failure to obtain the object is itself proof of its desirability.

Like Bakhtin, Girard has a social conception of self but draws attention to the similarity of peoples' desires rather than the differences between them. The more individualistic a society, the more that society will be in thrall to mimetic desire and the more fiercely will that desire be denied. Like Bakhtin, Girard draws attention to the ethical implications of interdependency but also demands that we acknowledge that the other is the source of our own desires and the extent to which the other is our potential rival, and therefore our own propensity for violence and self-deception. For Girard, the only solution to the problem of violence is absolute responsibility but this apparently harsh injunction does not seem to take account of the social and economic conditions that can exacerbate or ameliorate the spiritual suffering that can flow from mimetic desire.

Mimesis and the self

In his focus on the destructive aspects of mimesis, Girard can seem to underestimate the significance of mimesis as a means for cultural integration and social cohesion. Its importance in human culture is reflected in psychoanalytic theories of identification and particularly Lacan's "mirror stage", which cultural theorists have used in the elaboration of how identities related to gender, race or sexual orientation are acquired and performed (Potolosky, 2004). The research discussed in Chapter Six suggests that not only is the capacity to imitate present at birth, but that it is also essential for human learning and socialisation. Additionally it is, as Meltzoff (2003) suggests, fundamental to our capacity to recognise another as being similar to ourselves, to empathy and to understanding another's point of view, and as such is the essential precondition for all intersubjective dialogical relationships.

However, the links and possible mutual confirmation between these two different fields of study have hardly been explored. Girard does not adduce "scientific" evidence from outside the scope of his own, admittedly wide-ranging, enquiries and researchers of imitation have not greatly explored the social implications of their findings, particularly the role of reciprocal imitation in generating rivalry and conflict. Fleming's (2004) more recent book introducing Girard's ideas to a contemporary audience makes only passing reference to the research of Meltzoff and the significance of the discovery of the mirror neurons in footnotes.

Despite the growing awareness of the social nature of self and consciousness in the human sciences, the importance of imitation as reciprocal interaction is seldom recognised. Psychotherapy has also failed to be explicit about the role of imitation in either theory or practice, although concepts such as mirroring, empathy, reflection, and modelling all depend on it. It seems as though the comparatively recent emphasis on difference that has resulted from greater awareness of the prejudice, oppression, and discrimination suffered by minoritised groups in a global society has led to an unthinking neglect of the ways in which people are similar to each other and therefore both learn from each other and communicate with each other through imitation. Another obstacle is the psychobiological or innate aspect of the mechanisms involved in early infancy and possibly throughout life that sit uncomfortably with an entirely social account of consciousness. The recent findings of research into imitation suggest that, from birth, human socialisation and learning is dependent on reciprocal imitation and that this is crucial not only in childhood but also throughout adult life:

> Everyday life in human society is animated in mutual interest between persons who, in their conversations, and depending on their status and companionship, express reciprocity of intentions, interco-ordination of skilful movements, convergent imaginings and conscious recognition. [Trevarthen et al, 1999, p. 127]

Dialogical consciousness: semiotic mediation or mimesis?

As previously noted, some recent developments in dialogical psychotherapy have incorporated the concept of communication and internalisation through "sign mediation" (Ryle, 2000, Ryle and Kerr, 2002). Leiman (1992, 2002) argues against Bakhtin's use of the utterance as the basic unit of analysis and replaces it with Voloshinov's concept of the sign. For Leiman, dialogical consciousness and semiotic mediation are inseparable, but semiotic mediation still implies the notion of meaning being transferred from one consciousness to another separate consciousness by signs, leaving the thesis of somatic particularism intact. The findings of researchers related to imitation and the Mirror Neurons System discussed in Chapter Six suggest that responsive understanding in communication is *immediate* rather than *mediated* by signs and that, as Harris (2002) points out, the notion that ideas are conveyed through linguistic signs is not congruent with consciousness as a thoroughly social phenomenon. The accumulating evidence suggests that social consciousness is not primarily a cultural development or even a consequence of language but a pre-condition for survival that reflects the lifelong dependency of human beings on other human beings, and that language is not a separate ability but part of a continuum of dialogical communicative action.

That words are signs is not disputed, but the meaning of a word is entirely dependant on its context in the utterance. As shown in Chapter Six, the non-linguistic factors in any utterance by far outweigh the significance of the words that are used, thus reducing the relative importance of words as repositories of meaning. Hence, the importance that Voloshinov (1976) attaches to socially created signs in the formation of consciousness does not take account of what Lakoff and Johnson refer to as embodied conceptual reason; i.e. that consciousness is structured by embodied experiences that are probably universally shared but not socially created. The prevalence of primary and complex metaphors in speech strongly suggests that the body has a formative role in creating shared intersubjective meanings, as so many metaphors are grounded in embodied experience. Infants both imitate others and engage in conversational reciprocity a long time before they learn to use words.

Reciprocal imitation possibly has a far greater role in human interaction and communication than previously thought and could also replace or account for the metaphorical concept of internalisation, overcoming the problem that Henriques et al (1984) identify of how what happens "outside" gets "inside" and the dualism that this implies. Imitation based on the recognition that the other is both "the same as me and separate from me" is a more economical and observable explanation for the repetition of object relations and dialogic sequences than internalisation. Dialogical interaction is necessarily embodied activity in which physiological processes cannot be separated from perceptual, cognitive, and emotional responses. It is not therefore feasible to suggest, as Harré (1983) does, that conversation is social reality and physiology is individual reality. Although Leiman's concept of sign is flexible, socially contextualised and not confined to the linguistic realm, it still represents a need to impose a structure on complex phenomena that closes down other possible interpretations. To conceive of consciousness purely in semiotic terms could amount to what Makhlin (1999) and Morson (1988) refer to as a form of "semiotic totalitarianism" that is the antithesis of everything Bakhtin stood for.

Heteroglossia, mimetic desire and narrative identity

Girard is concerned with the nature of human desire but not how desire is expressed in discourse, while Bakhtin is concerned with the struggle between different styles of speech but is less concerned with the conflicting human desires that cause conflict. As Nickolas Coupland points out:

> Bakhtin's perspective, motivational as it is, is still text-focused. He argues that styles or registers are socially indexical and that heteroglossia conflicts are conflicts among styles and only indirectly among people. [2001, p. 197]

However, Bakhtin's linguistic approach captures the multiplicity and fragmentary nature of some contemporary experiences in a way that Girard's generalisations fail to do. Identity is not a given, as in more stable, less geographically and socially mobile societies, but has constantly to be renegotiated. Desire and identity are closely related and entangled in heteroglossia; the struggle to assert or construct a self-identity, or to reject an imposed one, in discourse. As Giddens (1991) implies, attempts to achieve a coherent self-identity through the narrative construction of a biography of the self is one way of resisting the fragmentation of identity that can result from shifting and unpredictable social environments. Each environment potentially provokes different kinds of desire so that desire is not consistent throughout social life but varies for each individual in ways that can be conflicting and confusing. Contemporary life forces us into proximal contact with many different models promoting different lifestyles and identities. Claiming a narrative identity that is less dependent on the immediate social situation is also an assertion of autonomy that could be seen as a narcissistic strategy to attract the desire of others, as well as a protection against the "enslavement" of what Girard refers to as metaphysical desire. So Bakhtin's heteroglossia can be understood as a struggle of mimetic desires conducted not between different linguistic styles but by people using language and employing different linguistic styles to assert or resist an identity. This could be understood as a variant of Leiman's (2004) description of how utterances are used to position and reposition interlocutors in dialogue with each other, in which intonation and other stylistic variants are inseparable from meaning.

Different styles are also expressions of power and assertions of social differentiation:

> "Heteroglossia" is the struggle—of people through language—to maintain, assume, or subvert positions and control. [Coupland, 2001, p. 196]

As Weigand (2002a, 2002b) reminds us, speech is always purposeful in complex and often ambiguous ways. A part of the ambiguity of meaning is due to the speaker's attempts to disguise the assertion of or resistance to an identity, by fulfilling other communicative purposes within the same utterance. Communicative purposes can be instrumental, relational or to claim or assert an identity, but words and syntax alone do not convey the complexity of meaning as so much is dependent on context. Coupland (2001) argues that use of a particular linguistic style and shifts in style are predominantly related to identity and relational goals. The modern preoccupation with identity, which is always accepted, claimed, fought for or resisted in relation to others, is closely related to Girard's "metaphysical" desire, since identity is arguably the most contested object of mimetic desire. In the absence of socially sanctioned violence, language becomes the primary, but not the only, means whereby mimetic desires are expressed, concealed, and fought over. However, it is important to remember that not all assertions of identity are conflictual and that style shifts can be motivated by, for example, a wish to convey humour, irony, empathy, friendship, consideration for others or submission to the will of others.

Heteroglossia complicates this picture further due to Bakhtin's insight that words have previously been spoken by others and are infused with other peoples' intentions i.e. desires, so that each utterance and each word is potentially riddled with internal contradictions. While it is important to remember that it is people who use words purposefully, their intended meanings and desires can be subverted by the desires of previous speakers. This gives a new depth of meaning to Girard's (1966) dictum that desire is according to the other, as well as a link to Weigand's (1996) emphasis on the potential of dialogical discourse for misunderstanding.

Chronotopic aspects of the self

Our sense of self and identity is bound up with our experience of embodied historical continuity and memory, however inaccurate, is always chronotopic. It is the chronotope that contextualises dialogue by grounding it in a temporal-spatial and therefore material reality. It is a reminder that dialogue, whether written or spoken, can only take place among embodied subjects. Our spatio-temporal perceptions rely on our physical senses and it is how our bodies are situated that defines our individual chronotopes and subjective positions. The co-existence of other embodied voices may be as important in subjective experience as the "voices" from the past that are inferred from inner dialogue. The passage of time is etched on the body as it evolves from birth to old age and death. The individual chronotope also limits the extent to which we can be aware of events that take place in different times and places, which can nevertheless have a profound impact on our own lives. An experienced lapse of temporal continuity due to injury, trauma or illness can be deeply unsettling to the sense of self, as can involuntary exile from or loss of a home or homeland, an experience Bakhtin was all too familiar with. As Ahmed Sa'di (2004) suggests in relation to Palestinian experience, questions of identity and self-hood are often discussed at a level of abstraction that ignore the specificity of a particular place, a particular community, and particular objects. However, the chronotopic dimensions of experience have rapidly changed and become infinitely more complex since Bakhtin's death in 1975. Although Bakhtin lived through some of the most historically significant events of the 20th century, he had little experience of the technologies that have had so much impact on contemporary chronotopes. He did not have a telephone and, according to one academic acquaintance who witnessed an unwilling Bakhtin being interviewed by journalists in the year of his death,

> In the world of newspaper correspondents and the spinning of microphones, Bakhtin looked ancient, outdated, lonely, and lost.[1]

For Bakhtin the auditory aspects of culture were primary. He was a listener (Emerson, 1997), hence the emphasis on language and words in the dialogical self. He never extended his analysis to film, fashion or television and the other visual phenomena that have become so pervasive in the 20th and 21st centuries.

Ursula Heise (1997) suggests that the spatial metaphors of postmodernism and computer technology such as "websites", "cyberspace" and "sites of resistance" are indicative of a crisis in the relationship between time and space. The erosion of spatial obstacles to global capitalism and the ever decreasing life cycles of products have produced a time culture of instant and ephemeral satisfaction and the discarding not just of products but of values, traditions, stable relationships, and attachments to people and places. Knowledge of previously local events becomes instantly available to millions of people and individuals are caught up in immense global networks of communication and information that are often beyond their understanding or control. Computer and telecommunications technology in particular have promoted temporal values of simultaneity and instantaneity.

Such rapid changes have influenced ideas about the nature of self and how self-hood changes in response to developments in science and technology that affect everyday life. From a Girardian perspective, the contemporary media offer a bewildering array of potential "models" to emulate, while Western societies, increasingly characterised by competitive and acquisitive individualism, exacerbate anxieties about the adequacy of the self in a way that fuels mimetic desire.

Conceptualising mental distress

A Bakhtinian understanding of subjectivity also involves rethinking how psychotherapists understand mental distress, even though Bakhtin did not directly address problems of mental ill-health and distress in his writing. Discussing these issues within a Bakhtinian framework necessarily involves applying his ideas to areas they were not intended to address, which can lead to accusations of misapplication and dilution. The justification advanced here is that, while his key concepts of responsibility, authoring, outsideness, participatory thinking, the chronotope, dialogism, and carnival were formulated in relation to "art" and literature, Bakhtin did not divorce art from life and mental distress is indisputably part of life.

The social causes of mental distress have been widely documented in recent years (Sennett and Cobb, 1972, Smail, 1993, Pilgrim and Rogers, 1993, James, 1998, Wilkinson, 2005). The experience of mental distress, which is often medicalised and diagnosed as depression or anxiety or, more pejoratively, as personality disorder, is adversely correlated with economic and social status; women, working class people, people from ethnic minorities, and other minoritised groups are disproportionately affected. Relative social and economic disadvantage is strongly associated not only with a reduced quality of life but also with a substantially reduced life expectancy (Wilkinson, 2005). As Wilkinson points out, people are members of the same species who have the same physiological and psychological needs and are therefore in competition with each other for the same scarce resources. The way societies deal with this relative scarcity of resources, either by co-operation and affiliation or by competition leading to the domination of hierarchical elites who command a disproportionate share of resources, has a profound effect on mental health. The lower down the social-economic scale, the greater the level of mental distress experienced throughout the lifespan. The significance lies not in absolute levels of wealth but in relative levels and the degree of inequality in its distribution and what this inequality signifies. Regardless of levels of absolute wealth, the most unequal societies have higher levels of poor health, relatively poor rates of social integration, and higher levels of violence.

Neglectful and abusive parenting, widely seen as the antecedent to mental ill-health, is symptomatic of societal pressures as they impact on families and individuals. In Bakhtinian terms these could be understood as the dominance of authoritative discourses that reflect and promote the socio-economic interests of the wealthier and relatively more powerful groups in society as well as their tastes in art and culture, at the expense of the relatively disadvantaged groups who not only experience relative material deprivation but experience themselves construed in the eyes of the Other as inferior, lacking in power and status and worthwhile cultural resources and acumen. So powerful are these adverse social influences on the health of the person that the death rates of those lower down the social pyramid according to age are three times higher that those at the top.[2] Wilkinson (2005) refers to this phenomenon as "social toxicity" in which the psycho-social stress suffered by relatively less advantaged groups leads to physiological illness and higher death rates.

The interaction between social conditions, psychological health and physiological illness are all aspects of the embodied nature of the self and the inseparability of experience. Social toxicity affects people at all levels of society where there is a hierarchical ranking of power and status. This can be understood as the negative aspect of Bakhtin's benign conception of the mutual co-creation of identity, which is particularly prevalent in societies characterised by high social mobility and individualism where there is considerably more anxiety about how others see us:

> Our reflexivity as human beings, the way we experience ourselves partly through each other's eyes, is . . . the highway through which the social gets into us. No wonder then that it is also the main gateway by which the psychosocial gets under the skin to exert such a powerful influence on health. [Wilkinson, 2005, pp. 92–93]

In societies characterised by relatively high levels of social mobility together with a steep hierarchy of wealth and status, levels of social insecurity are also higher and these are reflected in the priority given to various strategies to maintain or gain wealth and status, for example through the acquisition of educational or professional qualifications, conspicuous consumption, and the joining of exclusive clubs or professional associations. As Stallybrass and White (1986) point out, "bourgeois" identity is based on the exclusion of what is considered to be "low", "dirty", "noisy" or "vulgar".

As we have already seen, the medieval carnival allowed those lower down the social scale an opportunity to compensate for their "inferior" position by mocking and ridiculing those higher up. The comic rituals of carnival were also tolerated and even encouraged by those who were its targets, as their positions in the social hierarchy were unassailable. However as Stallybrass and White suggest, Bakhtin's *troublesome folkloric approach* (1986, p. 26) is inadequate when it comes to the political realities of contemporary class societies: in more socially mobile societies, such safety valves are less easy to employ due to the insecurities of those who are higher up the ladder and the aspirations of those lower down. Even so, despite the reduced power of carnival to sublimate the frustrations of social inferiority, the designation of the various cultural categories as high and low remains remarkably constant. Stallybrass and White's description of these phenomena, in which the categories of class, geographical space, and the human body are all conceived of in these terms, seems to bear out Lakoff and Johnson's (1999) thesis about the inescapability of embodied experience in shaping perception:

> ... cultural categories of high and low, social and aesthetic but also those of the physical body and geographical space are never entirely separable (and is part) of a much broader and more complex cultural process whereby the human body, psychic forms, geographical space, and the social formation are all constructed within interrelating and dependant hierarchies of high and low. The high low/opposition in each of our four symbolic domains—psychic forms, the human body, geographical space, and the social order—is a fundamental basis to mechanisms of ordering and sense-making in European culture. [Stallybrass & White, 1986, pp. 2–3]

They also suggest that these metaphorical categories play a profoundly influential role in the subjective experience of self and the perception of self in relation to other people. Those higher up the socio-economic scale have, in Bakhtin's terms, a more powerful surplus of vision that allows them to define, categorise, and condemn the less powerful. These categorisations and condemnations are often spoken from a conservative moral agenda, employing a complex metaphor of morality as strength (Lakoff, 1995).³ Academic journals and broadsheet newspapers regularly describe and categorise what is routinely regarded as the problematic behaviour of disadvantaged groups in society, usually in terms of excessive drinking, smoking, eating or teenage pregnancy; behaviours which in turn lead to problems of drunkenness, poorer health, obesity, and inadequate parenting. Peter Good (2001) vividly describes how psychiatry, a powerful middle class profession, employs this surplus in relation to those deemed to be mentally ill, thus compounding the problems they are charged with alleviating. On an international scale, Edward Said (1978) describes how the Occidental Judeo-Christian world has used its powerful surplus to both describe and pathologise the Oriental, Islamic world. Dominant discourses of inadequacy and inferiority become internalised discourses of self-doubt or self-loathing, which can be reflected in depression or violence.

A further burden carried by those deemed inadequate and morally inferior by the dominant discourses is that of being exoticised and exploited. As Stallybrass and White (1986) suggest, the bourgeois subject, which can be generally understood as the Western, white, male middle and upper classes, is defined by that which it attempts to distance itself from. This expulsion, which also demarcates what is forbidden, is a magnet for desire that leads to exploitation. The bourgeois subject is both fascinated and repelled by "low life", which it can sentimentalise, envy, and desire while simultaneously despising, abusing, and rejecting it. But while the complex psychology of the bourgeois who exploits is well documented, the psychological effects of such exploitation are considerably less well understood, particularly when compounded by economic and class exploitation.

Specialist works, such as those exploring the psychological impact of child sexual abuse, address these issues to a limited extent, but the voices of the most exploited and oppressed by definition have little power and, if they are heard at all, are usually represented in the discourses of the relatively powerful who have access to the media and communication. It is only through access to a wider social landscape that a surplus of vision can be gained that is sufficient to articulate a sense of self that includes an awareness of exploitation by and inferiority in relation to others, and of the social conditions that give rise to this. Neither Bakhtin nor Girard take sufficient account of what Voloshinov (1976), from a Marxist perspective, terms the "objective social conditions" that are pervasive in consciousness, i.e. the economic base that underpins class societies, that shapes desires and is reflected in both external and internal discourse.

Chronotopic aspects of mental distress

Bakhtin's concept of the chronotope can also help to illuminate the spatial dimensions of mental distress in unequal, although socially mobile, class societies. Traditional psychotherapy tends to emphasise the historical or temporal aspects of the chronotope neglecting spatial aspects that are also relevant. Bakhtin (1984) sees the consciousness of Dostoevsky's characters not as historically determined, but as simultaneously co-existing and interacting. An individual's point of view or position is profoundly influenced by their location in relation to other people and objects. The spaces we inhabit, whether interior domestic spaces, the semi-public spaces of the workplace, the grander spaces associated with public life or the more anonymous spaces of urban life, all have a profound affect on our sense of self and identity. Particularly important is our ability to control the spaces in which we live and the ease with which we can move between different spaces. Our sense of self is profoundly affected by involuntary confinement in a particular space, for example in a prison or a hospital.

Class is an issue here: our sense of control over or ownership of private space, and the freedom to move between different spaces, is largely a function of wealth. Nowhere is this more obvious on a global scale than the freedom conferred by ownership of the right passport. Gender is also crucial. Mary O'Conner (1990) draws attention to Bakhtin's failure to differentiate women's experiences from those of men:

> Bakhtin's universalising of human experience in historical space-time configurations contradicts his general theoretical position that the monological voice denies the voices that speak from alternative positions in the historical moment. [O'Conner, 1990, p. 139]

In a general sense, women's freedom of movement has historically been far more restricted. Women's lives have more frequently been defined by domestic spaces and, since the onset of capitalism, by the acquisition of commodities. Capitalism is also, though not exclusively, associated with the commodification of women's bodies with all the restrictions on freedom of movement that this entails.

Control over time is also class-related and the experience of time also varies considerably between people. Only people at the margins of contemporary society, such as the very young or the very old, the very poor or the very rich, seem to have enough or even too much time and yet their choices as to how to use or spend their time may be very restricted. The degree of control we feel we have over our time and how we spend it can have a significant effect on our sense of well-being. Control over time is a potential source of conflict between people at a societal and an individual level. In this sense time is another commodity that is not equally distributed.

Violence and scapegoating

Violence, actual or simmering beneath the surface, is a constant feature of societies where inequalities are institutionalised and justified by appeals to the market, or meritocracy or even freedom, but are in fact based on "sacred" social distinctions based on exclusion. As James Alison (2001) observes, once the essence of Girard's thought has been grasped, the scapegoat mechanism can be detected in every news bulletin. Negative, punitive, and blaming discourses are internalised and turned against the self in a way that saps confidence and self-esteem, leading to anxiety and depression or aggression and violence. If society blames its victims for their own misfortune, then some of the victims will inevitably blame themselves.

How the phenomenon of scapegoating is experienced as individual distress and constructed in discourse is apparent in the account of Capps and Ochs (1995) of a woman suffering from agoraphobia. In her speech she positions herself in relation to others as weak, passive, a failure, and irrational and others, who fail to validate her attempts to communicate how she feels, reinforce or are the co-authors of this view of herself. From this position of experiencing herself as inadequate and lacking, she feels unable to communicate her wishes to those around her, leading to feelings of being trapped, which leads to panic and desperate attempts to control those around her which are, in turn, resisted. Referring to Bakhtin, Capps and Ochs note how the words of others are reflected in her self-descriptions and how her interlocutors co-construct these accounts. They also note how her self-description of vulnerability and lack of control in a hostile world were echoed in her daughter's account of herself, which was then affirmed by the mother. This account, as well as illustrating, as the authors intend, how the woman is dialogically positioned in her own discourse and the discourse of others as weak and powerless and as a result, manipulative. It also illustrates how she blames herself and is blamed by others for her position of victim as a working class woman, how her position of helplessness is imitated by her daughter, and how her mimetic desire to achieve more control over her own life is both modelled on and thwarted by more powerful people around her.

Considerations for therapists

Models and theories of psychotherapy compete with other models, exclude other possible meanings and have profound ethical implications in terms of how they construe mental distress and position the participants in a therapeutic encounter. A truly Bakhtinian therapy would eschew models and theories, while opening itself up to as wide a range of ideas and influences as possible:

> Bakhtin's strong reservations about theoritism are reservations about the very possibility of considering art or culture or any other dimension of human life . . . without reference to their ethical value and their impact on the formation of social judgement. [Tihanov, 2000, p. 53]

A Bakhtinian approach would not train, evaluate or accredit therapists but invite them to think creatively about their stance in relation to their clients, the interventions they choose or choose not to make and the philosophies that guide them, so that hidden or unstated assumptions and desires can be brought to light, challenged and thought about. Rather than being either an alternative to or additional component in model-based psychotherapy, the Bakhtinian approach suggested here is an ethical position that could be taken in relation to theories and practices, personal assumptions, beliefs, and narratives as well as a discursive practice that can be cultivated in therapy.

The following are two different but inter-related frames of reference for moving towards a Bakhtinian approach.

"Insideness", outsideness, and use of the surplus

For psychotherapists, the knowledge that is brought to bear in practising therapy could be thought about in two ways. The first is the knowledge that, while it may or may not be innate, is acquired by the infant very early in life, i.e. that other people belong to the same "kind" as him or her self and have similar bodies and minds all of which can experience a similar range of sensations, feelings, and emotions. This early form of knowledge of others is acquired through nurturing interactive relationships. Deficits in the quality of these relationships and early trauma or abuse can interfere with the acquisition of this knowledge which, I would argue, is close to what is commonly referred to as intuition but is in reality the ability to recognise, anticipate, and respond appropriately to another person's state of mind. It involves a clear sense of self and the boundary between self and others in combination with recognition of the similarity of the other to the self. This form of knowledge gives rise to empathy, sensitivity, "kindness", the ability to mirror the other's feelings and bodily expressions of them and to respond in ways that create a sense of experiences and intentions being shared. It can also be used to manipulate other people and is also crucial to the phenomenon of mimetic desire and the consequent competition, rivalry, and violence that this can foster. Embodiment is crucial because this is how proprioceptive and exteroceptive phenomena are experienced and expressed. It is also the basis of the shared experiences that are the basis of primary metaphors, and seems to correspond to what Shotter refers to as "knowing of the third kind", a knowledge that we share with others but are mostly unaware of possessing:

> It is a kind of knowing that takes into account (and is accountable within) the social situation . . . within which it is known. It is a "practical" form of knowledge in terms of which

people are able to influence each other in their being not just in their intellects, i.e. to actually move them rather than just "giving them ideas." [Shotter, 1993, p. 463]

Application of this form of knowledge in psychotherapy is used to build and maintain the "therapeutic alliance". Paying too much attention to the therapeutic alliance or staying in the zone of similarity and empathic understanding, rather than exploring and challenging unhelpful and dysfunctional patterns of relating, is regarded in some models as collusive. In order to easily differentiate it from the Bakhtinian concept of outsideness, it will be referred to here as "insideness". Insideness presumes that there is such a thing as common humanity, that there is an essential similarity between any two human beings regardless of how great the differences between them might be. For Bakhtin, knowledge of ourselves can only be given to us from the outside perspective of other people, but insideness suggests that we can also potentially know other people from our "interior" knowledge of ourselves.

Outsideness, the second form of knowledge, is acquired through life experiences that serve to differentiate individuals from other individuals and that give each person a different and unique view of the world or a surplus of vision. The surplus, in Bakhtin's view, is not an elitist concept: everybody can potentially contribute to the self knowledge of anyone else, as well as being potentially able to learn from anyone else's surplus of vision. To deny the capacity that others have to help us could be considered a form of narcissism and, in Girardian terms, be a means of asserting "absolute difference". When understood as a capacity possessed equally by all, the surplus emphasises interdependency. Unfortunately, when there are differences of power and status between people the surplus is not always benevolent and can be used against people. As Good (2001) observes, people in relative positions of power and authority can use their surplus to manipulate or oppress the less powerful. Taken to an extreme, a powerful surplus could be used to assert an absolute difference between self and other that, through its denial of similarity, eliminates empathy and facilitates violence, cruelty, and even torture.

Psychotherapists, partly by virtue of the boundaries that govern the kind of relationships that they can enter into with their clients and partly due to their training and experience, have a particular kind of surplus in relation to their patients. The nature of this surplus and the degree of power claimed as a result of it (to see what the patient cannot see) depends to a certain extent on the theory or model being used. Psychoanalytic models that rely on interpretation of the unconscious confer a more powerful surplus of vision than humanistic models which have fewer preconceptions about the meaning of experience. While humanistic models give more priority to the knowledge that comes from human similarity, this kind of knowledge is less highly valued in models that give greater priority to complex theory and technique and the knowledge that is gained from education and training, in other words from outsideness. As well as being helpful, the surplus that is granted by outsideness can be both powerful and potentially damaging to the patient. Psychotherapists are, in Bakhtin's terms, "authors" of their patients' identities and their relative power can be used to "finalise" in ways that are distressing or unhelpful. As Tihanov (2000) notes, the use of the surplus from a position of outsideness demands a "moral guarantee" based on taking full responsibility for the uniqueness and insecurity of one's own position.

All psychotherapy involves a combination of insideness and outsideness, and could be characterised as a constant interchange and interaction between these two forms of knowledge. The relative weight accorded to each is an ideological consideration, regarding the causative mechanisms in mental distress. Insideness emphasises the human condition and the distress that individuals suffer from circumstances that are beyond their control, sometimes even outside of their awareness. The realisation that their suffering is a common response to particular circumstances that is shared by others can be immensely reassuring. Outsideness emphasises the part the individual usually unwittingly plays in the perpetuation of their own suffering and is therefore more concerned with individual pathology and less with the social factors that gave rise to it. The mental health professions could also be placed on a continuum according to the relative weight given to insideness and outsideness, with counselling and some schools of psychotherapy weighted towards insideness and clinical psychology and psychiatry weighted towards outsideness. This is reflected in their differing trainings; insideness focusing on "experiential" work and developing self-awareness, and outsideness focusing on theoretical knowledge and specific related skills.

As previously noted, Bakhtin apparently had little time for human similarity and the comfort that can be gained by human beings finding common ground with other human beings, for empathy or identification (Jacobs, 2001, Emerson, 2000), and believed that for dialogical consciousness to develop, there must be contact and conflict with different languages, cultures and world views: the only way human beings can help each other is from the outside. The healthy or robust self welcomes or even seeks feedback from the outsideness of others (Emerson, 1997) but people who seek psychotherapy are usually feeling far from robust and are frequently suffering from feelings of desperation or despair. Bakhtin seems to take too little account of differing degrees of power or of the possibility that peoples' intentions towards one another may be hostile or malevolent, so that in a fragile social world, outsideness may be used to defend or aggrandise the self rather than to genuinely benefit the other. He also takes no account of desire and that far from welcoming the outside response of the other to the self, such interventions may be resented or experienced as humiliating and disrespectful.

Cultivating internally persuasive discourse

A Bakhtinian approach to the "training"[4] or the preparation of therapists would encourage and facilitate internally persuasive discourse. This involves letting go of the certainties of authoritative discourses and truth claims and subjecting them to critical scrutiny. This inevitably raises questions, rather than providing answers, and leads to greater uncertainty rather than closure: the more strands of knowledge, viewpoints, and ideas that are admitted, the greater the potential for conflict and confusion as well as creativity.

Like Bakhtin, Girard (1987) warns against structure, the need to categorise and classify and, by implication, the foreclosure of meaning that results from medically derived models of research. The competition between different therapeutic models and the increasingly market-driven nature of health provision in the UK means that very little research into psychotherapy is open-minded or likely to lead to any serious interrogation of its own assumptions. Such research tends towards closed systems of thinking in which assumptions, open to a number of interpretations, are taken as facts that are then given retrospective credence by the findings that are themselves selected from any number of alternative outcomes. Internally persuasive discourse confounds any attempts to stand outside the object of enquiry as a neutral or objective observer because it insists that any point of view is merely one among many other possible points of view and that how we are positioned, or position ourselves, influences what we see. From a Girardian perspective, it also demands that the mimetic desires that motivate commitment to particular theories or models are revealed. In a pluralistic social world with many incompatible world views, it would be difficult to reach even a general agreement as to what constitutes mental health and mental illness. The sociological analysis of Wilkinson and Girard's interdividual psychology suggests that, like wealth, even precarious mental well-being in terms of identity and self-esteem is often acquired at the expense of the well-being of others and that, if a thoroughly social conception of mental health and well-being were to be taken on board, it should be defined in terms of the quality of social relationships throughout society.

Like Bakhtin, Girard undermines the notion of professionalisation in psychotherapy. While Bakhtin would refute the idea of a body of expert knowledge that therapists could lay claim to, Girard throws light on the mimetic desires that are revealed or concealed by the numerous competing theories, schools, professional bodies, and professions that have a stake in the field of psychotherapy, as well as in the "sacred" assumptions that justify exclusions. As discussed in Chapter Four, some psychotherapy organisations have devised ruthless, anti-social methods of sharing out the scarce resources of professional recognition and, for many practitioners, the means to earn a living. These processes inevitably affect the attitudes practitioners have towards each other and the nature of their relationships with their clients.

Furthermore, while Bakhtin would apparently see no conflict between the benefit an individual might gain from a therapeutic dialogical relationship with another and the general good, a Girardian analysis would suggest that there may well be circumstances in which the quest for individual fulfilment and autonomy may be detrimental to society as whole. Many contemporary societies that emphasise individual freedom no longer have in place the prohibitions and customs that constrain the individual pursuit of mimetic desires, while failing to offer positive alternatives to the individual goals of recognition, status or wealth (Ranieri, 2002). Girard (1987) recognised that prohibitions are partially protective and that they also provoke mimetic desires to transgress them so that a different model of social existence is needed that offers protection from mimetic rivalry without relying on prohibitions. In societies that both lack prohibitions and alternative protective mechanisms, individual psychological well-being can come overly reliant on achievement in relation to or even at the expense of others. As Wilkinson (2005) has demonstrated, overall health is adversely affected in people who are relative losers in this process, even those who have tried not to engage with it. Girard understood that the consequences of refusing violence when others do not can be highly detrimental. As well as facilitating greater self-awareness, most therapies work towards encouraging autonomy and often individual achievement. While this can be beneficial and life-enhancing for some individuals, it also represents an accommodation with the society that causes and maintains the distress that can lead people to seek therapy and also affects many others who do not.

Dialogical selfhood and internally persuasive discourse

Internally persuasive discourse is an ideology that can hold a belief or idea while simultaneously questioning it; that can tolerate ambivalence and complexity without being indecisive. It both opposes other voices and is opposed by them while also being penetrated by them (Tsitsipis, 2004). It is distinguished from a discourse that is merely contradictory by its aspiration to greater understanding. It is neither totalising nor does it exclude other viewpoints and other explanations. From a Girardian perspective, it moves away from unthinking imitation of another's discourse but does not rebel against it (reverse imitation), but strives toward real independence of thought. James Alison (2001) seems to describe such a process in his analysis of the story in St John's gospel of the "Man blind from birth". After being miraculously cured of his blindness, the man is drawn into a debate between the disciples and the Pharisees about the meaning of the miracle. He neither imitates the arguments of others nor is he seduced into an outright rejection of their words. Rather he listens to all speakers and allows himself to be influenced by them but then reaches his own independent interpretation of the meaning of events. Sight in this sense is also a metaphor for understanding and is reached through a process of disinterested involvement that mirrors the position a therapist might take in relation to the different voices in the dialogical self.

Internally persuasive discourse does not therefore take a position in the "battle" of ideas which demands that an inferior theory is sacrificed to its superior successor. It is a centrifugal process that moves towards increasing openness and diversity, which could include a greater variety of dialogical positions that allows for more flexible conversations between them. However, for radical as opposed to merely adaptive change to occur, the ideological as well as the emotional volitional influences that inform these positions needs to be brought into consciousness.

As therapists, cultivating our own internally persuasive discourse could involve questioning the authoritative discourses of therapeutic schools and professional bodies but more importantly our own presuppositions, beliefs, and the meanings attributed to past experiences. It means recognising that the constitutive effect of our practices may be very different from the intentions that gave rise to them (Richer 1992). From a Girardian perspective, it involves the potentially painful exercise of uncovering and acknowledging the desires and insecurities that underpin our adherence to certain beliefs and to particular practices and their mimetic origins. It means giving up the illusion of individual autonomy when it comes to desire but trying to maintain an independent and self-questioning approach to the theories and assumptions that inform practice. It involves the emotionally complex ability to hold a belief that may be crucial to one's identity as a therapist and a person, and entertain doubt about it at the same time.

In therapy it could also mean therapists giving greater and more explicit recognition to the social, rather than individual, pathological origins of mental distress and in so doing undermining the nature of their own knowledge and authority and the relative balance of power in the therapy relationship. This may imply a commitment to the struggle for social justice in acknowledgment of how psychotherapy, as an economic activity, is parasitic on the imperfections and injustices in our societies. In Girardian terms this means recognition of the constant stimulation of mimetic desires, alongside the obstacles that prevent such desires being realised and arguing against the "voices" that give rise to these desires from specific ideological positions in a way that allows a greater understanding of the social and political context that has given rise to distress.

It is here that the therapist's "outsideness" can help the client towards a greater awareness of the causes of their distress beyond their immediate personal experience, by bringing into the dialogue previously unheard or unrecognised voices. As previously discussed, Bakhtin does not take enough account of how the voices of some people and groups are marginalised or even excluded (Pechey, 1989, Crowley, 1998). However, psychotherapy is rarely a level playing field where therapist and client co-create shared meanings from positions of equality, and the positioning of the therapist can also reduce the chance of some voices being heard. Politically determined institutional chronotopes are likely to reinforce the relative power of the therapist but can also be a constraint on how both therapists and clients experience themselves and on what can be said and thought about. Psychotherapy has traditionally tended to focus on a spatially and temporally restricted chronotope of the individual life and has therefore taken less account of the what Smail (1993) refers to as the distal influences, the activities or events brought about by people who occupy different times and spaces and who are often characterised by greater power and authority.

Girard's non-sacrificial ethics and internally persuasive discourse

Attempting to bring Girardian ideas to bear on the Bakhtinian concept of internally persuasive discourse is potentially controversial as Girard can be perceived as a monological voice, out of step with a pluralistic and complex world. However, the prevalence of violence in contemporary societies suggests that internally persuasive discourses are losing out to authoritative discourses that do not tolerate disagreement or dissent and are backed by force. James Alison, a gay Catholic theologian and Girardian, apparently employs and also advocates a particularly nuanced form of internally persuasive discourse in his attempts to wrestle with the moral and theological problems of gay identity in a church where active homosexuality has traditionally been regarded as sinful. His analysis suggests that a truly internally persuasive discourse is far more than a liberal, enlightened critique that is in reality parasitic on what it criticises; it is a willingness to challenge authority from the point of view of the victim and risk being stripped of reputation, profession, and even labelled mad.

Internally persuasive discourse could also be envisaged as what Alison refers to as the ability to talk with distinctions that involve neither blanket condemnation nor adulation but perceives people and their actions as complex, in both intention and effect. It also means being prepared to openly disagree with authority while being prepared to take the risk of and to admit to being wrong. Silence or the failure to speak can also be active complicity:

> I may be wrong, and I certainly couldn't be right without running the risk of being wrong. [Alison, 2001, p. 183]

A characteristic of authoritative discourse is its incorrigibility; rather than be corrected it justifies its errors with new arguments, insisting more and more on its own rectitude, so that a small mistake escalates and becomes a defining feature of the person or institution and the possibility of being wrong is so unthinkable that the argument becomes totally irrational. A victim position is often used to justify such discourses which are beyond the possibility of rational discussion; Alison vividly describes this as looking like *a terminal disease* (2001, p. 176). Internally persuasive discourse is certainly not an intellectual pastime conducted at a serene distance but a real and possibly dangerous engagement with the power of authoritative discourses:

> ... the capacity to understand what is really going on becomes available in the midst of the extremely violent and muddled turbulence of human social structures, and it is usually made available by people who stand up for the apparently unacceptable when it is in no way fashionable, and are prepared to risk their reputation, and even their life, to do so. What it invariably comes down to is people suspecting the potential victims may after all be entirely innocent, or at least no more guilty than anybody else, and that the whole unified voice to the contrary is ravenous wind. [Alison, 2001, p. 160]

Challenging authority, however dangerous, is one thing and, as noted previously, it is so easy to detect the clash of opposing desires, violence, and scapegoating in almost every arena of life that it becomes tedious. A far greater challenge, implied in the passage quoted above, is to subject oneself to the same analysis. In his narratives of violence unleashed by church authorities against himself and others, Alison also turns the arguments back onto himself and his own role, exposing his own hypocrisy and his own manipulation of a situation to meet his own interests. It is much easier to criticise or challenge authoritative discourses from the position of the victim or by identification with the victim. It is much harder to look for and challenge our own complicity with the institutions and practices of which we may be critical and to acknowledge the extent to which we have also benefited from these. Alison's account also suggests that it is difficult, if not impossible, to be part of human social life and not be complicit in violence: a moral commitment to internally persuasive discourse demands that we acknowledge this.

Psychotherapy and its institutions are engaged in sacrificial politics, where the weapons of exclusion are research and regulation, from which many of its critics inside the professions benefit. Internally persuasive discourse implies a different stance to that of merely taking sides or demolishing one sacred institution or belief only to replace it with another. In this sense, the ethics of internally persuasive discourse could be said to coincide with Girard's non-sacrificial ethics in a way that involves

> ... the continuous deconstruction of the artificial sacred in all the forms of life in which we find ourselves, contributing in this way to a new form of human social life where every apparently sacred distinction begins to be knocked down leading to an as yet unimagined fraternity. [Alison, 2001, pp. 33–34]

A commitment to developing internally persuasive discourse alongside Girard's non-sacrificial ethics is a pre-condition for Bakhtin's ideal conception of embodied dialogical intersubjectivity and for the responsible use of the surplus from a position of outsideness. Both are continual processes rather than stable states of affairs that require a total immersion in the violence and chaos of human social life and a willingness to accept the emotional and moral consequences.

Summary

In this final chapter I have suggested a direction for a Bakhtinian practice of psychotherapy, not as a replacement for existing models but as a position that can be taken in relation to any theoretical model, institutional practice or professional organisation, as well as towards our own beliefs, values, and narratives of self. I have chosen a humanistic and holistic interpretation of Bakhtin that contextualises the dialogical conception of self in a wider ethical framework for human intersubjectivity. I have also attempted to further integrate Bakhtin's thinking with that of Girard, while recognising some of the difficulties and uncertainties that doing so entails.

The conception of self proposed is a thoroughly social one, as is the description of some of the causes of mental distress. The ascription of mental illness to pathological structures within the self or disordered personality is a particularly invidious form of scapegoating or blaming the victim, which psychotherapy has colluded with for too long. While conceptualising mental distress from a Bakhtinian perspective could risk the accusation of overextending Bakhtin, it also reveals gaps in his thinking about human consciousness and social life because, in focusing on texts, he did not account for emotional and mental distress, human desires, and the ubiquity of violence in human social life. Some of these gaps have been filled by Girard's thinking about human social relationships and these seem to be lent confirmation by Wilkinson's recent sociological analysis of the interaction between health and inequality. Similarly, in his emphasis on the uniqueness of each human being and the unrepeatability of each human encounter, Bakhtin overlooked the significance of human similarity.

As Bakhtin's thought does not propose a theory of human intersubjectivity but rather an ethical ideal through which to approach it, there could not conceivably be a Bakhtinian model of psychotherapy or even less a "training" which equips therapists with knowledge of particular theories and associated skills. A Bakhtinian approach would instead involve therapists cultivating internally persuasive discourse as far as possible in the context of equal relations with one another in which "sacred" social distinctions can be safely challenged and done away with.

In endeavouring to be guided by the principles of internally persuasive discourse, I have evaluated the Bakhtinian concept of outsideness in the light of the Girardian understanding of human sameness and proposed a new concept of "insideness", not in opposition to outsideness but as a potentially complementary concept that both clarifies outsideness and is in turn clarified by it.

As dialogism and internally persuasive discourse are processes that by definition have no end point or final meaning, this book offers no conclusions to the discussions that have been presented and leaves matters unresolved but, in the spirit of dialogism, open to further responses and further permutations of meaning.

Notes

1. B. F. Egorov, "Slovo o M.M. Bakhtin" (1975) cited in Emerson, C. (1997, p. 54).
2. Wilkinson (2005) cites the Whitehall Study of civil servants working in London which found that death rates were 3 times higher age for age amongst junior office workers than the highest ranking civil servants. In the UK these deaths do not reflect differences in medical care or material conditions that adversely affect health such as poor nutrition but high levels of psychological stress, associated with raised blood pressure and cortisol levels leading to increased risk of cardio-vascular diseases.
3. This metaphor is derived from a combination of goodness as being upright, doing evil is falling, being evil is low and evil, itself, is a force to be opposed.
4. In the author's view "training" or "being trained" as a psychotherapist is problematic with its implications that formally recognised structures and qualifications are guarantees of competence. In France, the emphasis is on the *formation* of therapists, in which the emphasis is on personal change rather than printed qualifications (Evans, 1996).

BIBLIOGRAPHY

Adlam, C. (1997). In the name of Bakhtin: Appropriation and Expropriation in Recent Russian and Bakhtin studies. In A. Renfrew (Ed.), *Exploiting Bakhtin*, Strathclyde, Strathclyde Modern Languages Series, No. 2.

Alison, J. (1997). The Man Blind from Birth and the Subversion of Sin: Some Questions about Fundamental Morals. *Contagion*, 4: 27–46.

Alison, J (2001). *Faith beyond Resentment: fragments Catholic and Gay*. London: Darton, Longman & Todd.

Anderson, P. (2000). Sacrificed Lives: Mimetic Desire, Sexual Difference and Murder. *Cultural Values*, 4 (2): 216–227.

Angus, L & Mcleod, J. (2004). Self-multiplicity and narrative expression in psychotherapy. In: H. J. M. Hermans & G. Dimaggio (Eds.), *The Dialogical Self in Psychotherapy*. Hove and NY: Brunner-Routledge.

Anspach, M. R. (2004). Introduction to Girard, R. (2004). In: M. R. Anspach (Ed.), *Oedipus Unbound, Selected Writings on Rivalry and Desire*. Stanford: Stanford University Press.

Arronowitz, S. (1994). *Dead Artists, Live Theories and other Cultural Problems*. London: Routledge.

Averintsev, S. (2001). Bakhtin, Laughter, and Christian Culture. In S. Felch & P. Contino (Eds.), *Bakhtin and Religion, A Feeling for Faith*, Evanston, Illinois: NorthWestern University Press.

Baker, H. D. (1995). Psychoanalysis and Ideology: Bakhtin, Lacan and Žižek. *History of European Ideas*, (20): 1–3, 499–504.

Bakhtin, M. M. (1981). *The Dialogical Imagination: Four Essays*, trans. C. Emerson & M. Holquist. Austin: University of Texas Press.

Bakhtin, M. M. (1984). *Problems of Dostoevsky's Poetics*, trans. C. Emerson. Minneapolis: University of Minnesota Press.

Bakhtin, M. M. (1984). Towards a Reworking of the Dostoevsky Book. In: Bakhtin, M. M. (1984). *Problems of Dostoevsky's Poetics*, trans. C. Emerson. Minneapolis: University of Minnesota Press.

Bakhtin, M. M. (1984b). *Rabelais and his World*, trans. H. Iswolsky. Indiana: Indiana University Press.

Bakhtin, M. M., (1985). A Critique of Marxist Apologias of Freudianism. *Soviet Psychology*, 23: 5–27.

Bakhtin, M. M. (1986). *Speech Genres and Other Late Essays*, trans. V. McGee. C. Emerson & M. Holquist (Eds.). Austin: University of Texas Press.

Bakhtin, M. M. (1990). *Author and Hero in Aesthetic Activity: in Art and Answerability, Early Philosophical Essays*, trans V. Liapunov. M. Holquist & V. Liapunov (Eds.). Austin: University of Texas Press

Bakhtin, M. M. (1993). *Toward a Philosophy of the Act*, trans V. Lipianov. V. Lipianov & M. Holquist (Eds.). Austin: University of Texas Press.

Balmary, M. (1986). *Psychoanalysing Psychoanalysis: Freud and the Hidden Fault of the Father*, trans. N. Lukacher. Baltimore: John Hopkins University Press.

Barsky, R.F. (1998). Bakthin as Anarchist? Language, Law and Creative Impulses in the Work of Mikhail Bakhtin and Rudolf Rocker. *South Atlantic Quarterly*, 97 (3/4): 623–641.

Bateson, G. (1972). *Steps to an Ecology of Mind*. New York: Ballantine Books.

Bender, C. (1998). Bakhtinian Perspectives on "Everyday Life" Sociology. In: M. M. Bell & M. Gardener (Eds.), *Bakhtin and the Human Sciences*. London: Sage.

Bernard-Donals, M. (1994). *Between Phenomenology and Marxism*. Cambridge: Cambridge University Press.

Bernard-Donals, M. (1998). Knowing the Subaltern: Bakhtin, Carnival and the Other Voices of the Human Sciences. In: M. M. Bell & M. Gardiner (Eds.), *Bakhtin and the Human Sciences*. London: Sage.

Bernstein, A. (1989). The Poetics of Ressentiment. In: G. Morson & C. Emerson (Eds.), *Rethinking Bakhtin, Extensions and Challenges*. Illinois: NorthWestern University Press.

Bertau, M. (2004). Developmental Origins of the dialogical self: some significant moments. In: H. J. M. Hermans & G. Dimaggio (Eds.), *The Dialogical Self in Psychotherapy*. Hove: Brunner-Routledge.

Bertonneau, T. (1987). The Logic of the Undecidable: An Interview with René Girard. *Parole gelees UCLA French Studies*, 5: 1–23.

Billard, A. & Arbib, M. (2002). Mirror neurons and the neural basis for learning by imitation: Computational Modeling. In: M. I. Stamenov & V. Gallese (Eds.), *Mirror Neurons and the Evolution of Brain and Language, Advances in Consciousness Research*. Amsterdam/ Philadelphia: John Benjamins Publishing Company.

Birkett, I. (1998). The Death and Rebirth of the Author: The Bakhtin Circle and Bourdieu on Individuality, Language and Revolution. In: M. M. Bell & M. Gardiner (Eds.), *Bakhtin and the Human Sciences*. London: Sage.

Bocharov, S. (1995). The Event of Being: On Mikhail Mikhailovich Bakhtin, trans. T. Cunningham. *Novyi Mir, 11*: 211–221, reprinted in C. Emerson (Ed.), *Critical Essays on Mikhail Bakhtin* (1999). New York: G. K. Hall.

Borch-Jacobsen, M. (1988). *The Freudian Subject*, trans. C. Porter. Stanford: Stanford University Press.

Bracher, M. (1993). *Lacan, Discourse and Social Change, A Psychoanalytic Cultural Criticism*. Ithaca & London: Cornell University Press.

Brandist, C. (2002). *The Bakhtin Circle, Philosophy, Culture and Politics*. London: Pluto.

Brandist, C., Shepherd, D. & Tihanov, G. (2004). *The Bakhtin Circle in the Master's Absence*. Manchester: Manchester University Press.

Broks, P. (2003). *Into the Silent Land*. London: Atlantic Books.

Bromberg, P. (2004). Standing in the spaces: the multiplicity of self and the psychoanalytic relationship. In H. J. M. Hermans & G. Dimaggio (Eds.), *The Dialogical Self in Psychotherapy*. Hove and NY: Brunner-Routledge.

Brouwer, S. (1999). Problems of Carnivalisation and Novelisation in Russian Literature. *Dialogism, 3*: 31–51.

Buccino, G., Binkofski, F., Fink, G. R., Fadiga, L., Fogassi, V., Gallese, V., Seitz, R. J., Zilles, K., Rizzollatti, G. & Freund, H-J. (2001). Action observation activates premotor and paretal areas in a somatopic manner: an fMRI study. *European Journal of Neuroscience, 13*: 400–404.

Capps, L. & Ochs, E. (1995). *Constructing Panic, The Discourse of Agoraphobia*. Harvard, London: Harvard University Press.

Cheyne, J.A. & Tarulli, D (1999). Dialogue, Difference and Voice in the Zone of Proximal Development. *Theory and Psychology, 9*: 5–28.

Chodorow, N. (1978). *The Reproduction of Mothering*. Berkeley: University of California Press.

Clark, K. & Holquist, M. (1984). *Mikhail Bakhtin*. Cambridge, MA: Harvard University Press.

Coates, R. (1998). *Christianity in Bakhtin, God and the Exiled Author*. Cambridge: Cambridge University Press.
Coates, R. (2001). The First and Second Adam in Bakhtin's Early Thought. In: S. Felch & P. Contino (Eds.), *Bakhtin and Religion, A Feeling for Faith*. Evanston, Illinois: NorthWestern University Press.
Cooper, M (2004). Encountering self-otherness: "I"-"I" and "I-Me" modes of self-relating. In: H. J. M. Hermans & G. Dimaggio (Eds.), *The Dialogical Self in Psychotherapy*. Hove: Brunner-Routledge.
Coupland, N. (2001). Language, Situation and the Relational Self: theorising dialect style in sociolinguistics. In: P. Eckert, & J. R. Rickford (Eds.), *Style and Sociolinguistic Variation*. Cambridge: Cambridge University Press.
Crossley, N. (2001). *The Social Body, Habit, Identity and Desire*. London: Sage.
Crowley, T. (1996). *Language in History*. London: Routledge.
Davies, C. (2000). Fathers, Others: The Sacrificial Victim in Freud, Girard, and Levinas. *Cultural Values*, 4 (2): 194–204.
Decety, J. & Sommerville, J. (2003). Shared representations between self and other: a social cognitive neuroscience view. *Trends in Cognitive Sciences*, 7 (12): 527–533.
Dentith, S. (1995). *Bakhtinian Thought, An Introductory Reader*. London: Routledge.
Derrida, J. (1978). *Writing and Difference*, trans. A. Bass. Chicago: University of Chicago Press.
DeSantis, A. (2001). Caught Between Two Worlds: Bakhtin's Dialogism in the Exile Experience. *Journal of Refugee Studies*, 14 (1): 1–19.
Dews, P. (1995). *The Limits of Disenchantment: Essays on Contemporary European Philosophy*. London: Verso Books.
Douchemel, P. (1988). *Violence and Truth, on the works of René Girard*. London: Athlone Press.
Dostoevsky, F. (1972). *Notes from Underground/The Double*, trans. J. Coulson. London: Penguin.
Dostoevsky, F. (2003). *The Brothers Karamazov*, trans. D. McDuff. London: Penguin.
Dupuy, J. (1984). Shaking the Invisible Hand. In: P. Livingstone (Ed.), *Disorder and Order, Proceedings of the Stanford International Symposium (Sept 14–16, 1981)*. Saratoga: Anma Libri.
Dupuy, J. (1995). The Self-Deconstruction of the Liberal Order. *Contagion*, 2: 1–15.
Eagleton, T. (2003). Pork Chops and Pineapples, Mimesis: The Representation of Reality in Western Literature, by Erich Auerbach. *London Review of Books*, 25 (20): 17–19.

Easthope, A. (1991). The Bakhtin School and Raymond Williams: The Subject and Signifier. *Critical Studies*, 3 (2)–4 (2): 116–123.
Emerson, C. (1984). Editor's Introduction. In: Bakhtin, M. M. (1984). *Problems of Dostoevsky's Poetics*, trans. C. Emerson. Minnesota: University of Minnesota Press.
Emerson, C. (1989). *Rethinking Bakhtin, Extensions and Challenges*. Evanston Illinois: NorthWestern University Press.
Emerson, C. (1991). Freud and Bakhtin's Dostoevsky: Is there a Bakhtinian Freud without Voloshinov? *Wiener Slawistischer Almanach*, 27: 33–44.
Emerson, C. (1996). The Kariakin phenomenon, *Common Knowledge*, 5 (1): 161–178.
Emerson, C. (1997). *The First Hundred Years of Mikhail Bakhtin*. Princeton: Princeton University Press.
Emerson, C. (1999). Introduction. In: C. Emerson (Ed.), *Critical Essays on Mikhail Bakhtin*. New York: G. K. Hall.
Emerson, C. (2001). Afterward: Plenitude as a Form of Hope. In: S. Felch & P. Contino (Eds.), *Bakhtin and Religion, A Feeling for Faith*. Evanston, Illinois: NorthWestern University Press.
Erwin, E. (1997). *Philosophy and Psychotherapy*. London: Sage.
Eisold, K. (1994). The Intolerance of Diversity in Psychoanalytic Institutes. *International Journal of Psychoanalysis*, 75: 785–800.
Evans, D. (1996). *An Introductory Dictionary of Lacanian Psychoanalysis*. London: Routledge.
Fadiga, L & Gallese, V. (1997). Action representation and language in the brain. *Theoretical Linguistics*, 23 (3): 267–280.
Falconer, R. (1997). Introduction to Face to Face Bakhtin in Russia and the West. In C. Adlam, R. Falconer, V. Makhlin & A. Renfrew (Eds.), *Face to Face Bakhtin in Russia and the West*. Sheffield: Sheffield Academic Press.
Finlay, M. & Robertson, B. (1990). Quasi-Direct Discourse in the Psychoanalytic Context: Dialogical Strategy/Strategic Dialogue. *Social Discourse International Resource Papers*, 3 (1–2): 57–78.
Fleming, C. (2004). *René Girard, Violence and Mimesis*. Cambridge: Polity Press.
Fogassi, L. & Gallese, V. (2002). The neural correlates of action understanding in non-human primates. In: M. I. Stamenov & V. Gallese (Eds.), *Mirror Neurons and the Evolution of Brain and Language, Advances in Consciousness Research*. Amsterdam/Philadelphia: John Benjamins Publishing Company.

Fogel, A. (1985). *Coercion to Speak, Conrad's Poetics of Dialogue*. Harvard, MA: Harvard University Press.

Fogel, A. (1989). Coerced Speech and the Oedipus Dialogue Complex. In: G. Morson & C. Emerson (Eds.), *Rethinking Bakhtin, Extensions and Challenges*. Evanston, Illinois: NorthWestern University Press.

Foucault, M. (1970). *The Order of Things*. New York: Vintage Books.

Freud, S. (1994). *Civilisation and its Discontents*. New York: Dover Publications.

Gallese, V., Fadiga, L., & Rizzollatti, G. (1996). Action recognition in the premotor cortex. *Brain, 119*: 593–609.

Gans, E. (2000). The Origin of Language: Violence Deferred or Violence denied? *Contagion, 7*: 1–17.

Gardiner, M. (1998). "The Incomparable Monster of Solipsism": Bakhtin and Merleau-Ponty. In: M. M. Bell & M. Gardiner (Eds.), *Bakhtin and the Human Sciences*. London: Sage.

Garrels, S. (2004). Imitation, Mirror Neurons, & Mimetic Desire: Convergent Support for the Work of René Girard, Fuller Theological Seminary Pasadena, Colloquium on Violence and Religion.

Gasparov, M. (1984). M. M. Bakhtin in Russian Culture of the Twentieth Century, trans. Ann Shukman. *Studies in Twentieth Century Literature*, 9 (1): 169–172, reprinted in C. Emerson (Ed.), *Critical Essays on Mikhail Bakhtin*. New York: G. K. Hall.

Georgaca, E. (2001). Voices of the Self in Psychotherapy: A Qualitative Analysis. *British Journal of Medical Psychology*, 74: 223–236.

Georgaca, E. (2003). Exploring Signs and Voices in the Therapeutic Space. *Theory and Psychology*, 4 (13): 541–560.

Giddens, A. (1991). *Modernity and Self-Identity, Self and Society in the Late Modern Age*. Cambridge: Polity Press.

Girard, R. (1966). *Deceit, Desire and the Novel, Self and Other in Literary Structure*, trans. Y. Freccero. Baltimore: The John Hopkins University Press.

Girard, R. (1977). *Violence and the Sacred*, trans. P. Gregory. Baltimore: The John Hopkins University Press.

Girard, R. (1978). *To Double Business Bound, Essays on Literature, Mimesis and Anthropology*. Baltimore: The John Hopkins University Press.

Girard, R. (1984). *Disorder and Order in Mythology, in Disorder and Order, Proceedings of the Stanford International Symposium (Sept 14–16, 1981)*. P. Livingstone (Ed.). Saratoga: Anma Libri.

Girard, R. (1987). *Things Hidden since the Foundation of the World*, trans. S. Bann & M. Metteer. London: Continuum.

Girard, R. (1996). Eating Disorders and Mimetic Desire. *Contagion, 3*: 1–19.
Girard, R. (2001). *I See Satan Fall like Lightening*. New York: Orbis.
Girard, R. (2004). *Oedipus Unbound, Selected Writings on Rivalry and Desire*. M. R. Anspach (Ed.). Stanford: Stanford University Press.
Good, P. (2001). *Language for Those Who Have Nothing, Mikhail Bakhtin and the Landscape of Psychiatry*. New York: Kluwer Academic/Plenum Publishers.
Goodchild, P. (2000). The Logic of Sacrifice in the Book of Job: Philosophy and the Practice of Religion. *Cultural Values, 4* (2): 167–193.
Hacking, I. (1999). *The Social Construction of What?* Cambridge, MA: Harvard University Press.
Handley, W. R. (1993). The Ethics of Subject Creation in Bakhtin and Lacan. In: D. Shepherd (Ed.), *Bakhtin, Carnival and other subjects: Selected Papers from the Fifth International Bakhtin Conference*. University of Manchester, July 1991.
Harré, R. (1983). *Personal Being: a Theory for Individual Psychology*. Oxford: Blackwell.
Harris, R. (2002). The Role of the Language Myth in Western Cultural Tradition. In: R. Harris (Ed.), *The Language Myth in Western Culture*. Richmond, Surrey: Curzon.
Heise, U. (1997). *Chronoschisms, Time, Narrative and Postmodernism*. Cambridge: Cambridge University Press.
Henriques, J., Hollway, W., Urwin, C., Venn, C. & Walkerdine, V. (1984). *Changing the Subject, Psychology, Social Regulation and Subjectivity*. London: Routledge.
Hermans, H. J. M. (1996). Voicing the Self: From Information Processing to Dialogical Interchange. *Psychological Bulletin, 119* (1): 31–50.
Hermans, H. J. M. (2004). The Dialogical Self—Between Exchange and Power. In: H. J. M. Hermans & G. Dimaggio (Eds.), *The Dialogical Self in Psychotherapy*. Hove: Brunner-Routledge.
Hirschkop, K. (1986). Bakhtin, Discourse and Democracy. *New Left Review, 160*: 92–113.
Hirschkop, K. (1989). Introduction: Bakhtin and cultural theory. In: K. Hirschkop & D. Shepherd (Eds.), *Bakhtin and Cultural Theory*. Manchester: Manchester University Press.
Hirschkop, K. (1997). Bakhtin Philosopher and Sociologist. In: C. Adlam, R. Falconer, V. Makhlin & A. Renfrew (Eds.), *Face to Face Bakhtin in Russia and the West*. Sheffield: Sheffield Academic Press.
Hirschkop, K. (1998). Bakhtin Myths, or, Why We All Need Alibis. *South Atlantic Quarterly, 97* (3/4): 579–598.

Hirschkop, K. (1998b). Is dialogism for real? In: D. Shepherd (Ed.), *The Contexts of Bakhtin, Philosophy, Authorship, Aesthetics*. Amsterdam: Harwood Academic Publishers.

Hirschkop, K. (1999). *Mikhail Bakhtin An Aesthetic for Democracy*. Oxford: Oxford University Press.

Hirschkop, K. (2001). Bakhtin in the sober light of day. In: K. Hirschkop & D. Shepherd (Eds.), *Bakhtin and Cutural Theory*, 2nd edition. Manchester: Manchester University Press.

Hirschkop, K. (2001b). Bakhtin's Linguistic Turn. *Dialogism*, 5/6: 21–34.

Hitchcock, P. (1997). Bakhtin, Marx and Worker Representation: An Architectonics of Answerability. In: C. Adlam, R. Falconer, V. Makhlin & A. Renfrew (Eds.), *Face to Face Bakhtin in Russia and the West*. Sheffield: Sheffield Academic Press.

Hitchcock, P. (1998). The Bakhtin Centre and the State of the Archive: An Interview with David Shepherd. *South Atlantic Quarterly*, 97 (3/4): 753–772.

Holquist, M. (1981). Introduction. In: Bakhtin, M. M. (1981). *The Dialogical Imagination: Four Essays*, trans. C. Emerson & M. Holquist. Austin: University of Texas Press.

Holquist, M. (1993). Foreword to Bakhtin, M. M. In: V. Lipianov & M. Holquist (Eds.), *Toward a Philosophy of the Act*, trans. V. Lipianov. Austin: University of Texas Press.

Holquist, M. (1990). *Dialogism, Bakhtin and his World*. London: Routledge.

Jackson, R. (1993). *Dialogues with Dostoevsky*. Stanford: Stanford University Press.

Jacobs, A. (2001). Bakhtin and the Hermeneutics of Love. In: S. Felch & P. Contino (Eds.), *Bakhtin and Religion, A Feeling for Faith*. Evanston, Illinois: NorthWestern University Press.

James, O. (1998). *Britain on the Couch, Treating a Low Serotonin Society*. London: Arrow.

Jefferson, A. (1989). Bodymatters: self and Other in Bakhtin, Sartre and Barthes. In: K. Hirschkop & D. Shepherd (Eds.), *Bakhtin and Cultural Theory*. Manchester: Manchester University Press.

Jones, M. V. (1990). *Dostoevsky After Bakhtin: Readings in Dostoevsky's Fantastic Realism*. Cambridge: Cambridge University Press.

Kagan, I. (1998). People Not of Our Time. In: D. Shepherd (Ed.), *The Contexts of Bakhtin, Philosophy, Authorship, Aesthetics*. Amsterdam: Harwood Academic Publishers.

Kearney, R. (1986). *Modern Movements in European Philosophy*. Manchester: Manchester University Press.

Kearney, R. (1995). Myths and Scapegoats: The case of René Girard. *Theory Culture and Society*, 12: 1–14.

Kinsbourne, M. (2002). The role of imitation in body ownership and mental growth. In: W. Prinz & A. Meltzoff (Eds.), *The Imitative Mind*. Cambridge: Cambridge University Press.

Knoblich, G. & Jordan, S. (2002). The Mirror system and joint action. In: M. I. Stamenov & V. Gallese (Eds.), *Mirror Neurons and the Evolution of Brain and Language, Advances in Consciousness Research*. Amsterdam/Philadelphia: John Benjamins Publishing Company.

Kop, E. (2000). A Dialogue Epistemology: Bakhtin on Truth and Meaning. *Dialogism*, 4: 7–33.

Kozhinov, V. (1999). Bakhtin and His Readers. In: C. Emerson (Ed.), *Critical Essays on Mikhail Bakhtin*. New York: G. K. Hall.

Koczanowicz, L. (2000). Freedom and Communication: The Concept of Human Self in Mead and Bakhtin. *Dialogism*, 4: 54–66.

Kristeva, J. (1980). *Desire in Language: A Semiotic Approach to Literature and Art*, trans. T. Gara & L. S. Roudiez. L. S. Roudiez (Ed.). Oxford: Basil Blackwell.

Kuhn, T. (1970). *The Structure of Scientific Revolutions*. Chicago, Illinois: University of Chicago Press.

Lacan, J. (1977). *The Four Fundamental Concepts of Psychoanalysis*, trans. A. Sheridan. J. A. Miller (Ed.). London: Karnac.

Lacan, J. (1977b). *Ecrits: a selection*, trans. A. Sheridan. London: Routledge.

Lacan, J. (2002). *Ecrits*, trans. B. Fink. London: Norton.

Lakoff, G. (1995). Metaphor, Morality and Politics, Or, Why Conservatives Have Left Liberals in the Dust, Graduate Faculty of the New School for Social Research. *Social Research*, 62 (2): 1–21.

Lakoff, G. & Johnson, M. (1999). *Philosphy in the Flesh, the Embodied Mind and its Challenge to Western Thought*. New York: Basic Books.

Lane, J. (1997). Sociology and Dialectics: Pierre Bourdieu and the Critique of Formalist Aesthetics. In: C. Adlam, R. Falconer, V. Makhlin & A. Renfrew (Eds.), *Face to Face Bakhtin in Russia and the West*. Sheffield: Sheffield Academic Press.

Leiman, M. (1992). The Concept of Sign in Vygotsky, Winnicott and Bakhtin: further integration of object relations theory and activity theory. *British Journal of Medical Psychology*, 65: 209–221.

Leiman, M. (1994a). The Development of Cognitive Analytic Therapy. *International Journal of Short-Term Psychotherapy*, 9 (2/3): 67–82

Leiman, M. (1994b). Projective Identification as early Joint Action Sequences: A Vygotskian addendum to the Procedural Sequence

Object Relations Model. *British Journal of Medical Psychology*, 67: 97–106.

Leiman, M. (1995). Early Development. In: A. Ryle (Ed.), *Cognitive Analytic Therapy: Developments in Theory and Practice*. Chichester: Wiley.

Leiman, M. (1997). Procedures as Dialogical Sequences: a revised version of a fundamental concept in CAT. *British Journal of Medical Psychology*, 70 (2): 193–207.

Leiman, M. (2000a). De Saussure's and Bakhtin's semiotic conceptions: contrasting positions for understanding the nature of psychotherapeutic discourse. Paper presented at the 3rd Nordic-Baltic Summer Institute for Semiotic and Cultural Studies, Imatra, Finland.

Leiman, M (2000b). Ogden's matrix of transference and the concept of sign. *British Journal of Medical Psychology*, 73: 385–397.

Leiman, M. (2002). Towards Semiotic Dialogism, The Role of Sign-Mediation in the Dialogical Self. *Theory and Psychology*, 12 (2): 147–280.

Leiman, M. (2004). Dialogical Sequence Analysis. In: H. J. M. Hermans & G. Dimaggio (Eds.), *The Dialogical Self in Psychotherapy*. Hove: Brunner-Routledge.

Leiman, M. & Stiles, W. B. (2001). Dialogical Sequence Analysis and the Zone of Proximal Development as conceptual enhancements the assimilation model: The case of Jan revisisted. *Psychotherapy Research*, 11: 311–330.

Livingstone, P. (1992). *René Girard and the Psychology of Mimesis*. Baltimore and London: The John Hopkins University Press.

Lock, C. (1991). Carnival and Incarnation: Bakhtin and Orthodox Theology. *Journal of Literature and Theology*, 5 (1): 68–82, reprinted in C. Emerson (Ed.), *Critical Essays on Mikhail Bakhtin* (1999). New York: G. K. Hall.

Lock, C. (1999). The Bakhtin Scandal/L'Affaire Bakhtine. *Literary Research/Recherche Litteraire*, 31: 13–19.

Lock, C. (2001). Bakhtin Among the Poets: Towards a History of Silence. *Dialogism*, 5/6: 44–64.

Lock, C. (2001a). Bakhtin and the Tropes of Orthodoxy. In: S. Felch & P. Contino (Eds.), *Bakhtin and Religion, A Feeling for Faith*. Evanston, Illinois: NorthWestern University Press.

Lock, C. (2001b). Double Voicing, Sharing Words: Bakhtin's Dialogism and the History of the Theory of Free Indirect Discourse. In: J. Bruhn & J. Lundquist (Eds.), *The Novelness of Bakhtin*. Copenhagen: Museum Tusculanum Press.

Lodge, D. (1990). *After Bakhtin, Essays on Fiction and Criticism*. London: Routledge.
Lodge, D. (2002). *Consciousness and the Novel*. London: Penguin.
Lodge, D. (2006). *The Year of Henry James*. London: Penguin.
Lorrigio, F. (1990). Mind as dialogue: The Bakhtin circle and pragmatist psychology. *Critical Studies*, 2 (1/2): 91–110.
Makhlin, V. (1997). Face to Face: Bakhtin's Programme and the Architectonics of Being-as-Event in the Twentieth Century. In: C. Adlam, R. Falconer, V. Makhlin & A. Renfrew (Eds.), *Face to Face Bakhtin in Russia and the West*. Sheffield: Sheffield Academic Press.
Makhlin, V. (1999). The Mirror of Non-Absolute Sympathy. In: C. Emerson (Ed.), *Critical Essays on Mikhail Bakhtin*. New York: G. K. Hall.
Malik, K. (2003). The dirty D word. *The Guardian*, 20th October.
Matejka, L. (1986). On the First Russian Prolegomena to Semiotics, Appendix 1. In: Voloshinov, V. N., *Marxism and the Philosophy of Language*, trans. L Matejka & I. R. Titunik. Cambridge, MA: Harvard University Press.
Meltzoff, A. & Moore, M. (1977). Imitation of Facial and Manual Gestures by Human Neonates. *Science*, 198: 75–78.
Meltzoff, A. & Moore, M. (1983). Newborn infants imitate adult facial gestures. *Child Development*, 54: 702–709.
Meltzoff, A. & Moore, M. (1989). Imitation in newborn infants: Exploring the range of gestures imitated and the underlying mechanisms. *Developmental Psychology*, 25: 954–962.
Meltzoff, A. & Moore, M. (1995). Infants' understanding of people and things: From body imitation to folk psychology. In: J. Bermudez, A. Marcel & N. Eilan (Eds.), *Body and the Self*. Cambridge: MIT Press.
Meltzoff, A. & Moore M. (1997). Explaining Facial Imitation: A Theoretical Model. *Early Development and Parenting*, 6: 179–192.
Meltzoff, A. (2002). Elements of a developmental theory of imitation. In: W. Prinz & A. Meltzoff (Eds.), *The Imitative Mind*. Cambridge: Cambridge University Press.
Meltzoff, A. & Decety, J. (2003). What imitation tells us about social cognition: a rapprochement between developmental psychology and cognitive neuroscience. *Philos. trans. R. Soc. London B. Biological Science*, 358: 491–500.
Miller, A. (1983). *For Your Own Good, The Roots of Violence in Child Rearing*. trans. H. & H. Hannum. London: Virago.
Morris, P. (1994). *The Bakhtin Reader, Selected writings of Bakhtin, Medvedev, Voloshinov*. London: Arnold.

Morrison, I. (2002). Mirror neurons and cultural transmission. In: M. I. Stamenov & V. Gallese (Eds.), *Mirror Neurons and the Evolution of Brain and Language, Advances in Consciousness Research*. Amsterdam/ Philadelphia: John Benjamins Publishing Company.

Morss, J. R. (1996). *Growing Critical, Alternatives to developmental psychology*. London: Routledge.

Morson, G & Emerson, C. (1989). *Rethinking Bakhtin, extensions and challenges*. Evanston, Illinois: NorthWestern University Press.

Morson, G. & Emerson, S. (1990). *Mikhail Bakhtin: Creation of a Prosaics*. Stanford: Stanford University Press.

Nadel, J. & Butterworth, G. (1999). *Imitation in Infancy*. Cambridge: Cambridge University Press.

Neilson, G. M. (2000). Action and Eros in the Creative Zone: Kant, Weber and Bakhtin. *Dialogism*, 4: 34–53.

Nikolaev, N. (1998). The Nevel School Of Philosophy (Baktin, Kagan and Pumpianshkii) Between 1918 and 1925: Materials From Pumpianskii's Archives. In: D. Shepherd (Ed.), *The Contexts of Bakhtin, Philosophy Authorship Aesthetics*. Amsterdam: Harwood Academic Publishers.

O'Conner, M. (1990). Chronotopes for women under capital: An investigation into the relation of women to objects. *Critical Studies*, 2 (1/2): 137–151.

Orlean, A. (1988). Money and Mimetic Speculation. In: P. Douchemel (Ed.), *Violence and Truth, on the works of René Girard*. London: Athlone Press.

Oughourlian, J. M. (1984). *Mimetic Desire as a key to Neurotic and Psychotic Structure in Disorder and Order, Proceedings of the Stanford International Symposium (Sept 14–16, 1981)*. P. Livingstone (Ed.). Saratoga: Anma Libri.

Oughourlian, J. M. (1991). *The Puppet of Desire, The Psychology of Hysteria, Possession, and Hynosis*, trans. E. Webb. Stanford, California: Stanford University Press.

Oughourlian, J. M. (1996). Desire is Mimetic: A Clinical Approach. *Contagion*, 3: 43–49.

Ouzgane, L. (2001). Desire, Emulation and Envy in the Portrait of a Lady. *Contagion*, 8: 114–118.

Packard, V. (1965). *The Pyramid Climbers*. London: Penguin.

Pankov, N. (2001). Bakhtin's Dissertation Defence. In: K. Hirschkop & D. Shepherd (Eds.), *Bakhtin and Cultural Theory*, 2nd edition. Manchester: Manchester University Press.

Parker, I. (1992). *Discourse Dynamics, Critical Analysis for Social and Individual Psychology*. London: Routledge.
Parker, I. (1999). *Deconstruction and Psychotherapy*. London: Sage.
Pechey, G. (1989). On the borders of Bakhtin. In: K. Hirschkop and D. Shepherd (Eds.), *Bakhtin and Cultural Theory*. Manchester: Manchester University Press.
Pechey, G. (1978). Philosophy and Theology in Aesthetic Activity. *Dialogism*, 1: 55–73.
Pechey, G. (2007). *Mikhail Bakthin, The Word in the World*. London: Routledge.
Piaget, J. & Inhelder, B. (1969). *The Psychology of the Child*. New York: Basic Books.
Pigalev, A. (1997). Bakhtin and Rosenstock-Heussy: "Absolute Need of Love" versus "Dative Thinking". In: C. Adlam, R. Falconer, V. Makhlin & A. Renfrew (Eds.), *Face to Face Bakhtin in Russia and the West*. Sheffield: Sheffield Academic Press.
Pilgrim, D. & Rogers, A. (1993). *A Sociology of Mental Health and Illness*. Buckinghamshire: Open University Press.
Pirog, G. (1987). The Bakhtin Circles' Freud: From Positivism to Hermeneutics. *Poetics Today*, 8 (3/4): 591–610.
Pollard R. (2003). Who was Bakhtin? Marxist materialist, Christian mystic or rampant plagiarist? *Reformulation*, May, 7–11.
Pollard, R., Hepple, J. & Elia, I. (2006). A dialogue about the dialogical approach. *Reformulation*, 25: 21–23.
Polledri, P. (2003). Envy Revisited. *British Journal of Psychotherapy*, 20 (2): 195–218.
Poole, B. (2001). From phenomenology to dialogue, Max Scheler's phenomenological tradition and Mikhail Bakhtin's development from "Toward a philosophy of the act" to his study of Dostoevsky. In: K. Hirschkop & D. Shepherd (Eds.), *Bakhtin and Cultural Theory*, 2nd edition. Manchester: Manchester University Press.
Poole, B. (1998). Bakhtin and Cassirer: The Philosphical Origins of Bakhtin's Carnival Messianism. *South Atlantic Quarterly*, 97 (3/4): 537–578.
Poole, R. (2001b). The Apophatic Bakhtin. In: S. Felch & P. Contino (Eds.), *Bakhtin and Religion, A Feeling for Faith*. Evanston, Illinois: NorthWestern University Press.
Postle, D. (1997). Counselling in the UK: Jungle, Garden or Monoculture? In: R. House & N. Totton (Eds.), *Implausible Professions, Arguments for Pluralism and Autonomy in Psychotherapy and Counselling*. Ross-on-Wye: PCCS Books.

Potolsky, M, (2006). *Mimesis*. Abingdon: Routledge.

Ranieri, J. (2002). Leo Strauss on Jerusalem and Athens: a Girardian Analysis, Colloquium on Violence and Religion, pp. 1–42.

Reed, N. (1994). Reading Lermontov's "Geroj nasego vremeni": Problems of poetics and reception, unpublished PhD thesis, Harvard University.

Reed, N. (1999). The Philosophical Roots of Polyphony: A Dostoevskian Reading. In: C. Emerson (Ed.), *Critical Essays on Mikhail Bakhtin*. New York: G. K. Hall.

Renfrew, A. (1997). Introduction: Bakhtin, Victim of whose circumstance? In: A. Renfrew (Ed.), *Exploiting Bakhtin*. Strathclyde: Strathclyde Modern Languages Series, No 2.

Richer, P. (1992). An Introduction to Deconstructionist Psychology. In: S. Kvale (Ed.), *Psychology and Postmodernism*. London: Sage.

Rizzolatti, G., Fadiga, L., & Gallese, V. (1996). Premotor cortex and the recognition of motor actions. *Cognitive Brain Research*, 3: 131–141.

Rizzolatti, G. & Arbib, M. (1998). Language within our grasp. *Trends in Neurosciences*, 21 (5): 188–194.

Rizzolatti, G., Craighero, L. & Fadiga L. (2002). The Mirror System in Humans. In: M. I. Stamenov & V. Gallese (Eds.), *Mirror Neurons and the Evolution of Brain and Language, Advances in Consciousness Research*. Amsterdam/Philadelphia: John Benjamins Publishing Company.

Rochat, P. (2002). Ego Function of Early Imitation. In: W. Prinz & A. Meltzoff (Eds.), *The Imitative Mind*. Cambridge: Cambridge University Press.

Ryle, A. (1990). *Cognitive-Analytic Therapy: Active Participation in Change, A New Integration in Brief Psychotherapy*. Chichester: Wiley.

Ryle, A (1991). Object Relations Theory and Activity Theory: A Proposed Link by way of the Procedural Sequence Model. *British Journal of Medical Psychology*, 64: 307–316.

Ryle, A. (1994). Consciousness and Psychotherapy. *British Journal of Medical Psychology*, 67: 115–123.

Ryle, A. (2000). Origins of CAT, ACAT website, www.acat.me.uk.

Ryle, A. (2001). CAT's dialogic perspective on the self, paper presented at the ACAT conference, March 2001.

Ryle, A & Kerr, I. B. (2002). *Introducing Cognitive Analytic Therapy, Principles and Practice*. London: Wiley.

Rzhevsky, N. (1994). Kozhinov on Bakhtin. *New Literary History*, 25 (2): 433–37.

Sa'di, A. H. (2002). Catastrophe, Memory and Identity: Al-Nakbah as a Component of Palestinian Identity. *Israel Studies*, 7 (2): 175–198.

Said, E.W. (1978). *Orientalism*. London: Penguin.
Said, E W. (2001). *Reflections on Exile*. London: Granta.
Samuels, A. (1997). Pluralism and Psychotherapy: What is a Good Training? In: R. House & N. Totton (Eds.), *Implausible Professions, Arguments for Pluralism and Autonomy in Psychotherapy and Counselling*. Ross-on-Wye: PCCS Books.
Sandywell, B. (1998). The shock of the old: Mikhail Bakhtin's contributions to the theory of time and alterity. In M. M. Bell; & M. Gardiner (Eds.), *Bakhtin and the Human Sciences*. London: Sage.
Selgado, J. (2004). Methodology and the Dialogical Self: Different ways of killing a metaphor, paper presented at 3rd International Conference on the Dialogical Self, Warsaw, 26–29th August.
Semerari, A., Carcione, A., Dimaggio, G., Nicolo, G. & Procacci, M. (2004). A dialogical approach to patients with personality disorders. In: H. J. M. Hermans & G. Dimaggio (Eds.), *The Dialogical Self in Psychotherapy*. Hove: Brunner-Routledge.
Sennett, R. & Cobb, J. (1972). *The Hidden Injuries of Class*. London: Norton.
Shepherd, D. (2004). Re-Introducing the Bakhtin Circle. In: C. Brandist, D. Shepherd & G. Tihanov (Eds.), *The Bakhtin Circle, in the Master's Absence*. Manchester: Manchester University Press.
Shotter, J. (1990). Social Individuality versus Possessive Individualism, The Sounds of Silence. In: I. Parker & J. Shotter (Eds.), *Deconstructing Social Psychology*. London: Routledge.
Shotter, J. (1993a). Bakhtin and Vygotsky: Internalisation as a boundary phenomenon. *New Ideas in Psychology*, 11: 61–75.
Shotter, J. (1993b). Harre, Vygotsky, Bakhtin, Vico, Wittgenstein: Academic discourses and Conversational Realities. *Journal for the Theory of Social Behaviour*, 23 (4): 459–482.
Shotter, J. (1995). In Conversation, Joint Action, Shared Intentionality and Ethics. *Theory and Psychology*, 5 (1): 49–73.
Smail, D. (1993). *The Origins of Unhappiness, A New Understanding of Personal Distress*. London: Harper Collins.
Shotter, J. & Billig, M. (1998). A Bakhtinian Psychology: From out of the heads of individuals and into the dialogues between them. In: M. M. Bell & M. Gardiner (Eds.), *Bakhtin and the Human Sciences*. London: Sage.
Stallybrass, P. & White, A. (1986). *Politics and Poetics of Transgression*. New York: Cornell University Press.
Stamenov, M.I. (2002). Some features that make mirror neurons and human language faculty unique. In M. I. Stamenov & V. Gallese

(Eds.), *Mirror Neurons and the Evolution of Brain and Language, Advances in Consciousness Research*. Amsterdam/Philadelphia: John Benjamins Publishing Company.

Stamenov, M. I. & Gallese, V. (2002). Mirror Neurons System, Past, present, and future of a discovery. In: M. Stamenov & V. Gallese (Eds.), *Mirror Neurons and the Evolution of Brain and Language, Advances in Consciousness Research*. Amsterdam/Philadelphia: John Benjamins Publishing Company.

Stiles, W. B. (1997). Signs and Voices: joining a conversation in progress. *British Journal of Medical Psychology*, 70: 169–176.

Stiles, W. B. (2002). Assimilation of problematic experiences. In: J. C. Norcross (Ed.), *Psychotherapy Relationships that Work: Therapist Contributions and Responsiveness to Patients*. Oxford: Oxford University Press.

Stiles, W. B., Osatuke, K., Glick, M. J. & Mackay, H. C. (2004). Encounters between internal voices generate emotion: an elaboration of the assimilation model. In: H. J. M. Hermans & G. Dimaggio (Eds.), *The Dialogical Self in Psychotherapy*. Hove: Brunner-Routledge.

Taylor, C. (2004). A Turk, a Turk, a Turk, (review of Snow, Orphan, Pamuk). London Review of Books, August, pp. 30–32.

Taylor, M. (2002). From Memetics to Mimetics: Richard Dawkins, René Girard, and Media-related Pathologies, Colloquium on Violence and Religion 2002, Judaism, Christianity and the Ancient World, Mimesis, Sacrifice and Scripture.

Tihanov, G. (2000). Culture, form, life. In: C. Brandist & G. Tihanov (Eds.), *Materialising Bakhtin: The Bakhtin Circle and Social Theory*. Basingstoke: Macmillan.

Tihanov, G. (2001). The Body as a Cultural Value: Brief Notes on the History of the Idea and the Idea of History in Bakhtin's Writings. *Dialogism*, 5/6: 111–121.

Titunik. I R. & Bruss, N. (1976). Introduction to Freudianism, A Marxist Critique. In: Voloshinov, V. N. (1976). *Freudianism: A Marxist Critique*, trans. I. R. Titunik. (Eds.) I. R. Titunik & N. Bruss (1927). Indiana: Indiana University Press.

Trevarthen, C., Kokkinaki, T. & Fiamenghi JR, G. A. (1999). What infants' imitations communicate with mothers, with fathers and with peers. In: J. Nadel & G. Butterworth (Eds.), *Imitation in Infancy*. Cambridge: Cambridge University Press.

Tsitsipis, L.D. (2004). A Sociolinguistic application of Bakhtin's authoritative and internally persuasive discourse. *Journal of Sociolinguistics*, 8 (4): 569–594.

Turkle, S. (1992). *Psychoanalytic Politics, Jaques Lacan and Freud's French Revolution*. London: Free Association Books.
Vice, S. (1997). *Introducing Bakhtin*. Manchester: Manchester University Press.
Voloshinov, V. N. (1986). *Marxism and the Philosophy of Language*, trans. L. Matejka & I. R. Titunik. Cambridge, MA: Harvard University Press.
Voloshinov, V. N. (1976). *Freudianism: A Marxist Critique*, trans. I. R. Titunik. I. Titunik & N. Bruss (Eds.) (1927). Indiana: Indiana University Press.
Voloshinov, V. N. (1976b). *Discourse in life, discourse in art*, trans. I. R. Titunik. Indiana: Indiana University Press.
Vygotsky, L. S. (1978). *Mind in society: The development of higher psychological processes*. M. Cole, V. John-Steiner, S. Scribner & E. Souberman (Eds.). Cambridge, MA: Harvard University Press.
Wall, A (1998a). Chatter, babble and dialogue. In: D. Shepherd (Ed.), *The contexts of Bakhtin, Philosophy Authorship Aesthetics, Studies in Russian and European Literature*, Vol. 2. Amsterdam: Harwood Academic Publishers.
Wall, A. (1998b). A Broken Thinker. *South Atlantic Quarterly*, 97 (3/4): 669–698.
Ware, T. (1997). *The Orthodox Church*. London: Penguin Books.
Watchtel, A. (2000). Not ready for Prime Time; The Prehistory of Bakhtin's Problems of Dostoevsky's Poetics in English. *Dialogism*, 4: 112–126.
Waterman Ward, B. (2000). Abortion as a Sacrament: Mimetic Desire and Sacrifice in Sexual Politics. *Contagion*, 7: 19–35.
Webb, E. (1991). Translator's Introduction. In: Oughourlian, J. M. (1991). *The Puppet of Desire, The Psychology of Hysteria, Possession and Hypnosis*, trans. E. Webb. Stanford, California: Stanford University Press.
Webb, E. (1993). *The Self Between, From Freud to the New Social Psychology of France*. Seattle and London: Washington University Press.
Weigand, E. (1990). The Dialogic Principle Revisited – Speech acts and mental states, Dialoganalyse 3, Proceedings of the 3rd conference, Bologna, 75–104.
Weigand, E. (1996). Emotions in Dialogue, Dialoganalyse 6, Proceedings of the 6th conference Prague, 34–48.
Weigand, E. (1999). Misunderstanding: The Standard Case. *Journal of Pragmatics*, 31: 763–785.
Weigand, E. (2002a). The Language Myth and Linguistics Humanised. In: R. Harris (Ed.), *The Language Myth in Western Culture*. Richmond, Surrey: Curzon.

Weigand, E. (2002b). Constitutive features of human dialogic interaction: Mirror neurons and what they tell us about human abilities. In: M. I. Stamenov & V. Gallese (Eds.), *Mirror Neurons and the Evolution of Brain and Language, Advances in Consciousness Research*. Amsterdam/Philadelphia: John Benjamins Publishing Company.

Wertsch, J. V. (1985). *Vygotsky and the Social Formation of Mind*. Cambridge, MA: Harvard University Press.

Wilkinson, R. G. (2005). *The Impact of Inequality, How to make sick societies healthier*. London: Routledge.

Winicott, D. W. (1971). *Playing and Reality*. Harmondsworth: Penguin.

Wohlschlager, A. & Bekkering, H. (2002). The role of objects in imitation. In: M. I. Stamenov & V. Gallese (Eds.), *Mirror Neurons and the Evolution of Brain and Language, Advances in Consciousness Research*. Amsterdam/Philadelphia: John Benjamins Publishing Company.

Young, R. (1999). Psychoanalysis and Psychotherapy: the grand leading the bland. *Free Associations*, 7 (43): 43–459.

Zbinden, K. (1999). Traducing Bakhtin and Missing Heteroglossia. *Dialogism*, 2: 41–59.

Zima, P.V. (1999). *The Philosophy of Modern Literary Theory*. London: Athlone Press.

Žižek, S. (2003). *The Puppet and the Dwarf, The Perverse Core of Christianity*. London: MIT Press.

Zwart, H. (1999). The Truth of Laughter: Rereading Luther as a Contemporary of Rabelais. *Dialogism*, 3: 52–77.

INDEX

active intermodal mapping (AIM), 126–127, 129
Alison, James, 203, 210, 212, 213–214
Anderson, Pamela, 118
Averintsev, Serge, 171, 176

Baker, Harold, 59
Bakhtin, Mikhail:
   Author and Hero in Creative Activity, 25, 26, 38, 54, 155, 163, 164, 182 n5, 185
   biographical details, 7–10
   Christian Orthodox faith, 26, 49–50, 51, 118, 156–158
   on dialogical consciousness, 143–144
   The Dialogical Imagination: Four Essays, 4, 30, 45, 69, 75, 79, 141, 142, 160, 162, 167–168
   Discourse and the Novel, 29
   disputed texts, 14–16, 49
   Draft Exercise Books, 83, 183 n10
   Forms of Time and of the Chronotope, 160
   and Girard, 82–87, 189
   and Lacan 53–60
   legacy, 10–14
   on meaning, 141–143
   Notes Made in 1970–1, 51
   Problems of Dostoevsky's Art, 15, 26, 27
   Problems of Dostoevsky's Poetics, 7, 33, 69, 71, 81, 83, 84, 85, 87, 165, 173, 174
   and psychotherapists, 16–18
   and psychotherapy, 2–7
   Rabelais and his World, 36, 172, 171, 174, 175
   Speech Genres and Other Late Essays, 45, 67
   Toward a Philosophy of the Act, 11, 23, 159–161, 163, 166
Balmary, Marie, 121 n12
Barsky, R.F., 186
Bateson, G., 98
Bernard-Donals, M., 12
Bernstein, Michael Andre, 67, 68, 71
Billard, A. & Arbib, M., 97
Birkett, I., 176
Bocharov, Sergei, 19 n3
body, the, 158–159, 169, 180, 184 n15, 187

235

and women, 175
see also grotesque body
Borch-Jacobson, Mikkel, 98, 108
Bosenko, A.V., 13
brain, 152 nn.2, 6
Broks, Paul, 124
Bromberg, P., 147–148
Brouwer, S., 184 n13
Bruss, Neil, 15
Buber, Martin, 25–26
  Dialogical Principle, The, 25
Bush, George W., 114

Capps, L. and Ochs, E., 203–204
carnival, 169–177, 179, 183 n11, 200
Cassirer, Ernst, 9, 16, 23, 27
Cheyne, J.A. & Tarulli, D., 48–49, 189
Christian Orthodox church, 156–160, 170, 182 n3
Christianity, 80–82, 83, 93–94, 120 n1, 182 n 3, 184 n15, 186
chronotope, the, 160–162, 182 n5
  and mental distress, 202–203
  and the self, 196–197
Clark, K. & Holquist, M., 7, 13, 14, 15, 49
Coates, Ruth, 13, 49, 157, 158, 167, 168, 181 n1, 183 n9
cognitive analytic theory:
  Leiman on, 41–42
  Ryle on, 39–40
  Voloshinov on, 41–42, 47–48
Cohen, Herman, 23–24, 25
communication, 65
Conrad, Joseph, 70, 71
Coupland, N., 194, 195
Crowley, T., 31, 80
Cultural Values, 121 n16

Davies, Colin, 118
Derrida, Jacques, 17, 27, 60, 108
Descartes, René, 27
desire:
  Dostoevsky on, 80
  internally and externally mediated desire, 98–100
  metaphysical desire, 105–106, 191
  triangular, 110–114
  see also mimetic desire
Deurzen, Emmy Van, 86
Dialogic Action Game, 132–135
dialogic patterns, 44, 45
dialogical consciousness, 136–144, 192–194
dialogical psychotherapy, 39–40, 60–61
dialogical self:
  and cognitive analytic theory, 38–51
  and collection of voices, 42–53
  and dialogical psychotherapy, 39–40
  and internally persuasive discourse, 210–212
  and the I-Thou relationship, 38–39
  and metaphor, 144–148
dialogical sequence analysis (DSA), 44, 46–48
dialogism, 21–32, 77
dialogue:
  coerced, 70–77
  limitations of, 66–68
  and truth, 66–68
  unfinalisability of, 74–75, 77
differentiation, 55
discourse, 168–169, 189
Dostoevsky, Fyodor M., 35, 67
  Brothers Karamazov, The, 91, 102, 165–166
  Christian beliefs, 88 n2
  and desire, 80
  Idiot, The, 84
  Notes from the Underground, 84
  polyphony, 73–77
  Poor Folk, 144
  and psychology, 59–60
  Underground Man, 71, 84–85, 90–91, 113
double bind, 82, 99
Dupuy, J., 78, 107–108. 115

Eagleton, Terry, 72
Easthope, Anthony, 27
embodied conceptual systems, 145–147, 162, 180–182, 184, 200

Emerson, Caryl, 175
  Bakhtin's faith, 26, 67
  dialogue, 70, 72–74, 88, 169
  disputed Bakhtin texts, 15
  ethics, 156
  on outsideness, 164
  semiotics, 51
ethics, 62 n4, 156–159

Falconer, Rachel, 10–11
Fleming, C., 117, 192
Fogel, Aaron, 70
Foucault, Michel, 17, 60
Freud, S., 27, 108
  consciousness, 109–110
  on narcissism, 104–108
  on the Oedipus Complex, 101–104
  on violence, 120 n2

Gans, Eric, 82
Gardiner, Michael, 65
Garrels, S., 125
Gasparov, M., 13
Georgaca, Eugenie, 57–59
Girard, René, 5, 66, 118–119, 166, 196
  and Bakhtin, 82–87, 189
  internally and externally mediated desire, 98–100
  and internally persuasive discourse, 212–215
  interpretation of Dostoevsky's *Underground Man*, 90–91
  on narcissism, 104–108
  non-sacrificial ethics, 212–215
  on the Oedipus Complex, 101–104
  and the scapegoat mechanism, 92–95, 113
  on the self, 108–110, 190–191
  universalism, 117
  on violence, 92–95
  see also interdividual psychology; mimetic desire
Good, Peter, 86, 172, 201, 205
grotesque body, 169, 173–175, 176

Hacking, Ian, 153 n9
Handley, William, 54, 55, 63 n12
Harré, R., 194

Harris, R., 130, 131, 186
Heise, Ursula, 197
Henriques, J. *et al*, 63 n 13, 193
Hermans, H.J.M., 35, 70
heteroglossia, 28, 29–31, 58, 59, 194–196
  and mimetic desire, 195–196
  and polyphony, 77–80
heteroglossic self, 78–79
Hirschkop, Kenneth, 3, 8, 21, 31, 31 n1, 174, 187
  on Bakhtin's legacy, 12
  Dialogical Imagination, The, 8, 9
  on dialogism, 24, 26, 29, 77
  on heteroglossia, 78, 79
  on intersubjectivity, 162–163, 178–179
  on language, 26–27
  on the modern novel, 36
Hitchcock, P., 14
Holquist, M., 13, 23, 67, 77, 156, 179, 183 n8
  on the chronotope, 161
  see also Clark, K. & Holquist, M.

I-Thou relationship, 25–26, 38–39
imitation, 125–128, 152 n2, 179
  see also internally and externally mediated desire; mimetic desire
insideness, 206, 207, 266
interdependency, 162–166
interdividual psychology, 95–98, 110–114
  limitations of, 116–118
  and psychotherapy, 114–116, 209
internally and externally mediated desire, 98–100
internally persuasive discourse, 4, 208–210
  and dialogical selfhood, 210–212
  and Girardian non-sacrificial ethics, 212–215
interpersonal relatedness, 155
intersubjectivity, 12, 23, 178–180
  Hirschkop on, 162–163, 178–179
intertextuality, 59
Ivanov, V.V., 14

Jackson, R., 88 n1
Jacobs, Alan, 165–166, 183 n9
Jakobson, Roman, 32 n6, 63 n9
Jefferson, Ann, 163

Kagan, Iudif, 9, 32 n3
Kagan, Matvai, 9, 23–24
Kant, I., 21–22, 23, 24, 32 n1, 182 n4
Kinsbourne, M., 127
Klein, M., 41, 42, 43, 47
Koczanowicz, Leszek, 39
Kozhinov, Vadim, 13, 14
Kristeva, J., 57

Lacan, J., 27, 53–60, 62 n9, 95, 100, 121 n13
 and Bakhtin 53–60
 differentiation, 55
 language, 55–57
 mirror stage, 53
 on speech, 53
Lakatos, I., 107, 121 n14
Lakoff, G. and Johnson, M., 144, 150, 152 n7
 embodied conceptual systems, 145–147, 162, 180–181, 193, 200
 primary metaphor, 159
language, 26–31, 41–42, 53, 82, 129–132, 153 n9
 allegorical, 69
 Lacan on, 57–59
 misuse of, 168–169
 see also dialogical consciousness; heteroglossia
language myth, 130–131
laughter, 169–172, 176–177, 184 n13
Leiman, M. and Stiles, W., 46, 57, 59
Leiman, Mikael, 14, 22, 59, 194
 cognitive analytic theory, 43–44
 dialogic patterns, 44
 dialogical sequence analysis, 46, 47
 semiotics, 49, 50–52, 62 n6
 utterance, 44, 48, 195
Levi-Strauss, Claude, 95
Lock, Charles, 10, 18, 49–50, 169, 175, 182 n7

Lodge, David, 37, 170
Luther, Martin, 172, 174, 184 n16

madness, 115–116
Makhlin, Vitalli, 11, 12, 18, 19 n2, 194
Malik, K., 69
Marxism, 52
metaphor, primary, 159
Matejka, L., 19 n4
Mead, James, 33
meaning, 139–143, 195
Meltzoff, A., 125, 126, 128, 149, 152 n1, 191, 192
Meltzoff, A. & Decety, J., 126
Meltzoff, A. & Moore, M., 120 n5, 125–126
menippea, 61 n1, 172–173
Menippus, 184 n17
mental distress:
 and the chronotope, 202–203
 and social conditions, 198–202
metaphysical desire, 105–106, 191
Miller, Alice, 103
mimesis, 109, 112–114, 120 n3, 130, 190
 and the self, 95–98, 117–119, 191–192
mimetic desire, 84, 85, 90–91, 117, 128, 209–210, 211–212
 and discourse, 189
 and heteroglossia, 195–196
 Oughourlian on, 113–113
 and the self, 81–82, 95–98, 108, 118, 119
 and triangular desire, 110–114
 types, 98–100, 190
 and violence, 92–95
mirror neurons system (MNS), 97, 125, 128–135, 151, 179
mirror stage, 54
Morson, G. and Emerson, C., 26, 157
Morson, Gary, 15, 194

Nadel, J. and Butterworth, G., 126
narcissism, 104–108, 190–191
Neilson, Greg, 22–23
novel, modern, 36–38, 61 n.1, 72

Object Relations theories, 39–40,
    43–44, 101, 104–105, 147
O'Connor, Mary, 202
Oedipus Complex, 40, 101–104
Orlean, A., 112
Oughourlian, Jean-Michel, 96–97,
    101, 118, 120 n5
  on Freudian consciousness,
    109–110
  on madness, 115–116
  on mimetic desire, 113–114
  and universalism, 117
outsideness, 162–167, 180, 205–208,
    215

Packard, Vance, 111
Pamuk, Orhan, 113
Pan'kov, Nicolae, 9
Parker, I., 69
Pechey, Graham, 1, 30, 31, 157
phenomenology, 27, 52
Piaget, J., 125
Pirog, Gerald, 52, 53
polyphonic novel, 34
polyphonic self *see* dialogical self
polyphony, 72
  applied to Dostoevsky's novels,
    73–77
  and heteroglossia, 77–80
  and moral purpose, 73
Poole, Brian, 9, 14, 16, 18, 26
Poole, Randall, 32 n1, 158
projective identification, 42–43, 47
Proust, Marcel, 106–107
psyche, dialogical views of, 43–44

Rabelais, François, 171, 183 n11
Reed, Natalia, 66, 73–77, 85, 107, 176,
    189
reflexivity, 58–59
Republic (Plato), 120 n3
Rizzolatti, G., Craighero, L. & Fadiga
    L., 97
Rochat, P., 127
Roman Catholicism, 170, 172
Rorty, Richard, 146
Ryle, Anthony, 42, 43, 47, 48, 109
  on cognitive analytic theory, 40–41

on consciousness, 110
on psychoanalysis, 108

sacrifice *see* scapegoat mechanism
Sa'di, Ahmed, 196
Said, Edward, 1, 201
Samuels, A., 86
Saussure, Ferdinand de, 27, 53
scapegoat mechanism, 92–95, 200,
    203–204
Scheler, Max, 9
self, 24, 188–190
  and the chronotope, 196–197
  Girard on, 108–110, 190–191
  ideological model of, 6
  and mimesis, 95–98, 117–119,
    191–192
  and mimetic desire, 81–82, 95–98,
    108, 118, 119
  see also dialogical self; dialogism
self state, 46, 61 n3
semiotics, 49, 50–51, 62 n6, 136,
    192–194
Shepherd, David, 8, 9
Shotter, J., 50, 62 nn4, 7, 146, 205–206
Shotter, J. & Billig, M., 67
signs *see* semiotics
Smail, David, 46–47, 212
social conditions, 198–202
social toxicity, 199
speech, 54, 62 n5
  see also language
Stallybrass, P. and White, A., 189,
    199–200, 201
Stamenov, M.I. and Gallese, V., 129
Stiles, William, 34, 42–43
Strawson, Galen, 153 n8
structuralist approach, 95
surplus of vision, 163, 164, 200, 201,
    206–207
Symbolic Order, 56

theory of mind (ToM), 127
Tihanov, G., 169, 204, 207
Titunik, I.R., 15
training of psychotherapists, 206–207,
    208, 215, 216 n4
transference, 57–58

Trevarthen, C., Kokkinaki, T. & Fiamenghi JR, G.A., 192
Trinity, the, 157, 182 n2
Turkle, Sherry, 56

universalism, 117
University of Marbourg, 23
utterance, 44–46, 47–48, 50, 51, 139, 193

Veblen, Thorstein, 110–111
Vice, S., 30, 77
violence, 83, 203–204
    Freud on, 120 n4
    and mimetic desire, 92–95
    and women, 113, 118
voices, 33–34, 42–43, 58
Volkova, Elena, 164
Voloshinov, Valentin, 6, 9, 14–16, 26–27, 136, 193, 202
    allegorical language, 69
    cognitive analytic theory, 41–42, 47–48
    communication, 65
    determinism, 52–53
    on dialogical consciousness, 143–144
    Freudianism, a Marxist Critique, 14, 15, 19 n4
    on language, 19 n4, 131, 136, 137
    Marxism and the Philosophy of Language (*MPL*), 14, 15, 25, 19 n4, 32 n6
    meaning, 139–141
    semiotics, 49, 51, 69, 136
    utterance, 44–46, 50, 139
Vossler, Karl, 131
Vygotsky, L.S., 41

Wall, Anthony, 3, 4, 11
Ware, Timothy, 158
Waterman Ward, Bernadette, 105
Webb, E., 93, 116
Weigand, Edda, 129–130, 131, 132, 144, 149–150, 179
    and the Dialogic Action Game, 132–135
    and embodied dialogical consciousness, 136–144
    meaning, 139–141, 195
Wilkinson, R.G., 198, 199, 209, 210, 215, 216 n2
Winnicott, D., 41
women:
    and the body, 175
    and freedom, 202–203
    and narcissism, 105
    roles of, 40, 46
    status of, 198
    subjugation of, 189
    and violence, 113, 118
words *see* language; speech; utterance

Zbinden, Karine, 78
Zizek, Slavoj, 68
Zwart, Hub, 172, 177

For Product Safety Concerns and Information please contact our EU
representative GPSR@taylorandfrancis.com
Taylor & Francis Verlag GmbH, Kaufingerstraße 24, 80331 München, Germany

www.ingramcontent.com/pod-product-compliance
Lightning Source LLC
Chambersburg PA
CBHW051354290426
44108CB00015B/2006